Modern
Safety
Practices

RUSSELL DeREAMER

Corporate Safety Manager

International Business Machines Corp.

NEW YORK • JOHN WILEY & SONS, INC.

London

MODERN
SAFETY
PRACTICES

SECOND PRINTING, MAY, 1961

Library of Congress Catalog Card Number: 58–12708

Printed in the United States of America

To Faye

Phyllis

and Carol

PREFACE

This book provides managers and supervisors, safety engineers and students of management a comprehensive and an integrated coverage of modern safety practices. Text material is written to pinpoint the relationship between safety and good management—safety and human relations. The need is stressed for designing safety programs to conform to modern management practices and newly developed and tested concepts of safety organization and administration.

It is a well-established fact that outstanding safety performance can be achieved in those industrial establishments and businesses where not just the safety engineer is doing a good accident-prevention job, but the entire supervisory force has assumed full responsibility for safety—where safety performance is a positive factor in a supervisor's chances for an increase in pay and advancement—where safety is built into each job.

This, of course, is merely applying to safety the sound principles of management which apply to all other important functions in organizing and motivating human endeavor. This entails placing responsibility and authority for making safety decisions at points as near as possible to where the action takes place—in the hands of the first-line supervisor. Hence it is perhaps of primary significance that this book is directed toward motivating line supervisors to a more active role in accident prevention.

Several new approaches to the problems of industrial safety are discussed, including a new personalized approach to employee safety training that has produced rather spectacular results, a step-by-step program for getting employees to follow safety rules, and a supervisor-employee oriented program for developing safety awareness and employee safety participation. These safety concepts and practices have been applied successfully. They would be effective in any type of business, large or small.

It is hoped that *Modern Safety Practices* will become a practical guide to supervisors and safety engineers, enabling them to examine their respective safety responsibilities and safety functions in the light of up-to-date knowledge. This book is recommended as a text for supervisory safety training. It can be given to supervisors for individual study. This can then be followed with well-organized and directed group discussions of the subject matter, enabling supervisors to relate what they have read to their individual safety experiences and objectives.

This book also can be a useful text for college-level students, especially those in schools of business administration, industrial management, and engineering. Students, too, need to have a clear understanding about safety: what it is, what it will do, and what they can rightfully expect from it. They need to have an appreciation of the dividends of successful safety efforts, particularly as these dividends relate to management practices and the operation of profitable businesses.

For the safety engineer, *Modern Safety Practices* outlines a consultative approach to safety organization and administration. The need is stressed for getting results through the power of well-marshaled facts, persuasion, teaching, and advising, rather than the power to command and direct. The book contains sound, management-oriented knowledge on the development of safe working conditions, human factors in machine and equipment safety, the reduction of noise, safety appraisals, and the measurement of safety performance. In addition, selected accident case histories, steps for organizing a supervisor-centered safety-observer program, new ideas on the teaching of safety key points instead of details, and the outline of a complete safety program found in the appendix should be of special interest and help to safety engineers. The techniques and procedures which are discussed can be put right to work. They get close to the practical problems faced by safety engineers each day.

Finally, no attempt is made to avoid controversial subjects. An orderly program is suggested for disbanding safety committees, a "sacred idol" of the safety movement. Facts and fiction concerning the accident-prone theory are discussed. New material is presented on the use of total injury frequency rates rather than disabling-injury frequency rates in measuring supervisory safety performance.

Modern Safety Practices is a product of many years of industrial safety experience and rewarding associations with safety and management leaders in the United States and Canada. In retrospect it becomes evident that many persons have contributed directly or indirectly to the writing of this book. It would not be practical to attempt to name all of them. However, those who have read *Industrial Accident Prevention* by H. W. Heindrich will recognize the influence of this pioneer and leader in the safety movement. Others who have contributed by their friendliness and willingness to share their safety knowledge include: H. Gene Miller, Arthur Kelly, Glen Griffin, and Norval Burch, National Safety Council; Henry Lamb, American Standards Association; Everett Martin and Leroy Faulkner, Liberty Mutual; L. R. Morrison, ACF Industries; Leroy McCarty, Remington Arms; Earl Shedd, U.S. Rubber; Asa Lombard, Bullards; Harley Trice and Donald Ankeny, Mine Safety Appliances Company; H. B. Duffus, Westinghouse; F. T. Clarke, G. Roy Fugal, Dr. B. L. Vosburgh, Harold Vann, Herschel Smith, Harold Oaklander, Alan Jones, F. A. Gass, William Prout, Charles Harper, W. H. Evans, Howard Fawcett, Margaret Stewart, and Fred McKinnon, General Electric Company.

To Louis E. Newman, President, A. L. Smith Iron Company, and formerly Manager, Health and Safety Services, General Electric Company, a special note of gratitude is due. He fostered the idea that this book should be written. He gave freely of his advice and counsel. If it had not been for his encouragement and confidence, there is much doubt this book would have been completed.

RUSSELL DEREAMER

Dobbs Ferry, New York
July, 1958

CONTENTS

PART I

SAFETY PHILOSOPHY AND PRINCIPLES

PART II
CREATING AND MAINTAINING SAFETY AWARENESS

PART III
DEVELOPING SAFE WORKING CONDITIONS

PART I

SAFETY PHILOSOPHY AND PRINCIPLES

CHAPTER

1

Safety – a management practice

The experienced plant manager knows that safety is good business. He knows that it is good business to accept safety as a management responsibility, to establish policies, procedures and practices under which every member of management will clearly understand that the safety of employes is a primary responsibility at all times and that it is not to be sacrificed or jeopardized in any way.

HARRY W. ANDERSON
General Motors

There was a time when a supervisor's concern for safety might have been limited to an occasional personal appearance at a monthly safety meeting or the investigation of a serious accident. That this is no longer the case requires little emphasizing, but the reasons that supervisors must have a key role in modern safety programs deserve careful study.

Forty years ago, when formalized safety programs became a part of the industrial scene, the concerted efforts of one man, the safety engineer, produced outstanding reductions in the work-injury rate. Maximum attention was given to the elimination of hazardous conditions. Guards and protective devices were placed on machines where there had been no guards before. Personal protective equipment was developed and put into use. Work methods that were often back-breaking and dangerous were made less arduous and much safer by the introduction of conveyors, hoists, motorized trucks, and other labor-saving equipment. Thus, largely through the efforts of the safety engineer, working conditions were improved and the injury rate reduced. In the past, a safety program built around one man, the safety engineer, could be justified. Today, the picture is vastly different. Guards and safety devices are incorporated in the design of many machines. Large sums are spent each year on personal protective devices. Management is meeting its responsibility for a safe work environment. But the elimination of the physical hazards is just one part of a modern safety program. Safety men are concerned because where the safety record is good it is becoming increasingly more difficult to achieve a further reduction in work-injury rates.

From 1926 to 1932 a rapid reduction in the frequency of disabling injuries occurred. As reported by industrial members of the National Safety Council, rates in this six-year period dropped from a high of 31.87 disabling injuries per million manhours worked in 1926 to a low of 12.46 in 1932. This was nearly a 60 per cent improvement. However, in the following twenty years the rates improved only 38 per cent, and in recent years there has been a leveling-off of the downward injury-rate trend. Exhibit 1–1 provides a graphic presentation of these data.

Because of the outstanding improvements in industrial-disabling-injury rates that have occurred in the last forty years, the safety job is a lot tougher today. A low accident rate will not respond to the efforts of just one man. Today, the outstanding safety records are being recorded in plants where the entire supervisory staff is doing a good accident-prevention job. Much more effort is needed to make a good record better than to obtain a good record in the first place.

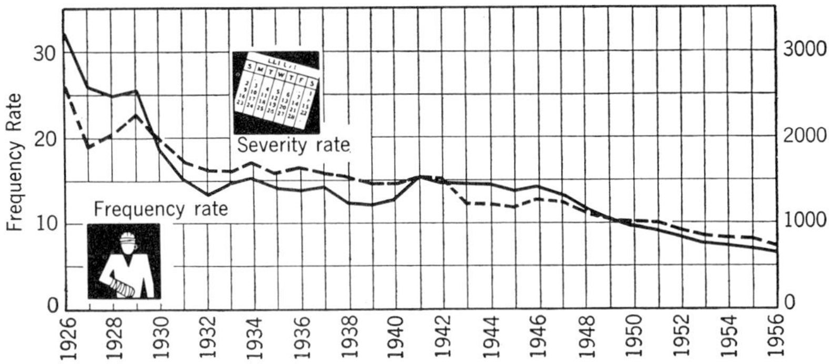

Exhibit 1–1. Injury frequency and severity rates from 1926 to 1956 of firms reporting injury statistics to the National Safety Council. (Source: *Accident Facts,* 1957 edition.)

The supervisor's role in safety

A study of accident case histories reveals why a supervisory approach to accident prevention is so effective. A lot of accidents are occurring because of a lack of safety awareness. Men fall from ladders, operate their machines without a guard, drop objects on their toes, or cut their hands because of misuse of a tool. These accidents are obviously the result of unsafe acts, not unsafe conditions. But it is not implied that the worker intentionally acted unsafely. Perhaps there had not been complete instructions on safe practices. Perhaps the need for working safely had not been stressed. Perhaps the desire for working safely had not been created. An effective means of eliminating this garden-variety type of accidents is discussion with the worker. Safety must be put on a personalized basis. This being the case, supervisors and not the safety engineer are in a better position to do something about accidents. The supervisor is the only person who can control men, machines, and working conditions on a daily, full-time basis. The supervisor is closest to the person most likely to get hurt. He can take direct action. Therefore, where safety has been given a high priority among management activities and supervisors have fully discharged their responsibilities for safety, the results have been outstanding. This is now the way it should be.

But in some cases the claim may be made that supervisors are responsible for safety although there is no valid basis for the assertion. If employees rush to put on their safety glasses or replace a machine guard when they see the *safety engineer* but feel free to work without their safety glasses or to remove a machine guard in the presence of their supervisor, obviously responsibility for safety has not been assumed by the supervisor. Likewise, when the safety man signs and issues all safety instructions, prepares all injury reports, conducts all safety meetings, *he*, and not the supervisor, is doing the safety job. Such a situation is unfortunate for two reasons. By not assuming full responsibility for safety, the supervisor gives up some of his rights to manage, and he overlooks an important part of his job—a part which will help him win greater acceptance of his leadership and improve production.

A supervisor's safety check list

A supervisor who wants to check the quality of his safety efforts can use the Safety Check List on the next page. His answers will tell him how good a safety job he is really doing.

It is clear that supervisors must concentrate on the development of the proper "safety awareness." They must continue, of course, to fulfill management's responsibility for providing safe working conditions. But mostly, the emphasis must be on the development of a healthy safety climate. Safety is contagious (it is caught as well as taught), and the best carrier of the contagion is the boss and the boss's boss. Thus, because of their close association and frequent contacts with the people in their work groups, first-line supervisors have an indispensable part in the plant safety program.

This does not mean, of course, that the safety engineer's job has become less important. Actually, to fill the requests for safety services which come from an alert safety-minded line organization, the safety engineer must increase his competence and scope of knowledge. Modern manufacturing methods, the use of new materials, high-speed machine tools, the use of high voltages, high pressures, electronics, and the use of radioactive materials have increased the technical aspects of the safety job. Line supervisors must look to the highly qualified safety engineer for assistance.

There are other reasons for the increased emphasis of the supervisor's role in the safety program. Today enlightened management recognizes that the benefits of its accident-prevention efforts can be measured in both human and economic gains. These gains are best achieved where supervisors assume their full responsibility for safety, where safety is a practice of good management. Thus, the supervisor and other members of the management team in companies with successful safety programs are playing dominant roles in accident-prevention activities.

SUPERVISOR'S SAFETY CHECK LIST

	My Practice Is Adequate	My Practice Needs Attention
1. I accept safety as just as much a part of my job as production, quality, and cost.	( )	( )
2. I recognize the relationship among good safety, good housekeeping, and good management.	( )	( )
3. I give adequate safety instruction to every new employee and to every old employee starting a new job.	( )	( )
4. I impart to all employees the understanding that the violation of standard safe work practices is just as serious as the violation of any other company rule—I am taking corrective action when safety rules are ignored.	( )	( )
5. I see that necessary personal protective equipment is provided.	( )	( )
6. I always set a good safety example myself.	( )	( )
7. By personal contact and group discussions, I make it possible for each employee to take part in the safety program.	( )	( )
8. I do not release new or relocated machines or equipment to an employee until I am satisfied that the necessary protective devices have been provided and the employees have received instructions regarding its safe operation.	( )	( )
9. I investigate and determine the cause of *all* injuries, even the minor cases.	( )	( )
10. I am constantly watchful for and I take immediate steps to correct unsafe work conditions and unsafe work procedures.	( )	( )
11. I see that all injuries are reported and promptly treated.	( )	( )

Dividends of supervisory safety effort

It is apparent that real accomplishment in safety brings *benefits* far beyond those detected by casual observation. Safety need not be a welfare or employee-benefit activity. It need not be an expense item, except through misdirected or half-hearted effort. Where safety is a major, full-time, day-to-day responsibility of each supervisor; where safety performance is a positive factor in a man's chances for an increase in pay and advancement; where safety is built into the equipment, the machines and tools, and the employee-supervisor relationships at the workplace—there the money and time spent on the safety program become investment dollars with a high return in dividends.

The first-line supervisor is the key man in any successful safety program. Safety or accident prevention requires his concentrated and conscientious effort. Because it does, it is logical for a supervisor to ask, "What's in it for me?" These are the dividends.

Through his safety efforts the supervisor gains from his people a greater acceptance of his leadership. Each employee wants recognition, he wants to be considered as an individual, he wants his feelings to be respected. On the other hand, he resents any action or comment of his supervisor that might be regarded as a lack of consideration for his welfare, his comfort, or his safety. A safe place to work and a safety-conscious management rank high among the things an employee looks for in his job. Likewise, his family has an equal concern for his safety while at work. Conditions are such today that competition among employers in offering better wage rates, security, and employee benefits has been largely eliminated, but there is still a basis for keen competition—the offer of "a healthier and safer place to work."

It is apparent that the safety efforts of a supervisor can play a constructive part in shaping the emotional attitude of the employees toward himself and his company. To be a leader, the supervisor must have the respect of his people. To win respect, he must first show respect. The concern he demonstrates for the safety of the man on the job is a sensitive indicator of the respect he has for his people. But, this concern must be full-time and sincere. It must be a demonstration of the kind of personal interest the supervisor would have in accident prevention if his son were working in the plant. An employee will not buy the lip-service kind of safety that he sometimes receives. To win acceptance, the supervisor must really want to operate a safe plant and, by the example he sets, must let his people know that he expects them to work safely, too. This matter of a supervisor's winning leadership through his safety efforts has important by-products because employee safety awareness is so closely related to:

An employee's temperament.
His attitude toward his work.
His ideas of obedience.
His sense of responsibility.
His respect for his boss.

Thus, through the safety program, management can demonstrate its concern for human values. Placing a guard on a machine and insisting on its use is tangible evidence that management cares about its people. A good safety program is a combination of a lot of little things that do so much to create employee satisfaction and loyalty.

Through his safety efforts the supervisor improves his production, quality, and cost performance. Many plant managers are aware that the supervisor with the best safety records usually have good production, quality, and cost records, too. This relationship between safety, production, and cost has been known for a long time. It is easily understood. An employee may perform an unsafe act several times without being hurt—but most likely not without costing the supervisor's section money in terms of slipshod work, damaged material, or delays in production. A tool or a part falling from a table and crushing a worker's toe is a dramatic reminder that many parts or tools have fallen without hitting a foot, but nevertheless adding to expense in terms of damaged material, reduced quality, and delay.

The high cost of accidents

A review of just a few accidents reveals many interesting highlights on the high cost of an inadequate safety program.[1] A commercial aircraft taxiing into a runway struck the tail cone of another aircraft with its wing tip. The total repair bill for both planes was $93.05—rather insignificant in a multi-million-dollar business. But, one of the airline's safety-minded executives was not satisfied that this had been the total cost of the accident. He decided to find out just how much the smashup had really cost.

The answer he got may surprise a lot of people who think accidents do not cost much. Two flights were inmmediately canceled with a

[1] C. M. Christenson, "Management's Economic Interest in Safety," a paper presented at The Institute of Aeronautical Sciences, January, 1954.

revenue loss of $2000. Two other trips had to be canceled later to balance equipment from Seattle to Los Angeles and from Seattle to San Francisco at an estimated revenue loss of $6000. The equipment damage involved an out-of-service for two airplanes for a total of twenty hours at an average of $550 per hour, or a total of $11,000. The incident also caused a loss of flight time to crew members and stewardesses and an additional loss of $400 for dead-head costs to balance crews. Thus, this one accident, a so-called minor one, involving no injuries cost $19,400 instead of the $93.05 originally reported.

Here is another example: A machine operator slipped on a oily spot while running to extinguish a fire—not the type of accident that reaches the local newspapers. At first glance, it looked like the back injury sustained by the employee would require one or two trips to the dispensary. Another minor case, but complications set in. A second look revealed these facts. Because of a permanent partial disability and several weeks away from work, the injured employee received $10,300 in workmen's compensation payments. Hospital and doctor bills soared to $4525. Other expenses amounted to $491.18. Thus, the total bill for extingiushing one small fire was over $15,000. Scores of cases are on record in which the total compensation and medical expenses for one injury have exceeded $100,000, and one company has reported that it is still paying compensation on an injury sustained in 1928.

Even the minor injury, the small cut or bruised finger, sends profit dollars down the drain. A drill-press operator used his hand instead of a brush to clear away chips and cut his index finger. Time spent in the dispensary was eighteen minutes. Travel time to and from the dispensary added twelve minutes more to the down-time of his machine. Medication and dressing cost 10 cents. Forms required for reporting the injury and for medical records cost 15 cents. The drill-press operator's hourly rate was $1.82. Thus, a quick calculation revealed that it cost $1.06 to treat the minor injury. This cost estimate might be considered low. Estimates made by various safety engineers of the cost of first-aid cases average about $4.50 per case. These additional costs could logically have been added to the injury bill:

1. Nurse's time.
2. Cost of the delay in production.
3. Cost of preparing state reports.
4. Hospital overhead.
5. Return trips to the dispensary for redressing, which average about three trips per injury.
6. Additional medicine and dressings required.

The disabling injury and the so-called minor injury that are multiplied hundreds of times in the course of a year add materially to the total cost of industrial accidents. The bad ones magnify the problem. Following a fatal accident in a metal-working plant, the plant manager said, "The accident was the most upsetting thing to the plant's productivity that has ever happened within my experience." A fatality, of course, brings the loss of productivity into sharp focus, but every accident interferes with production, and anything that slows production and increases cost should be the concern of all supervisors. To ignore even the minor accidents is like carrying water in a leaky pail.

Finally, through his safety efforts, the supervisor can help improve the community relations of his company. A high accident rate in any community would decrease the earning power of some, add to the number of handicapped and totally disabled, and leave some families without support, in turn increasing taxes and the costs of operating the community welfare department and hospitals. Thus, the community-conscious company, the organization that is eager to justify its existence by contributing to the community welfare, would want to discharge its responsibility as a good neighbor by helping to reduce accidents on and off the job.

An off-the-job accident study

Competent safety engineers have been aware of the carry-over value of good industrial safety training. They have recognized that a person who has been trained in the plant to think of his safety is more likely to avoid accidents when away from the plant, too. The General Electric Company has obtained some encouraging statistical data on this important by-product of industrial safety training. A three-phase study was made for the company by Mr. James Rowan, partner in Mellott, Pitney, Rowan and Company, New York City, to determine the relationship between a good in-plant safety program and off-the-job accidents of employees and their families. The study was made at Coshocton, Ohio, the location of General Electric's Laminated Products Department. This plant was selected because it is isolated from other General Electric Plants and because the plant safety record there is outstanding.

Some of the significant findings of the research study were:

1. General Electric employees and their dependents driving automobiles have one-sixth as many accidents on the highways as other residents of the city and county of Coshocton.

2. All types of accidents off the job being considered, the average family in the United States has more than twice as many accidents as the average General Electric family at Coshocton.

3. Ninety-five per cent of the families of General Electric employees know something about the plant safety program as compared to 55 per cent of the families of non-General Electric industrial employees.

4. Fifty per cent of the General Electric families use plant safety ideas at home as contrasted to 25 per cent of other industrial worker's families.

To discover these facts, a three-phase study was made. The phases are listed below in chronological order:

1. A study of the traffic accidents in the city and county of Coshocton that had occurred in a prior twelve-month period.

2. A survey using a modified depth-interview technique among (*a*) a representative cross-section of G-E wage-earning families, (*b*) a comparable group of wage-earning families in other companies, and (*c*) a sampling of families in occupations other than manufacturing.

3. An analysis of non-occupational accident cases treated at the general hospital in a twelve-month period.

The following significant guides to supervisors and other management people emerged:

1. Provide employees and families with specific ideas on home and traffic safety.

2. Emphasize fully the dramatic, colorful features of the plant safety program especially in media reaching families.

3. Establish a system for compiling statistics on off-the-job accidents in plant communities.

4. Consider plans to show how schools in plant communities can cooperate effectively in improving community safety.

The results of the study tend to confirm the belief that a relationship does exist between the plant safety program and off-the-job accident experience of employees and their families. There is little doubt that safety programs that are being successfully conducted by American industry are contributing to the reduction of injuries on highways, in the home, and in the community.

The Coshocton study may well be a significant indication of a direction plant safety programs should take in the future. It seems reasonable to conclude that the safety efforts of the plant supervisor will contribute to the building of a better community.

In summary then, these are the dividends of a supervisor's safety efforts:

1. A greater acceptance of supervisory leadership—better employee relations.
2. Improved production, quality, and cost performance.
3. Improved community relations.

Conclusions

Busy supervisors can hardly be expected to fulfill various safety functions which take even a little additional time unless they can see a good reason and a need for the activity. Because past practices may have convinced many supervisors that the safety function could be left to the safety engineer or a safety committee, much re-education may be necessary. Hence the number-one job of safety engineers in large and small industrial plants, in the insurance companies, in state labor departments, in associations and safety councils is to teach all supervisors that safety is a practice of good management.

Of course, any successful safety program starts from the top of the organization and works down. The company president or the plant manager passes the responsibility for safety down through the levels of management to the first-line supervisor. And for reasons that are now obvious, the first-line supervisor becomes the focal point of all safety functions. To assure future progress in work-accident prevention, supervisors must be convinced that the sincere efforts they make to prevent work-accidents will cause employees to more readily accept supervisory leadership. In a sense a safety program which is built around the supervisor is a cornerstone of good employee relations.

Likewise, supervisors must be convinced by the tangible evidence which is available that their safety efforts will help improve production, costs, and quality and that the end result will be better profits. Compensation and medical payments, damaged equipment and products, and production delays resulting from accidents all subtract directly from profits. Thus, a company making 10 per cent net profit faces this kind of problem: Every time 1 dollar is spent because of an accident, 10 additional dollars of product must be produced or 10 additional dollars of services must be sold just to get the 1 dollar back. To the operator of any business, the costs of one accident could be the difference between a profit and a loss in any one year.

Mr. J. T. Rossello, superintendent at the Chelsea plant, Chemical Division, General Electric Company, has a clear vision of the supervisor's safety responsibility. Here is how he put it in a letter to his supervisory staff:

> Anyway we look at it, safety responsibility is ours. Our operators are trained and guided by us. We must hold them accountable for doing the job right and in turn we are accountable for the guidance, teaching, discipline and correction needed for a safe plant. You cannot be a "good Joe" in this area and ignore safety violations. In the end we'll get no thanks and probably a set back by being soft so let's not entertain the thought.

Good community relations, lower employee turnover and absenteeism, better employee morale, and steadier work are other gains which flow from a good safety effort. Because of these many benefits, supervisors must agree that the safety function ranks high among their various responsibilities requiring full and unqualified support and daily personal attention. What is needed is a safety program which in all phases promotes and implements the basic principle that the supervisor has responsibility for the safety of his people. Such a program starts with the basic concept that safety and good management go hand in hand.

SELECTED REFERENCES

"A Human Relations Program," the results of a National Association of Manufacturers safety survey, *Occupational Hazards,* June, 1954.

Anderson, H. W., "Safety is Good Business," *National Safety News,* July, 1952.

MacDonald, J. Carlisle, "Safety Helps Public Relations," *National Safety News,* July, 1952.

MacMillan, C., *Foremanship and Safety,* John Wiley and Sons, New York, 1943.

Simonds, R. H., *Estimating Costs of Industrial Accidents,* U.S. Department of Labor, U.S. Government Printing Office, Washington, D.C., 1955.

Walton, A., *New Techniques for Supervisors and Foremen,* McGraw-Hill Book Co., New York, 1940.

CHAPTER 2

Basic principles of accident prevention

Accident prevention is both a science and art. It represents, above all other things, control—control of man performance, machine performance, and physical environment. The word "Control" is used advisedly because it connotes prevention as well as correction of unsafe conditions and circumstances.

H. W. HEINRICH

Uniform Boiler and Pressure Vessel Laws Society

There are some who believe the type of industry, the kind of product being manufactured, the size of the plant, the composition of the work force, or the nature of the hazards involved have a considerable bearing upon safety performance. The facts, however, do not support this view. There are foundries and steel mills filled with hazardous equipment that have outstanding safety records. On the other hand, there are light-assembly plants with only minor hazards that have poor safety records, although it might be assumed that a good record could be achieved rather easily. What is lacking is sincere desire to make the plant a safe place to work. Regardless of the size of the plant, large or small, or the type of product, steel rails or pills, the key to a better safety record is the existence of a proper safety awareness. Safety must become a matter of habit in the plant.

Developing safety awareness

In the development of "safety awareness" the aim is to condition a person's mind so that whenever there is an element of danger present, a sixth "safety" sense will cause him to react the safe way. Awareness for many things is an inborn trait. A person can walk into a room and immediately sense if joy or sorrow prevails. Likewise the presence of an influential person can be felt. A young man sitting in the lobby of a hotel or in the waiting room of a railroad station might continue reading his paper undisturbed as several men walk directly in front of him. But if suddenly he hears the click of high heels and the rustling of a dress and smells the scent of "Temptation" perfume, he looks up from his paper. This is "awareness." No development was required. However, safety awareness must be developed. Fortunately it can be by training, repetition, and by constant correction. The notice given to red and green traffic lights, the skull and crossbones on the medicine bottle, and the white X at a railroad crossing is an example of developed awareness. These symbols might have no meaning to a small child, but by training and repetition they can become meaningful. Take another example; training and repetition have conditioned the operator of an automobile to know a red light means stop. But training and repetition was not enough. A certain amount of correction or enforcement, symbolized by the traffic policeman, was also required. Likewise, by (1) *training,* (2) *repetition,* and (3) *correction* a line supervisor can achieve success in the reduction and control of accidents. The will and desire to work safely can be created in the minds of all workers.

Unfortunately, a great deal of complacency exists concerning safety simply because many people believe accidents just happen. Even a President of the United States once said, "It doesn't matter where you are, flying in a plane or asleep in your bed, when your number comes up, that's it." This opinion is shared by a large group of people. Of course, if there were any basis for the "*your number is up*" *theory,* there would be no need for life guards on the beach, protective devices on machines, or the numerous other measures that are taken to control accidents. Another group is content to attribute all accidents to the *price of progress.* This group recognizes that the construction of the tallest building, the spanning of the widest river, the testing of the fastest plane, or the development of the most destructive weapon requires exposure to certain dangers. They conclude that such exposure must inevitably lead to accidents. But, exposure to danger does not mean that safety cannot be a part of the process. Lindbergh exposed himself to dangers when he crossed the Atlantic. The atomic scientists exposed themselves and thousands of workers to danger when they developed the atomic bomb. In each case a calculated risk was involved, but the end result was progress with safety. Still another group accepts the theory that accidents are a result of the *law of averages.* They use this concept as an argument against giving safety much thought. Finally there are some who feel all accidents are *acts of God* destined to occur regardless of the steps that might be taken to prevent them. This theory, of course, is not supported by any religion common in the Western World.[1]

Accidents are caused

The real fact is this: Accidents are caused; they do not just happen. Thus, by finding the causes of accidents, steps might be taken to prevent them. This basic safety principle is relatively simple and easily understood. But apparently the simplicity of the statement creates doubt in the minds of some that the real basis for preventing accidents can be found in a principle so elementary as the "accidents are caused" theory. This doubt is evidenced by the reams of statistics and reports which attempt to associate injuries with accident proneness, psychosis, alcoholism, childhood backgrounds, and a multitude of other factors and conditions other than a lack of safety awareness, the safety performance of supervisors, and unsafe acts and unsafe conditions. Many reports and conclusions, especially those on accident proneness, have been harmful to the safety movement because they mislead the industrial supervisor and others into thinking that safety is a matter for the industrial psychologists or the medical department rather than a matter that the supervisor is the better qualified to handle by application of accepted methods of good supervision.

Basically, what is required is an acceptance of and a firm belief in these three fundamental safety concepts:

1. Accidents are caused.
2. Steps must be taken to control accidents.
3. Without correction, the same type of accident will re-occur.

---

[1] Ned Dearborn, "Six Murderous Beliefs," *National Safety News,* October, 1947.

These fundamental safety principles are by no means new. The following excerpt from a lecture before the Harvard National History Society, which was published in *The Atlantic Monthly* of October, 1880, contains these three basic concepts of accident prevention stated in the eloquent style of writing that characterizes the nineteenth century:

> We might say with perfect legitimacy that a friend of ours, who had slipped on the ice upon his doorstep and cracked his skull, some months after dining with thirteen at the table, died because of that ominous feast. I know, in fact, one such instance; and I might, if I chose, contend with perfect logical propriety, that the slip on the ice was no real accident. "There are no accidents," I might say. "The whole history of the world converged to produce that slip. If anything had been left out, the slip would not have occurred just then and there. . . ."
>
> If in the case of the unfortunate man we lose ourselves in contemplation of the thirteen-at-table mystery, and fail to notice the ice on the step and cover it with ashes, some other poor fellow, who had never dined out in his life, may slip on it in coming to the door, and fall and break his head too.

Although present-day supervisors might not be so disengaged as to lose sight of the cause of an accident in contemplation of the thirteen-at-the-table mystery or the position of the stars, it is not unlikely that corrective action has been postponed following some accidents because "It was the first time in twenty years anyone ever got hurt on that machine," or "It was really an unlucky accident; it couldn't happen again in one hundred years." The fact an accident occurred once is convincing evidence that it might occur again. Hence, the conviction that accidents are caused must be strengthened in the minds of everyone, and the need for immediate corrective action emphasized and re-emphasized. To make a plant a safe place to work and the world a safe place to live, everyone must understand the principles of accident prevention and the terminology associated with the principles.

Definitions

Accidents, injuries, unsafe acts, and *unsafe conditions* are terms common to all safety work. Their definitions should be known.

Accident may be defined as an unplanned, non-controlled, and an undesirable event or a sudden mishap which interrupts an activity or a function. In applying this definition to the accident-prevention program the supervisor should keep in mind that all accidents do not result in an injury. As a matter of fact, only a few of them do. Depending upon the activity involved, the ratio of accidents producing injuries to those producing no injury varies over a considerable range. Accidentally touching a high-voltage bare conductor might produce an injury in each accident, but a worker could drop a heavy object hundreds of times without succeeding in hitting his toe. However, although an injury is not involved, a delay in production, damaged material, reduction of quality, or additional wear on equipment may be a product of the accident. Hence, the need for checking the no-injury accidents as well as those which produce an injury should be evident.

Injury may be defined as the bodily hurt sustained as the result of the accident, such as a laceration, abrasion, bruise, puncture, wound, foreign body, fracture, etc.

Unsafe act may be defined as a departure from an accepted, normal, or correct procedure or practice, an unnecessary exposure to a hazard, or conduct minimizing the degree of safety normally present. Not every unsafe act produces an accident. This is an important consideration in safety work. Generally a supervisor has ample opportunity to correct the unsafe act before an accident occurs.

Unsafe condition may be defined as any physical condition that if left uncorrected may lead to an accident. Again it is well to keep in mind that most unsafe conditions have been observed before the accident occurs. Thus, the supervisor has numerous opportunities to correct the unsafe condition before the accident.

Ratio of unsafe acts to unsafe conditions

One of the outstanding contributions to industrial-safety literature has been the book by H. W. Heinrich, *Industrial Accident Prevention,*[2] published by McGraw-Hill in 1931. Most of the principles formulated by the author more than a quarter century ago still apply and are the basis of most industrial accident-prevention programs.

In his book Heinrich establishes the theory that 88 per cent of all accidents result primarily from unsafe acts, 10 per cent from unsafe conditions, and 2 per cent from acts of God. These ratios have done much to establish the importance of the human element in accident prevention. However, literal acceptance of the theory without consideration of prevailing conditions in a particular plant or industry could be detrimental to successful safety performance. It might lead to a de-emphasis of the need for developing safe working conditions

---

[2] H. W. Heinrich, *Industrial Accident Prevention,* third edition, McGraw-Hill Book Co., 1950.

by good housekeeping and adequate machine guarding—why spend much time and money correcting conditions that will prevent only 10 per cent of the accidents?

Actually the percentage of accidents which are triggered by either an unsafe act or an unsafe condition varies considerably from plant to plant. In an establishment where a great many unsafe conditions prevail and there is a high percentage of heavy machine work performed, it is likely that the unsafe condition will be the predominant factor in a large number of accidents. In a plant with the maximum of machine guarding and a high percentage of light assembly operations, the unsafe act will prevail as the principal cause of accidents. Maximum results in safety will be achieved by concentrating on those factors which are causing accidents in a particular plant, unsafe acts, unsafe conditions, or both. National averages or percentages are at best unreliable guides.

Also, over-emphasis of the concept that 88 per cent of all accidents are attributable to unsafe acts can lead to trouble because many of the so-called unsafe acts might turn out to be unsafe conditions when all the facts are thoroughly examined. Evidence exists which indicates that many worker errors have been touched off by faulty design, inadequate guards, poor working conditions, a lack of standardization and identification—in short, unsafe conditions that actually trapped the worker into performing the so-called unsafe act. Perhaps a close examination would reveal that many accidents result from a combination of unsafe acts and unsafe conditions rather than solely from an unsafe act or an unsafe condition.

The anatomy of an accident

There is a consensus among safety engineers that there are four distinct parts in the anatomy of an accident:

1. Contributing causes.
2. Immediate causes.
3. The accident.
4. The results of the accident.

These four parts of the accident may be outlined as follows:

I. Contributing Causes of Accidents

A. Supervisory safety performance
   1. Safety instruction inadequate

2. Safety rules not enforced
3. Safety not planned as part of the job
4. Infrequent employee safety contacts
5. Hazards not corrected
6. Safety devices not provided

B. Mental condition of person
1. Lack of safety awareness
2. Lack of coordination
3. Improper attitude
4. Slow mental reaction
5. Inattention
6. Lack of emotional stability
7. Nervous
8. Temperamental

C. Physical condition of person
1. Extreme fatigue
2. Deaf
3. Poor eyesight
4. Physically unqualified for job
5. Heart condition
6. Crippled

II. Immediate Causes of Accidents

A. Unsafe acts
1. Protective equipment or guard provided but not used
2. Hazardous method of handling (failure to allow for sharp or slippery objects and pinch points, wrong lifting, loose grip, etc.)
3. Improper tools or equipment used although proper tools were available
4. Hazardous movement (running, jumping, stepping on or climbing over, throwing, etc.)
5. Horseplay

B. Unsafe conditions
1. Ineffective safety device
2. No safety device although one is needed
3. Hazardous housekeeping (material on floor, poor piling, congested aisles)
4. Equipment, tools, or machines defective
5. Improper dress or apparel for job
6. Improper illumination, ventilation, etc.

III. The Accident

A. Fall
B. Slip
C. Slide
D. Strike against
E. Caught in or between
F. Erupt or explode
G. Burn

IV. Results of the Accident

A. Annoyance
B. Production delays
C. Reduced quality
D. Spoilage
E. Minor injuries
F. Disabling injuries
G. Fatality

Contributing and immediate accident causes

For a complete understanding of the anatomy of an accident, a full knowledge of the contributing and immediate causes of accidents is essential. The focal point in accident-prevention activities in the past has been the immediate causes of accidents—unsafe acts and unsafe conditions. Additional information that is now available indicates that progress in accident prevention can be accelerated by a shift in the emphasis to the contributing causes of accidents—the mental and physical condition of the worker and supervisor safety performance.

Some safety programs have become accident- or even injury-*observation* programs rather than true accident-prevention programs. That is, steps are not taken to correct a condition until an accident occurs that indicates the problem. The emphasis is all on the elimination of unsafe working conditions instead of the *development* of safe working conditions and safe work habits. In true safety work unsafe acts and unsafe conditions must be considered only as end-products or symptoms. The unsafe acts and unsafe conditions are not what is wrong; they are only the results. It is the factors which contribute to unsafe acts and unsafe conditions that are wrong. Control these contributing factors and the need for eliminating unsafe acts and unsafe conditions is minimized.

Of course, supervision must continue to deal effectively with the immediate causes of accidents, but much more time and attention must be given to the contributing causes. This means giving more attention to the relationship between men and machines, laying out the plant to meet the mental and physical needs of the operator, and including safety training in all job training. With this approach both operator safety and operator efficiency should improve.

Accident-control steps

When an accident does occur, it is an indication that something has gone wrong. Somewhere along the line someone has not done a good job of accident prevention and unsafe acts and unsafe conditions have been created. The supervisor who is sincere in his efforts to prevent accidents will want to have a working knowledge of the fundamental steps he can take to control the contributing causes of accidents—the mental and physical condition of the worker and his own safety performance. These are the steps:

I. Supervisor Safety Performance

A. Job-hazard analysis
B. Enforcement of safety rules
C. Adequate safety knowledge
D. Promotion of employee participation in safety
E. Proper job placement
F. Development of safe working conditions

II. Mental Condition of Person

A. Regular safety contacts by supervisor
B. Adequate safety indoctrination and on-the-job safety training
C. Safety promotions and publicity
D. Employee participation in safety program
E. Regularly scheduled safety meetings
F. Adequate supervisor-employee communication on all matters concerning the employee

III. Physical Condition of Person

A. Preplacement physical examinations
B. Periodic re-examinations
C. Proper job placement
D. Adequate medical facilities
E. Careful check of physical condition of worker on all transfers and changes in jobs
F. Recognition of the physical limitations of workers new to a job, especially if heavy work is involved

The accident flow chart

A flow chart (Exhibit 2–1) shows graphically the anatomy of an accident. The contributing causes of accidents, the sources of unsafe acts and unsafe conditions, are shown at the top of the chart. From each of the three sources the flow is into a central reservoir labeled unsafe acts and unsafe conditions—the immediate causes of accidents. The position of the overflow on the reservoir indicates that an accumulation of unsafe acts and unsafe conditions leads to accidents, which in turn account for production delays, spoilage, and injuries. The flow chart illustrates these basic accident-prevention fundamentals:

1. The supervisor's safety performance, the physical condition of the worker, and the mental condition of the worker are the main sources of unsafe acts and unsafe conditions. These three factors should be the focal points of accident-prevention work.

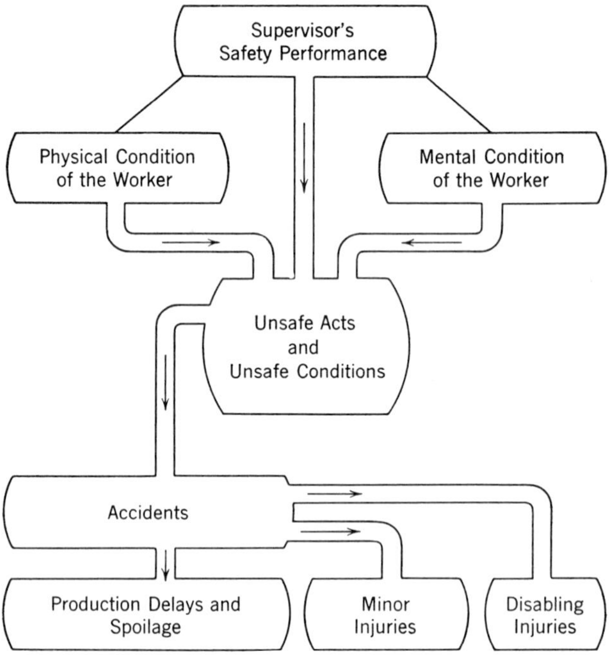

Exhibit 2–1. A flow-chart presentation of the anatomy of an accident.

2. Not all unsafe acts and unsafe conditions result in accidents, but all accidents result from unsafe acts and unsafe conditions, usually in combination.

3. All work accidents cause a delay in production, spoilage, or waste.

4. Some accidents cause injuries, and in a small percentage of the cases, the injury is disabling.

Ratio of minor and disabling injuries

A check of the injury records of several different types of industries indicates that the ratio between minor injuries and disabling injuries is not constant. This conclusion might be contrary to the commonly accepted theory that there is a direct fixed ratio among no-injury accidents, minor-injury accidents, and major-injury accidents. Table 2–1 gives the ratios of minor-injury accidents to disabling-injury accidents of various plants in several industries.

TABLE 2–1

	Frequency Rate	Minor Injuries	Disabling Injuries
Small machine shop	8.07	14	1
Foundry	9.15	96	1
Heavy equipment manufacturing	5.23	121	1
Aircraft engine	2.15	226	1
Appliances	2.33	312	1
Lamp	2.18	540	1
Atomic products	0.35	880	1
Electronic equipment	1.13	1160	1
Chemical	0.77	1850	1

Several factors might influence these ratios, such as the type of work being done, the composition of the work force (that is, the ratio between men and women), the injury-reporting habits of various employees, the time it takes to get to the dispensary, the personality of the nurse, and so forth. Reference to Table 2–1 indicates that in general, heavy industries with relatively high frequency rates have the lower ratios between minor injuries and disabling injuries. This is in part an arithmetical normality. The high frequency rate means total minor injuries are spread over several disabling injuries. However, there are other reasons why the ratios are low in heavy industry. Men who do heavy work are less likely to report all minor injuries. Also, the nature of the work provides greater opportunity for a serious injury. On the other hand, a light bench assembly operation presents relatively few opportunities for a serious injury, and employees on such operations, especially women, are much more likely to report the minor cuts, burns, and bruises. For example, the chemical plant in the table has a minor-disabling injury ratio of 1850 to 1 and a disabling frequency of only 0.77. In this particular plant, the work is light, the hazards are minor, and the workforce is mostly women.

It is safe to conclude that there is no fixed or constant ratio that can be applied to minor-disabling-injury experience. As a matter of fact, the ratios do not remain constant even in a specific plant, but vary from period to period. On the basis of these observations, it would be wrong to conclude that the occurrence of a given number of minor injuries (for example, 29 minor injuries to 1 serious injury[3]) is an indication that a disabling injury is about to occur. On the other hand, it would be correct to conclude that an increase in the usual minor-injury rate in a plant or in any section of a plant is a good indication of a need for increasing the accident-prevention effort. A higher minor-injury rate over a previous period should be taken as a warning signal that accidents are not being controlled.

Supervisors must be taught to give attention to all types of injuries, regardless of their severity. Although *X* number of minor injuries do not equal a major injury like 10 dimes equal 1 dollar, it is true that some minor injuries might have been disabling injuries except for the matter of luck involved. A scaffold collapses and two men fall to the ground. One man is killed and the other walks away with minor injuries. One man falls from a loading platform and gets up unhurt. Another man has the same accident and breaks his arm. Even the minor cut can lead to an infection and in some cases death. As one supervisor said, "There is no such thing as a minor accident; just some of them result in minor injuries." Thus, it is important for a supervisor to give personal attention to all types of injuries regardless of their severity. Also, it should be evident that each minor injury is an indication that a number of no-injury accidents are occurring with resultant delays in production and waste. Perhaps the ratio between no-injury accidents and the injury producing accidents is high, but what this ratio is could be anybody's guess. The important point to recognize is that the no-injury accidents also deserve the prompt personal attention of supervisors.

Conclusions

From the basic principles and philosophies of accident prevention are evolved the elements of effective safety effort. Many experts in the field of industrial safety will agree that in order to achieve good results in accident prevention, line supervisors must include these four elements in their safety programs:

1. Development of safe working conditions.
2. Creation of safe work habits on a personalized basis.

[3] As expressed by H. W. Heinrich, in a unit group of 330 similar accidents, 300 will produce no injury, 29 will result in minor injury, and 1 will result in a serious injury. This is usually called the 300-29-1 ratio. It was not intended that these statistics should be used as a fixed ratio that would apply to any one plant.

3. Promotion of employee participation in safety.
4. Corrective action when safety rules are ignored.

Because of his direct control over the people in his section and the direct action he is able to take to maintain safe working conditions, the first-line supervisor is in a key position to prevent accidents. The significance of supervisory safety performance in the control of accidents is indicated by the results of a study made by the Corps of Engineers during the Second World War. More than 1700 injury cases involving civilian employees were analyzed to determine the extent and type of supervisor failure involved in each accident. Here is what was found:

Three out of five accidents occurred when the supervisor was not at the scene of the accident.

Where supervisor failure was indicated, the types of failures were:

1. Failure to enforce safety rules, 29 per cent.
2. Failure to inspect for hazards, 22 per cent.
3. Insufficient safety instructions, 20 per cent.
4. Other reasons, 2 per cent.

Undoubtedly a large percentage of the 1700 injuries would not have occurred if safety rules had been enforced, safe working conditions had been developed, and workers had been trained to do the job safely. These are the elements of the safety program that need to be stressed. But regardless of the soundness of an organized approach to accident prevention, any attempt to control accidents without first creating a proper safety philosophy, teaching safety principles, and eliminating misconceptions about the causes of accidents would be relatively ineffective. Supervisors, safety engineers, and workers must believe that accidents are *caused* and they can be *prevented.*

CHAPTER

3

Accident proneness - facts and fiction

An early and still existing view in safety literature has been that a number of people are accident prone. This view has led to the labeling of "accident proneness" as the cause of accidents in a significant percentage of cases. In reality, it is not the cause at all. Where a person does experience repeated accidents, the cause generally is a number of inherent conditions related not only to his physical or mental make up, but also to the environment in which he works. The real challenge is to identify these causes and to take corrective action.

JOHN V. GRIMALDI
General Electric Company

Everyone is subject to accidents, and having them or not having them usually depends upon the number of unsafe acts committed and unsafe conditions exposed to in a given period. Yet, in the past fifty years numerous studies have been made which associate a large percentage of accidents with a so-called accident-prone group of people. These studies, of course, should have been made. Such research is a proper function of the industrial psychologist and others. However, misconception and over-emphasis of the accident-prone theory by industrial safety engineers and supervisors could lead to a lot of misdirected safety effort. Industrial management must be convinced that lack of supervisory safety direction, the employee's physical condition, and the employee's mental condition cause accidents, and that any attempt to control work injuries by the elimination of the accident prone would be sure to fail.

Definition of accident proneness

Usually "accident proneness" is described as a combination of human abilities which make a person highly proficient in bringing about accidents, regardless of his environment, at a rate higher than could be statistically expected by chance alone. Perhaps it will suffice to describe the accident-prone individual as a person who will have an abnormally high rate of injuries, regardless of his job, work environment, age, or length of service. However, there is a great deal of disagreement in the literature regarding the number of injuries an employee must have to be considered accident prone.

It is a matter of record that the accident-prone concept originated following the discovery that a small percentage of the population had a high percentage of the injuries. However, this discovery has little significance. Assume, for example, that a group of 1000 workers have 250 injuries in one year. By allowing 1 injury to a worker, only 250 workers could be injured. Thus, 25 per cent of the workers have 100 per cent of the injuries. Actually, fewer than 250 workers will have all of the injuries because some workers in the group will be injured two or more times before others have any injuries at all. Hence, the fact that a small percentage of the work group has a high percentage of the accidents does not mean necessarily that the existence of accident proneness has been demonstrated. It might mean only that the number of injuries reported was much less than the number of workers included in the study.

To avoid any misunderstanding, it may be helpful to point out that no attempt is being made here to disprove the existence of accident-prone persons. The goal is to convince managers, supervisors, and safety personnel that only a very small percentage of the population could possibly be identified as truly accident prone. Therefore, at the moment the accident-prone concept has little value in an industrial safety program. Attention must not be diverted from the tangible elements of accident prevention to such an intangible as accident proneness.

So much is being written about accident proneness that it is likely that the reader of this book will, within the next month, find in a magazine article, in his daily newspaper, or in a supervisory newsletter the statement, "Between 20 and 30 per cent of workers cause 60 to 85 per cent of all accidents." Obviously, it would not be wise to jump to the conclusion that accident proneness is the problem. Likewise, in any discussion of accident proneness, it is likely that someone will tell about the worker who is always getting hurt. In the mind of the story teller this single case appears to furnish a convincing example of an "accident prone" employee. The story of Jim Brown is a case in point. Jim had nine injuries in a four-month period. One day, he had two accidents within an hour. He fell over a skid and bruised his leg. Returning to work following treatment, he fell over the same skid. Accident prone? Probably not. Any competent supervisor will look for the causes of Jim's accidents. Jim fell over a skid which had been left in a main aisle and at a blind corner. Following the first accident, no one moved the skid. Jim had his attention diverted while explaining his injury to a fellow employee, and he fell over the skid again. Now, what about the other seven injuries? Two of them were eye injuries. Jim got sand in his eyes, because his safety glasses had been improperly fitted. One injury was a small laceration of Jim's little finger. He did not know how it happened. The four remaining injuries were burns on his right forearm. Investigation revealed that a protective flap had been removed from Jim's automatic welder. The purpose of the flap was to protect Jim from flying sparks. When asked why he had not reported the condition at least after the first burn, Jim said, "Oh, I don't like to bother my boss with such little things."

Jim's story is typical of the type of case which is used presumably as a good example of the accident-prone employee. As a matter of fact, the case was taken from a recent report on an accident-prone study conducted in a large manufacturing plant. Salient facts are unchanged, but the account of the case has been altered to avoid identification of the researcher. Jim was called accident prone. Accident prone or not, certainly no one will deny that eight of Jim's accidents could have been prevented by the development of safe working conditions—keeping skids out of main aisles and keeping flaps of the welder in place. Of course, it is pretty difficult to keep the work place in A-1 shape at all times. Occasionally, a guard will be removed, safety glasses will be bent out of shape, and skids will be left in aisles. Hence, it would be a pretty tough job to stop all injuries. However, if Jim's supervisor had investigated each of Jim's injuries, it is reasonable to assume one eye injury, one skid injury, and three burns would have been avoided. Then, Jim would have been the victim of an accident just four times instead of nine. In other words, he had five injuries because the conditions which caused the first injuries were not corrected. Look at it like this. A supervisor who believes Jim is accident prone is likely to assume the case is out of his hands. It is a matter for the medical department or a psychologist. On the other hand, a supervisor who believes Jim's accidents had a cause is likely to take positive action and look for the cause. This positive approach is the one which produces tangible results.

Normal distribution of injuries

In the above case, Jim was considered accident prone because he had nine injuries. Perhaps his injury experience followed a normal experience pattern for the work group. Putting the matter in the form of a question, would it be possible for Jim to have incurred nine injuries without violating any of the laws of probability? Many of the ideas of probability are familiar. For example, the probability that the toss of a coin will result in a head is one out of two, and if the coin is tossed the second time after coming up heads, the probability remains the same. Likewise, it can be predicted that if the coin is tossed 100 times, it is a mathematical probability the 100 tosses will result in 50 heads and 50 tails. This is a simple application of the theory of probability. There are many applications. For example, insurance companies rely upon theories of probability to compute mortality tables. Of course, a general treatment of this interesting subject is beyond the scope of this chapter. It will suffice to point out that given a relatively small number of injuries and a large group of workers, statisticians are able to compute a normal distribution of injuries among the group. This point has significance because it is apparent that many researchers, in assuming the existence of "accident proneness," have at times failed to compare the actual injury experience of their test groups with the normal distribution that would be expected if all individuals in the group were equally liable to injuries and pure chance determined who would be hurt how many times.

The fact that a head comes up on the first toss of a coin does not preclude a head appearing again on the second toss. Likewise, having one injury does not immunize a worker from having another injury. Thus, if accident liability is unchanged by injuries already had, some workers in a group may have two, three, or more injuries before others have any, without any of the theories of probability being violated. Nevertheless, in a group of 10,964 workers, 90 of them were labeled accident prone because they had had five or more injuries. The statistics from this particular study are found in Table 3–1.

TABLE 3–1

Workers		Injuries per Worker	Total Injuries
8189		0	0
1834		1	1834
550		2	1100
212		3	636
89		4	356
43	Total of 90 workers each with 5 or more injuries	5	215
26		6	156
14		7	98
3		8	24
3		9	27
0		10	0
1		11	11
0		12	0
10,964			4457

At first glance, it is not surprising that the 90 workers each with five or more injuries were identified as supposedly accident prone. By comparison with the 8189 workers having no injuries the 90 workers stand out. The statistics appear pretty convincing. But the picture changes when a statistician computes the normal distribution of 4457 injuries had by 10,964 workers, based on chance alone. A comparison of this computed theoretical distribution and the actual injury experience of the group raises some doubts that the 90 workers are all accident prone.

In computing a normal distribution of injuries based on a mathematical probability, it is assumed all workers in the study group have an equal liability to injuries. Admittedly, production workers actually do not have this equal injury liability. Working conditions vary, age and work experience vary, the calibre of supervision differs, and there is a variation in the amount and quality of job training received. Yet these variations do not preclude a comparison of the two sets of statistics in Table 3–2.

TABLE 3–2

Actual Injury Experience of Group, Number of Workers		Number of Injuries per Worker	Computed Theoretical Injury Distribution	
8189		0	8256	
1834		1	1698	
550		2	594	
212		3	237	
89		4	100	
43	90 workers	5	44	79 workers
26		6	19	
14		7	9	
3		8	4	
3		9	2	
0		10	1	
1		11	0	
10,964			10,964	

In Table 3–2, column 1, 90 workers had five or more injuries. As indicated in the third column, 79 workers would have had five or more injuries on the basis of chance alone. The difference in these two figures indicates that factors other than chance had their influence. The conclusion might be made that accident proneness accounts for the variation in the two figures. But why accident proneness? Would it not be reasonable to attribute the difference to such factors as temporary changes in working conditions, temporary changes in the mental or physical condition of the workers, the quality of supervision received, or the training previously received by the workers, etc. These are factors over which supervisors have some control. They provide a positive approach to accident prevention.

Psychological tests

Finally, assuming the 11 workers (90 minus 79) are accident prone, 0.1 per cent of the total work force—just who are the really accident prone among the 90 persons with five or more accidents? There is no clean-cut answer available. Numerous tests and a wide variety of methods have been suggested for detecting the accident-prone worker. To name a few, sensory-motor, manual-dexterity, mechanical-aptitudes, vocational-interests, emotional-stability, cultural-interests, intelligence, personality, eye, blood, and combinations of these tests have been recommended by various investigators as a means of predicting accident proneness.

Also, accident proneness has been associated with a person's credit rating, court record, visits to venereal-disease clinics, and acquaintance with social workers—with a revolt against authority, an unconscious need for punishment, a desire for sympathy, an estimation of unworthiness, feeble-mindedness, and uninhibited expressions of hostility. All these things cannot apply to any one person, and some of them can apply to all people. In short, nobody is accident prone or everybody is accident prone, at least part of the time.

Accident proneness not a fixed condition

Presumably, errors are being made in the identification of the accident-prone employee. Use of certain tests, including personality and interests tests, may actually be compounding this error. Interest and personality tests have limited reliability. Thus, a researcher using these tests is, in effect, attempting to identify accident proneness, a condition of nebulous description, with a measuring tool that has limited reliability. It is no wonder that the end result is one of confusion. Dr. Herbert H. Meyer and Joseph M. Bertotti bring the point concerning personality and interests tests into sharp focus with the following statement:

> Tests are used quite often to measure interests and personality characteristics. In these areas a great deal of caution must be exercised in interpreting test results. While interests and "personality" are usually important factors in determining job success, psychologists have not been as successful in developing valid measures of these characteristics as they have been in developing measures of abilities.
>
> The scale below presents a summary picture of the accuracy with which the different human characteristics can be measured. [See Exhibit 3–1.] As the scale shows, certain physical characteristics can be measured with a fair degree of confidence. As we proceed down the scale, we find that interest measures are less accurate, and, finally, personality traits can be assessed least accurately.
>
> One reason why personality tests generally do not provide valid predictions is probably the fact that personality "traits" themselves are not always highly consistent. Our personalities vary somewhat with situations in which we are placed. We are all "retiring" in some situations and "aggressive" in others. We may show great "perseverance" in one kind of activity and very little in another.

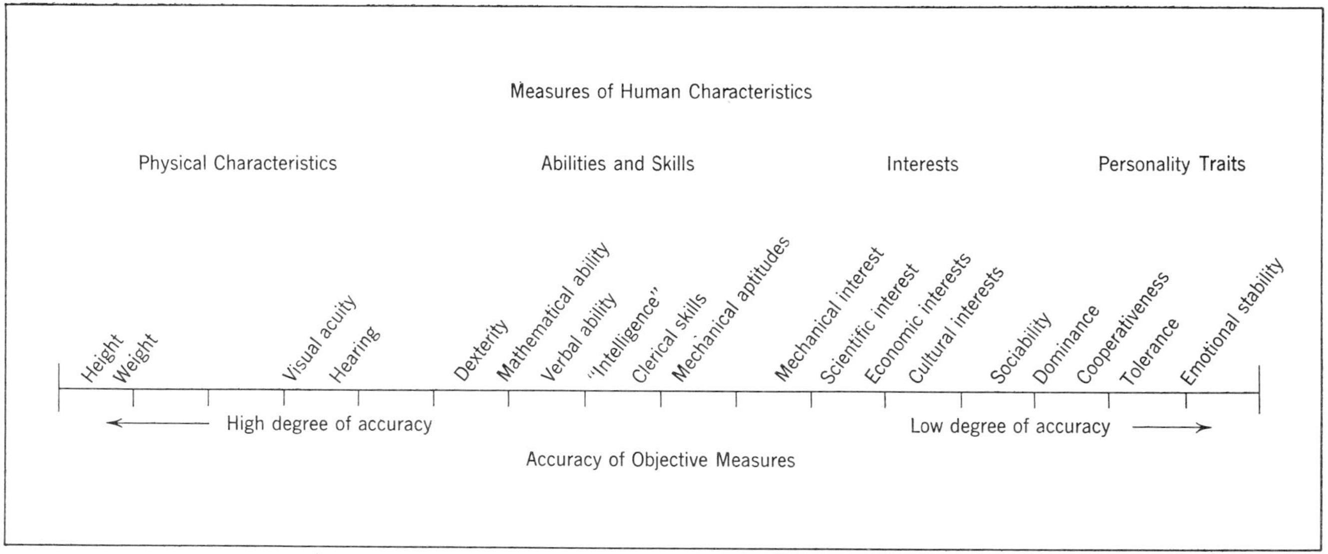

Exhibit 3–1. A scale indicating the relative accuracy of various measures of human characteristics. (Source: Herbert H. Meyer and Joseph M. Bertotti, "Uses and Misuses of Tests in Selecting Key Personnel," *Personnel*, November, 1956.)

Their closing remarks, which indicate that personality traits are not always highly consistent, have an appropriate relationship to a statement made by M. S. Schulzinger, M. D., Cincinnati, Ohio. Dr. Schulzinger has analyzed a consecutive series of 35,000 injury cases studied in private practice over a twenty-year period. These cases included 27,000 industrial injuries and 8000 non-industrial injuries. In brief, this is Dr. Schulzinger's conclusion:[1]

> The currently accepted theory that most accidents are sustained by a small fixed group of "accident prone" individuals is open to question. On the basis of clinical experience and studies, the writer suggests that most accidents are due to relatively infrequent solitary experiences of large numbers of individuals. The total number of accidents suffered by those who injure themselves year after year, over a period of three or more years, is relatively small. The frequently observed unequal distribution of accidents appears, among other things, to be due to the unequal liability to accidents to the basis of age and sex, to transient or prolonged states of physical, physiological or psychological stress, to chronic "accident proneness" and to chance. The evidence indicates that if the period of observation is sufficiently long, the "small group of persons who are responsible for most of the accidents" is essentially a shifting group of individuals with new persons constantly falling in and out of the group. It seems to be more nearly correct to speak of varying degrees of "accident-proneness" rather than of the presence or absence of proneness.

As Dr. Schulzinger points out, most people move in and out of the so-called accident-prone group depending upon age, mental and physical state, environmental factors, and other conditions that vary with the passage of time rather than remaining fixed with the individual. His study, and other like studies, pin-point factors that might increase the likelihood of an accident and deserve the attention of the industrial supervisor.

Psychological factors of safety

From Dr. Schulzinger's reports and the reports of other researchers, these conclusions are significant:

1. Young males have had almost twice as many injuries as young females.
2. More injuries are sustained in summer than in winter. The highest number occur in June, July, and August, and the lowest in February. (This conclusion may not hold for a particular plant or company; nevertheless, a fruitful area for investigation is suggested.)

[1] M. S. Schulzinger, *The Accident Syndrome,* Charles C Thomas Co., Springfield, Ill., 1956.

3. Accidents often occur in chain fashion, as if one injury acted as trigger mechanism for another injury or series of injuries to the individual or the group. (Many safety engineers have observed a chain-fashion occurrence of a particular type of injury. For example, a plant will experience a series of fractured toes or a succession of

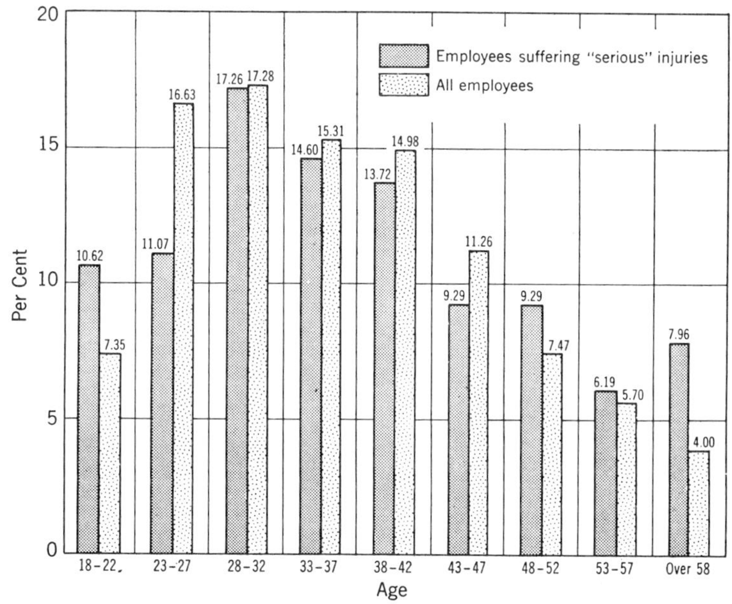

Exhibit 3–2. Age distribution of employees suffering "serious" injuries. (Source: Fred McKinnon and L. W. Smith, General Electric Company, Hanford Atomic Products Operation, Richland, Washington.)

hernias within a short period. There is no logical explanation for the phenomenon except perhaps that the unsafe condition or unsafe act that caused the first injury was not corrected.)

4. Youth is undoubtedly a factor which increases the likelihood of accidents. A statistical analysis of 227 serious injuries, those requiring extended treatment, has been made by Fred McKinnon and L. W. Smith, Hanford Atomic Products Operation, General Electric Company, which indicates that workers in the age groups of 18 to 22 and over 58 have more injuries than would be expected if age were not a factor. It is also interesting to note that workers in the age group of 23 to 27 had fewer injuries than expected. (See Exhibit 3–2.)

The statistical analysis also indicated that length of service and time of shift were factors influencing the occurrence of accidents which

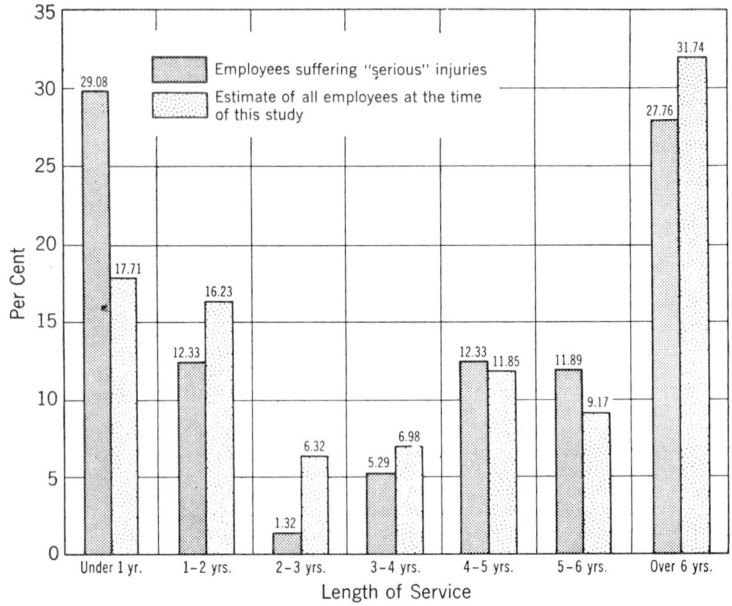

Exhibit 3–3. Distribution of length of service of employees suffering "serious" injuries. (Source: Fred McKinnon and L. W. Smith, General Electric Company, Hanford Atomic Products Operation, Richland, Washington.)

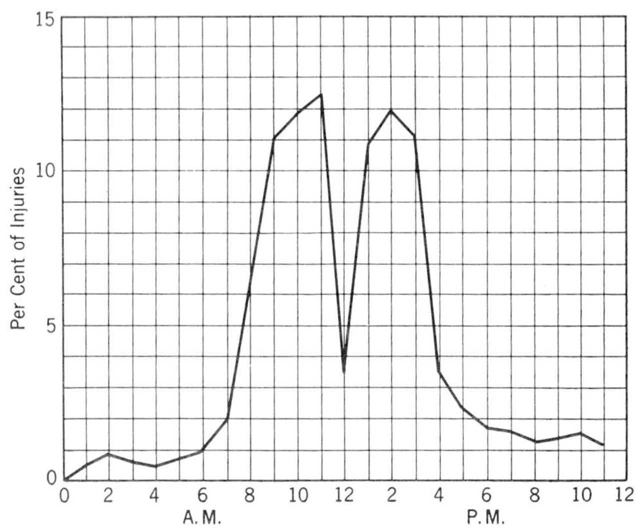

Exhibit 3–4. Time at which injuries occurred (data on 4348 injuries). (Source: Fred McKinnon and L. W. Smith, General Electric Company, Hanford Atomic Products Operation, Richland, Washington.)

result in injuries. Exhibit 3–3 indicates that workers have more than one and a half times as many injuries during the first year of service as would be expected. Exhibit 3–4 indicates that the time at which injuries occur comes pretty close to following a normal work curve. Peak injury rates occur at 10:00 to 11:00 A.M. and 2:00 to 3:00 P.M., on a first-shift operation.

The conclusions made in these studies provide significant guides for the industrial supervisor. These key points emerge:

1. Any attempt to control accidents by identification and elimination of the so-called accident prone would be of little value. Only a very small percentage, if any at all, of the population can be identified as accident prone.
2. Accident-prevention efforts should be intensified rather than relaxed during the summer months and during the third and sixth hours of an eight-hour shift.
3. More attention should be given to the indoctrination, safety training, and supervision of new employees in view of the high percentage of injuries that occur during the first year of service.
4. Efforts to improve on-the-job safety should be greatest in those areas where there are many young people, especially males.
5. To prevent the same type of injury from re-occurring, each injury should be investigated by supervision and immediate steps taken to correct the contributing and immediate causes of accidents.
6. Supervisors must be alert to radical changes in a worker's temperament and attitude, physical condition, and job satisfaction. Negative changes in any one of these factors might trigger an accident.
7. The physical condition and mental stability of a worker should always be a factor in job placement. Visual acuity, stature, sensitivity to certain chemicals, hearing ability, or physical deformations may affect a worker's ability to do certain jobs and therefore either increase or decrease the probability of an accident.

Many companies throughout the United States have achieved outstanding safety records. These excellent safety performances provide convincing evidence that elimination of the so-called accident-prone worker is not a material factor in future progress in the prevention of industrial accidents.

It would appear reasonable to ask, "Would the safety records shown in Exhibit 3–5 be possible if accident proneness were a problem in industry?"

Best No-Injury Records Known in Industry

The following list represents the best all-time no-injury records known to the National Safety Council. Each record consists of the number of continuous man-hours worked without a disabling injury. The list includes only the best record for each of the major industrial classifications.

Industry	Company, and Plant or Location	Man-Hours
Chemical	E. I. DU PONT DE NEMOURS & CO., Old Hickory Plant	28,743,768
Aircraft Mfg.	CONVAIR, San Diego, California	21,814,875
Electrical Equipment	WESTINGHOUSE ELECTRIC CORP., TV-Radio Div., Sunbury, Pa.	19,409,656
Communications	SOUTHWESTERN BELL TELEPHONE CO., St. Louis, Mo.	18,624,242
Machinery	INTERNATIONAL BUSINESS MACHINES CORP., Plant No. 2, Poughkeepsie, N. Y.	17,604,263
Textile	CHEMSTRAND CORP., Pensacola, Florida	15,156,411
Automobile	GENERAL MOTORS CORP., A. C. Sparkplug Div.	15,071,464
Tobacco	BAYUK CIGARS, INC., Philadelphia, Pa.	14,314,436
Sheet Metal	REMINGTON ARMS CO., Bridgeport Plant, Bridgeport, Conn.	12,701,206
Rubber	U. S. RUBBER COMPANY, Naugatuck Footwear Plant	10,250,040
Iron & Steel Products (Misc.)	REMINGTON ARMS CO., Ilion, N. Y.	9,152,494
Steel	BETHLEHEM STEEL COMPANY, Johnstown Plant	8,241,906
Petroleum	ESSO STANDARD OIL CO., Baton Rouge, La.	7,506,711
Foundry	UNION CARBIDE & CARBON CO., Haynes Stellite Div., Kokomo, Ind.	7,407,010
Glass	OWENS-ILLINOIS, Vineland Plant, N. J.	7,378,622
Leather	GENERAL SHOE CORP., Cowan, Tennessee	7,310,972
Construction	E. I. DU PONT DE NEMOURS & CO., Chambers Construction	6,732,783
Printing & Publishing	WESTINGHOUSE ELECTRIC CORP., Printing Plant, Trafford, Pa.	5,379,446
Cement	UNIVERSAL ATLAS CEMENT CO., Northampton Plant, Northampton, Pa.	5,333,434
Railroad Equipment	GENERAL MOTORS CORP., Electro-Motive Div., Cleveland, Ohio	5,294,960
Meat Packing	WILSON & CO., INC., Los Angeles Plant	5,051,451
Non-Ferrous Metals & Their Products	ALUMINUM COMPANY OF AMERICA, Alcoa, Tenn.	4,955,909
Food	SCHENLEY INDUSTRIES INC., Albert B. Blanton Plant	4,898,680
Electric Utilities	FALL RIVER ELECTRIC LIGHT CO., Fall River, Mass.	4,337,640
Service	BRUNSWICK LAUNDRY CO., Jersey City, N. J.	4,174,257
Pulp & Paper	DIXIE CUP CO., Easton, Pa.	3,770,076
Wood Products	CURTIS COMPANIES, INC., Clinton Division, Clinton, Iowa	3,634,107
Transit	HARRISBURG RAILWAY COMPANY, Harrisburg, Pa.	3,541,203
Gas Utilities	HOPE NATURAL GAS & SUBSIDIARY COMPANIES, Clarksburg, W. Va.	3,167,788
Air Transport	PHILIPPINE AIR LINES, Ground Operations	3,159,535
Shipbuilding	PHILADELPHIA NAVAL SHIPYARD, Naval Base, Philadelphia, Pa.	2,914,519
Clay Products	GLADDING, McBEAN & CO., Southern Division	2,887,000
Mining	PICKANDS MATHER & CO., Mahoning Mine, Hibbing, Minn.	2,875,085
Quarry	INTERNATIONAL MINERAL & CHEMICALS CORP., Florida Phosphate Div.	2,093,383
Marine	ERIE RAILROAD CO., Marine Dept., Jersey City, N. J.	1,525,140
Lumber	KOPPERS CO., Texas Wood Preserving Div.	1,128,357

Exhibit 3–5. (Source: *Accident Facts,* 1957 edition, National Safety Council, Chicago, Illinois.)

None of the companies listed in Exhibit 3–5 made a serious attempt to eliminate the "accident prone" from the work force, either before or after a bad individual accident and injury record. Of course, one reason for this is the lack of a reliable test or procedure for identifying the accident prone before employment. Also, assuming a bad accident record is made following employment, it is often impractical to transfer an employee from job to job. Union contracts, the employee's skills and interest, the unavailability of other jobs are all factors which would make it difficult to find a new job for an employee suspected of being "accident prone." Hence, it is highly reasonable to assume that good safety records can be achieved without any particular reference to the accident prone. It is not implied, of course, that the study of accident proneness is being ignored by progressive companies. Research is a normal function of medical and safety departments. Safety engineers and medical directors who are leaders in their fields have conducted numerous research projects in an effort to learn more about human behavior and the mental and physical characteristics of workers which might contribute to accidents. Much good has been gleaned from many accident-prone studies made by these competent people. Much additional knowledge is undoubtedly forthcoming.

But rather than considering "accident proneness" a constructive approach is to consider work habits and work attitudes which seem undesirable and then attempt modification, substitution, or elimination of such habits and attitudes through proper training (discussed in Chapter 4). A major source of work habits and work attitudes is the early experience of a worker on a new job. If job training is largely the result of trial and error, it is likely that several unsafe acts will become part of the normal job cycle. Thus, good job training dictates that the correct and the safe job method be taught the first few days a worker is placed on a new job. But supervisors can't stop here. Bad work habits of older workers must be replaced with good work habits. This is a harder job because habits once formed become difficult to change. Moreover, all of this training, no matter how good, will be of little value if the work habits and the work attitude of the boss does not conform to an acceptable pattern. This is true because work habits and attitudes of the boss have a way of transmitting themselves to the entire organization. Thus, in the formulation of good work habits and attitudes among workers, some changes in the work habits and attitudes of supervisors might be required. The first trap to avoid is not to lapse into traditional thinking that workers with three or more accidents are "accident prone."

SELECTED REFERENCES

Arbaus, A. G., and J. E. Kerrick, "Accident Statistics and the Concept of Accident Proneness," *Brometrics,* December, 1951.

Miller, H. Gene, "Accident Repeaters May Not Be Accident Prone," *National Safety News,* March, 1953.

Mintz, Alexander, and Milton L. Blum, "A Re-examination of the Accident Proneness Concept," *Journal of Applied Psychology,* Vol. 33, No. 3 (June, 1949).

Schulzinger, Morris S., "Accident Proneness," *Industrial Medicine and Surgery,* April, 1954.

———, *The Accident Syndrome,* Charles C Thomas Company, Springfield, Ill.

PART II

CREATING AND MAINTAINING SAFETY AWARENESS

CHAPTER

4

Personalized safety training

Modern job training has acquired another dimension —not only does an employee learn how to do a job but he learns how to do the job the safe way. He learns to recognize and to avoid hazards. It is useless to talk only in generalities about the need to be safe. Employees must be taught what to do and what not to do on an individualized basis if safety training is to be effective.

GLENN GRIFFIN
National Safety Council

Perhaps to better understand the need for a change in approach to present-day safety problems, a look at the past will help. Organized safety programs are not new. Early in the twentieth century, industry took positive steps to prevent accidents. At first, emphasis was on the elimination of physical hazards. Machine guards, safety devices, and personal protective equipment came into use. As a point of human interest, in 1912 a swing guard was installed on a kick press to protect the operator's hands. After the installation, a young girl factory worker remarked, "My machine is now almost human, for if I were to forget and leave my hand in the danger zone, I would not only be saved from injury, but likewise slapped on the wrist for my inattention." Three years later, the development of safety goggles was announced. The goggles had been designed with lenses of great "clearness" and "toughness" and with an elastic fastened to the goggles so they could be lifted and carried conveniently on the forehead. This latter innovation undoubtedly saved a lot of foreheads, but few eyes. Safety shoes, respirators, non-sparking tools, face shields, safety caps and hats, limit switches, and a large variety of safety devices are just a few of the developments in the last fifty years that have helped to eliminate or control physical hazards in the plant.

But it soon became apparent that just taking care of the physical hazards contributing to accidents was not enough. Attention was then directed to various training methods for the development of safety awareness. Slogans, safety posters, films, and safety booklets became a part of the accident-prevention program. "Personal Caution Is The Greatest Safe-Guard" was as popular forty years ago as "Be Careful, The Life You Save May Be Your Own" is today. Safety-poster subject matter has changed though. The hazards of celluloid collars, the extravagance of drink, the bad habit of spitting are no longer popular poster subjects. Likewise, safety messages and film material have progressed from the gruesome negative approach to the more pleasant positive approach used commonly today.

Mass safety training not adequate

Obviously, the various safety-training techniques mentioned constitute a mass educational approach to the plant safety problem. However, now there are indications that this mass approach may not be adequate. Many leading safety specialists will admit the conventional type of safety training cannot be expected to produce the same results in the next ten years as were produced in the last decade. Carefully conducted tests[1] reveal that some mass training methods, including class-room training and films, apparently have little effect on the frequency of injuries, especially in plants with good records. These studies reveal that mass or group training does help to maintain safety awareness, but group training does not become effective until each employee knows the hazards of his job and how to avoid them.

This means techniques must be developed so that each worker is told exactly what the hazards are on his job and is shown how to

[1] G. Roy Fugal, *The Relationship of Safety Education to Industrial Accidents,* Yale University Library, May, 1950.

avoid them. This means putting job safety training on a personalized basis as contrasted to the usual mass training methods commonly used. This approach will, of course, take more of the supervisor's time. But the increased time required pays off in continuous production, improved employee morale, and greater acceptance of the supervisor's leadership.

Group or mass training has a place in the complete safety program. However, accidents usually happen to people one at a time, so it would appear to be a natural step to carry the accident-prevention program to the individual employee one at a time, too. The advantages of the personalized approach are many. Hazards vary on each job and because of individual differences might even vary for employees on the same job. These individual differences can be considered if the safety training is personalized. Personalized safety training permits consideration of the worker's rate of learning, his interests, his natural ability, and his physical limitations. Personalized safety training can be specific. Group training must be general. The key to successful job safety training is *telling* the employee what the hazards are and *how* to avoid them. The evidence indicates that industry can cut total injury rates in half by using this personalized safety-training approach. This is so because a large percentage of industrial accidents are due to poor work habits and a lack of knowledge or skill about the job. Mass training tells what the hazards are—personalized training tells what the hazards are and *how to avoid them.*

Job-hazard analysis

Admittedly, the conventional mass approach to safety training takes little of the supervisor's time. Group training sessions, safety posters, films, and booklets are handled by the plant safety specialists or other staff people. On the other hand, where safety training is carried out on a personalized basis, the first-line supervisor must necessarily do the training. This will take more of his time and require more attention to detail, but this additional effort pays off because of the increased effectiveness of the training method. In launching a personalized safety-training program, the first step is the preparation of a job-hazard analysis for each job in the plant. To make the job-hazard analysis in an organized manner, a form similar to the one shown in Exhibit 4–1 is suggested.

JOB HAZARD ANALYSIS

Job Description: Three Spindle Drill Press - Impeller 84C6   Job Location: Bldg. 19-2, Pump Section

Key Job Steps	Tool Used	Potential Health and Injury Hazard	Safe Practices, Apparel, and Equipment
Get material for operation.	Tote Box	Dropping tote box on foot.	Wear safety shoes. Have firm grip on box.
		Back strain from lifting.	Stress proper lifting methods.
		Picking up over-loaded boxes.	Tell employee to get help or lighten load.
Inspect and set up drill press.	Drill Press	Check for defective machines.	Do not operate if defective. Attach red or yellow "do not operate" tag.
		Chuck wrench not removed.	Always remove chuck wrench immediately after use.
		Making adjustments when machine is running.	Always stop spindle before making adjustments.
Drilling		Hair, clothing, or jewelry catching on spindle.	Wear head covering, snug-fitting clothing. No loose sleeves. Avoid wearing rings, bracelets, or wrist watches.
		Spinning work or fixture.	Use proper blocks or clamps to hold work and fixture securely.
		Injury to hands--cuts, etc.	NEVER WEAR GLOVES. Use hook, brush, or other tool to remove chips. Use compressed air only when instructed.
		Drill sticks in work.	Stop spindle, free drill by hand.
		Flying chips.	Wear proper eye protection.
		Pinch points at belts.	Always stop press before adjusting belts.
		Broken drills.	Do not attempt to force drill, apply pres-

USE JOB HAZARD ANALYSIS CHECK LIST ON BACK OF THIS FORM.

Signature: James Black

Date: 4/22/54   Page: 1 of 3

(over)

Exhibit 4–1. (Courtesy of the General Electric Company.)

The key elements of the form are:

1. Job description.
2. Job location.
3. Key job steps.
4. Tool used.
5. Potential health and injury hazards.
6. Safe practices, apparel and equipment.

A review of the form will indicate the steps in making a job-hazard analysis. To start an analysis, the key steps of the job are listed in order in the first column of the form. Where pertinent, the tool used to perform the job step is listed in the second column. Then, in the third column opposite each job step the hazards of the particular step are indicated. Finally, in the fourth column of the form are listed the safe practices the employee must be shown and told, and the safety knowledge the employee must acquire. Here the supervisor lists the safe work habits which must be stressed and the safety equipment and clothing required for the job. In making the analysis, an organized approach is required so the less obvious accident hazards will not be missed. This means going out on the floor and actually watching the job being performed and jotting down key steps and hazards as they are observed. Supervisors who make such a job-hazard analysis are often surprised to find hazards in the job cycle they had missed seeing in the past. Thus, their original negative reaction to the thought of additional paper work soon disappears. In the long run, supervisors realize that proper hazard analysis will help them do a better training job.

As previously stated, a job-hazard analysis is made for each job. In most cases, each supervisor will have to make from five to ten different analyses. Of course, in maintenance and construction work, the variety of jobs will cover a much wider range. Fortunately, these jobs can be grouped by the type of work performed and a job-hazard analysis can be made for each category of work, rather than for each job. For example, repair, installation, relocation of equipment, cleaning motors, and unloading cars might be a few of the various categories of maintenance work to be analyzed.

The Supervisor's Guide to Job-Hazard Analysis which follows will provide a step-by-step procedure for planning a job-hazard analysis, making the analysis, and applying the results.

SUPERVISOR'S GUIDE TO JOB-HAZARD ANALYSIS

I. Three Basic Approaches:

A. Job-hazard analysis by machine or equipment.
B. Job-hazard analysis by jobs: assembly, welding, etc.
C. Job-hazard analysis by occupation: painter, steamfitter, carpenter, etc.

II. Suggestions for Making Job-Hazard Analysis:

A. Make a list of all jobs to be analyzed. Set a target date for completion of the jobs listed.
B. Analyze job while it is being performed and determine key job steps, potential hazards, and safe practices.
C. Make certain that potential health and injury hazards are described so as to indicate clearly the steps employees must take to avoid them.
D. Where safe apparel and equipment are designated, give detailed description.
E. Use check list on the back of the form as a reminder of things to be considered in making the analysis.

III. Suggested Use and Follow-Up:

A. Check analysis with employees to see if they can make any additions or corrections.
B. Have completed analysis checked by boss.
C. Go over completed analysis with employees presently on the payroll to make certain they understand hazards and means for protecting themselves against them. Always explain "Why."
D. Correct unsafe work habits. Use job-hazard analysis as a guide to train all new employees as well as present employees transferred to a new job.
E. Make analysis available so that employees may refer to it readily; keep a copy of each analysis.
F. Check employees' performance regularly to make certain that necessary precautions are being taken.
G. Make analysis of all new operations.

Job-hazard-analysis check list. In making a hazard analysis, a supervisor will use a check list to remind him to consider in his analysis such factors as: Clothing that would be considered safe for the job, the Protective Equipment required, Work Habits to be stressed, Health Hazards requiring explanation, and specific Work Rules that apply to the job. When a supervisor makes a job-hazard analysis, he is in effect studying each key step of the job in terms of things about the job that must be discussed with the employee to ensure safe job performance. Failure to cover even one or two factors, such as proper clothing for the job or the use of a dust respirator, might lead to an unsafe job performance. Hence, reference to a check list before making the job-hazard analysis should help set the stage for a complete coverage of the various safety aspects of the job, provided, of course, that each of the items contained in the check list is understood.

Although check lists should be tailor-made for each plant, some of the items contained in the check list shown in Exhibit 4–2 are of sufficient general application to warrant the detailed discussion which follows.

CLOTHING. For example, various types of clothing may be unsafe or unsuitable for certain jobs. Thus, points to be covered on clothing are included in the job-hazard-analysis check list. By referring to the check list, the supervisor is reminded that ties, long sleeves, and loose or baggy clothes would create a hazard around drill presses, lathes, and other equipment with exposed revolving parts. Girls may require safety caps to protect their hair. Jewelry, especially finger rings, constitute a real danger to machine operators. The handling of heavy objects may suggest the need for safety shoes. Fire-resistant clothing might be required because of high temperatures. Including pertinent points regarding proper clothing in the analysis provides a valuable reminder for the supervisor of points to cover during the actual job-instruction session.

PROTECTIVE EQUIPMENT. A worker handling rough bronze castings might need gloves to protect his hands. A drill-press operator, on the other hand, would face a serious hazard if he wore gloves. A new worker must be told about these hazards. A notation in the job-hazard analysis reminds the supervisor to cover such points in the job instruction. Likewise, the need for respirators, safety glasses, aprons, boots, and other protective equipment must be covered during the job training period. Where such equipment is required, a notation is made on the job-hazard-analysis form. But, it is not enough to just mention the need for protective equipment; supervisors must also explain the purpose and the function of the protective equipment. A demonstration of the impact strength of safety glasses, like driving a nail into a soft board with the glasses as a hammer, might help convince an employee the glasses really will protect his eyes. An explanation of the various types of respirators available and their purposes might help an employee put up with the discomfort such equipment creates. Also, if an employee understands the difference between

Job Hazard Analysis Check List

WHEN YOU MAKE A JOB HAZARD ANALYSIS STUDY EACH KEY STEP OF THE JOB IN TERMS OF THINGS ABOUT THE JOB THAT MUST BE DISCUSSED WITH THE EMPLOYEE TO ENSURE SAFE JOB PERFORMANCE.

TELL THE WORKER WHAT THE HAZARD IS AND HOW TO AVOID THE HAZARD.

Use this list as a reminder of things to be considered in your analysis.

WORK HABITS

LIFTING	HOUSEKEEPING
HOLDING	CARE OF TOOLS
WALKING	HORSEPLAY
SITTING	RUNNING

PROTECTIVE EQUIPMENT	HEALTH HAZARDS
GLOVES	SOLVENTS
RESPIRATORS	DUSTS
EYE PROTECTION	GASES
SAFETY SHOES	CHEMICALS

WORK RULES	CLOTHING
RED AND YELLOW TAGS	HEAD COVERING
NO-SMOKING AREAS	TIES, LONG SLEEVES
TREATMENT OF INJURIES	FINGER RINGS

WORKING CONDITIONS

(ARE THERE CONDITIONS LIKELY TO CAUSE ANY OF THE FOLLOWING TYPES OF ACCIDENTS?)

CAUGHT IN OR BETWEEN	STRUCK BY OR AGAINST
FALL TO SAME OR LOWER LEVEL	A CONTACT—ELECTRICAL CONDUCTOR, A CAUSTIC OR ACID, RADIOACTIVE PARTICLE, HOT OBJECTS, ETC.
AN ABRASION, LACERATION, OR PUNCTURE WOUND	
A SPRAIN OR STRAIN	

INCLUDE SAFETY INSTRUCTION IN ALL JOB INSTRUCTION

ALWAYS SET A GOOD SAFETY EXAMPLE YOURSELF

Exhibit 4–2. A job-hazard-analysis check list.

respirators, it is unlikely he will be found using a dust filter for protection against solvent vapors. This does happen.

HEALTH HAZARDS. Various solvents, dusts, and other chemicals might create conditions injurious to the health of employees. In many cases, an understanding of these health hazards is all the safeguard required. The check list reminds the supervisor to look for these hazards when he makes his analysis, and a notation reminds him to discuss the health hazard with the employee. Worker knowledge and understanding of the hazard becomes a built-in safeguard. Likewise, fire hazards and explosion hazards deserve an equal share in the discussion. What are the hazards? Where are the hazards? How can the hazards be avoided?

SAFETY RULES. It is easy to assume that a "No Smoking" sign on the wall and an arrow pointing to the dispensary are adequate instructions for the new employee. Cigarette butts under the "No Smoking" sign and the warehouse man who ended up in the president's office for treatment of a cut finger might be an indication that these matters need to be discussed in detail with new employees. Although the location of the dispensary and related subjects are usually covered in the employee-orientation session, just to be sure there is no misunderstanding, such matters should be reviewed in individual discussions with employees. It would be well for supervisors to keep in mind that plant safety rules will not be followed unless they are understood. Explaining the rules and telling the employee the reasons for them are a definite part of job safety training.

Making the job-hazard analysis. After a review of the check list, the supervisor is ready to go out on the floor and make a job-hazard analysis. His principal objective is to prepare himself to do a better training job—to include safety training in job training. The supervisor looks at the job in terms of the tools being used, the movements of the workers, and other conditions in the work area that might have a bearing on the performance of the job in a safe manner. Because some jobs might present hazards that are hard to locate, materials of unknown composition or in other conditions concerning the employee's safety, supervisors should not overlook the help available from the plant safety specialist, the plant physician, and outside sources. National Safety Council Instruction Cards, like the one shown in Exhibit 4–3, and National Safety Council Data and Detail Sheets, for example, are useful guides for supervisors.

In making the job-hazard analysis, the supervisor must strive to identify all of the hazards and conditions which ought to be covered in the job training. In addition to a study of the job as it is being performed, the supervisor will also find that a review of injury reports for his department will reveal the more illusive hazards. In planning the job-hazard analysis program, a logical place to start is with the jobs that have caused the most difficulty in the past—with the ones where the most accidents have occurred. Some target date should

DRILL PRESS OPERATORS

1. Use drills properly sharpened to cut to the right size.
2. Never attempt to hold the work under the drill by hand; clamp it securely to the table before starting the machine.
3. Run the drill only at the proper speed; forcing or feeding too fast may result in broken or splintered drills and serious injury.
4. If the work should slip from the clamp, never attempt to stop it with your hands. Stop the machine to make any adjustment or repair.
5. Do not leave the chuck wrench in the chuck.
6. Use a stick or brush to remove chips from the drill — never your fingers, cotton waste or a rag. File or scrape all burrs from the drill hole.
7. Be extremely careful when reaching around the revolving drill; wear snugly fitting clothing, and keep the sleeves short so they cannot catch in the drill. Wear a cap if your hair is long.
8. Do not wear gloves while operating the drill; if handling rough material use gloves only when the drill is not running.
9. Always stop the drill if you leave the machine.

SAFETY INSTRUCTION CARD No. 87

National Safety Council PRINTED IN U. S. A.

Exhibit 4–3. Instruction cards are helpful guides in making a job-hazard analysis.

be set however, for completing a job-hazard analysis for all jobs. To do a competent training job—to include safety training in all job training—the supervisors must know:

1. The hazards in each job.
2. The hazards in the work area.
3. The safety habits that must be taught.
4. The safety equipment required.

Adequate coverage of each of these four factors can be accomplished by using an organized approach to the problem—job-hazard analysis.

Retraining workers

The first step following completion of a job-hazard analysis is to retrain all workers presently on the payroll. It is best to set a target date for completion of this segment of the program, too. The objective is to review the job-hazard analysis with each worker. A good step prior to the review is to watch the worker go through the job cycle two or three times. What unsafe work habits has he acquired? During the review, the supervisor then makes a special effort to correct any unsafe work habits he has observed. This usually requires follow-up because acquired habits, good or bad, are not changed easily. At the conclusion of the review, the worker should be asked for his suggestions. Have any hazards been missed in the review? Is there a safer way to do the job? What additional safety equipment is needed? The job-hazard analysis can now be put into final form incorporating any suggestions that might have been received from experienced employees, the safety engineer, and outside sources.

The discussion to this point has covered a method for making a job-hazard analysis. A supervisor must know the hazards involved in each job in order to make his personalized safety training effective. In summary, there are four steps to remember:

1. Prepare for job-hazard analysis by reviewing a carefully prepared check list.
2. Go to the job and make a thorough safety analysis.
3. Review the completed analysis with workers presently on the job.
4. Make a job-hazard analysis of all jobs, any new job, and whenever a job method is changed.

Four steps have been reviewed above. The fifth step, the use of a job-hazard analysis as a tool for training all new workers, can now be discussed.

Integration of safety training and job training

In preparing the new worker or the worker transferred to a new job, the supervisor will appreciate that personalized safety training is best accomplished by the integration of safety instruction and job instruction. The problem of training the employee to work safely is not so much the act, for example, of teaching him to put on his safety glasses. It is more than that. There is the additional factor of establishing in the worker's daily conduct the *habit* of wearing his safety glasses. Supervisors must recognize that safe work habits, safe skills, and an understanding of the need for safety equipment and devices must be taught. To do a good teaching job requires adequate preparation (job-hazard analysis), patience, and diligence. Such training naturally takes time. Supervisors must discard the idea that employees can be prepared to perform their jobs safely and that the proper work habits will be acquired through the garden-variety "shot in the arm" job training that might be conventional.

During World War II, the Training within Industry Division of the War Manpower Commission sponsored a ten-hour Job Instruction Training Program. The many supervisors who had an opportunity to take the course will recall a four-step method of job instruction.

1. Prepare the worker.
2. Present the job.
3. Try out the performance.
4. Follow up.

By an organized and a planned approach to job training, supervisors found that the quality of their job instruction improved, it took less time in the long run to complete the training, and employees were doing a better job. Good job instruction is essential to safety. Hence, the four-step method of training is an important part of personalized safety training. In effect, all that is required is an adequate integration of safety training with job training following the prescribed four-step approach.

Preparing the worker

During the first step in job training—preparing the worker—the supervisor can take the opportunity to tell the worker about the safety equipment required for the job, like safety glasses, safety shoes, respirators, gloves, and so forth. An effort can be made to convince the employee that the safety equipment is necessary. The purpose and the function of the safety device can be explained. The location of the dispensary and fire equipment and the procedure for getting first-aid can be covered.

Especially where a new employee is involved, the initial warm-up period can be used to determine the employee's attitude about safety. Does the new employee think safety is something that is good for the *Other Fellow?* Does he think accidents occur because *Your Number Is up,* because of *The Law of Averages,* or because most people are *Accident Prone?* These negative beliefs must be purged. The supervisor must demonstrate a constructive and positive faith in the basic principle which characterizes all accident-prevention work—*accidents are caused and they can be prevented.* A strong desire in the mind of the employee to work safely must be developed.

Presenting the job

In the second step of the job instruction—presenting the job—the supervisor (The Boss) sets the style. Here, the sincerity and the thoroughness of the job instruction is important. Here, the employee is told the hazards in each step of the operation, and how to avoid each hazard. As the supervisor demonstrates the job, he is careful to perform each step exactly as he wants the new employee to repeat it. If safety glasses are required, the supervisor wears safety glasses. If gloves are required, he wears gloves. Thus, the employee sees his new job performed exactly as it should be. It is during this second step of job instruction that safe work habits are taught. At times the instruction must become detailed. For example, safe methods for holding an object, grasping a handle or part, walking, sitting, and lifting must be taught. No detail should be regarded as unimportant. At times the apparently trivial detail causes the most trouble. It may be the grip on the chisel that saves a skinned knuckle, the use of a hand rail that prevents a fall. Illustrated in Exhibit 4–4 are a few of the thousands of different hand operations Du Pont workers perform each day. Outlined in black is the safe method which employees are painstakingly taught. In gray is the wrong way. Arrows indicate danger points. This approach to personalized safety training can be duplicated in other industries and on hundreds of jobs.

The method taught for cranking the old Model-T Ford is a good example of *telling* what the hazard is and *how* to avoid it. The fact that so many supervisors still remember the safe method of grasping the crank handle with the thumb extended may be an indication of the effectiveness of the personalized-safety-training approach. Some supervisors may also recall that a firm footing and a strong arm against the radiator were also necessary to keep the Model T from running over the man at the crank. These simple safety suggestions were followed because the benefits could be seen—a broken arm was a dramatic indication that the rules had not been followed. Unfortunately, in many situations where safe work habits must be taught, the benefits are less obvious. Failure to follow the safe method for picking up a piece of paper might result in just a small cut, or an improper lift in a backache. These injuries are not so drastic as a broken arm; hence, the benefits of teaching proper methods for picking up an object or lifting may not be immediately apparent either to the employee or to the supervisor.

The extra time required to teach an employee to avoid a minor injury might appear not to be worthwhile. But minor injuries are a large part of the accident problem. The brief, to-the-point instruction "Pick up the tote box" might appear to be adequate directions to a new worker with normal intelligence. But is it? Actually most people must be taught to lift properly. There is a natural tendency to lift with the weaker back muscles. Therefore, instead of telling the new worker to "Pick up the tote box," the alert safety-conscientious supervisor goes into more detail. He teaches the proper methods for safe lifting. He shows the new worker how to use the stronger leg muscles, how to keep the back straight. He says, "Be sure to have a firm grip." "Don't lift an over-loaded box; get help." This is personalized safety training. This is integration of safety training and job training. After the training session, the worker knows what the hazards are and how to avoid them. Nothing has been taken for granted.

The personalized-safety-training approach when applied to all jobs provides employees with convincing evidence that supervisors are sincerely interested in safety and in the personal welfare of each em-

IN FEEDING moving machinery, trick is to avoid dangling fingers, most frequent cause of accidents. Employee is taught to hold fingers together.

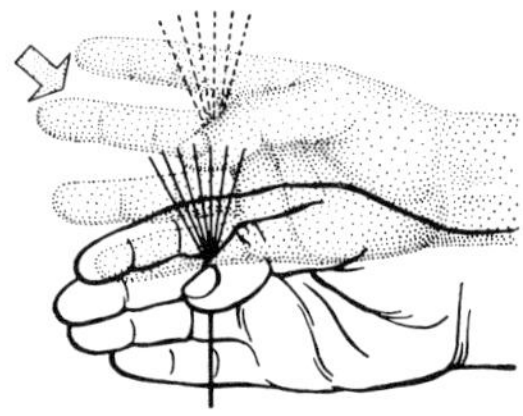

IN THREADING nylon yarn over guide before it enters steam conditioner, operator keeps fingers together. Spread out, they may touch hot parts.

IN PUSHING bobbin-filled carriers, employees are taught to turn knuckles inward to avoid the danger of scraping them against walls, other obstacles.

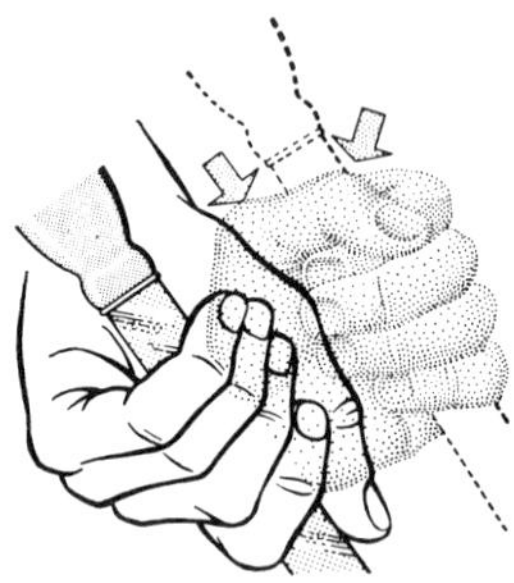

IN HOLDING chisel to be hit by hammer, thumb should be down and away from striking hammer. Heel of hand is fleshier, can take punishment better.

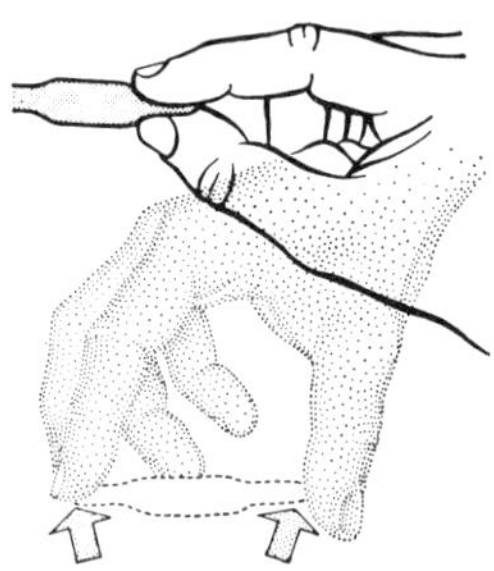

IN LIFTING paper wrapping for dental X-ray film, fingers should converge from top and bottom. Grasping edge produces painful paper cuts.

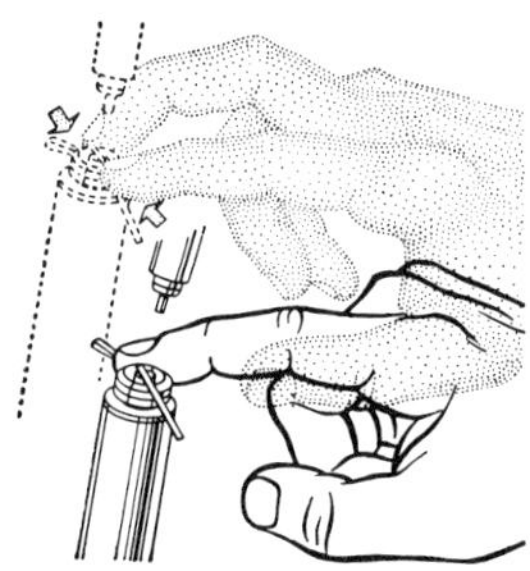

IN STEADYING wire for shaping by plunger in coal-blasting device, one-fingered jab is called for. Natural impulse to use two causes trouble.

Exhibit 4–4. No detail should be considered too trivial for inclusion in the job safety-training session. For example, using an incorrect method to grasp a sheet of paper could be a source of numerous minor but annoying finger lacerations. (Courtesy of E. I. du Pont de Nemours and Company.)

ployee. In addition, the employee is helped to realize that safety is an important matter to his company and of value to himself.

Trying out the performance

After an adequate presentation of the job including all of the safe habits that must be learned and the safety rules that must be followed, the supervisor is ready to *try out the performance.* He should keep foremost in his mind his goal to make working safely a matter of habit. Improper methods, movements, and positions should be corrected promptly. If not corrected, any unsafe method that creeps into the job cycle can become a matter of habit. Once a habit has formed, it is difficult to break.

A supervisor may feel that if he tells a man what he is to do and how he is to do it, and then gives him a demonstration, that the training job is complete. Unfortunately, this is not generally the case. The learner's ability to pay attention, his interest in the new job, his knowledge of shop terms and shop customs, the breadth of his experience are all important factors which determine the amount of instruction he will absorb. Hence, the need for a careful try-out of the job cannot be passed over lightly. Two factors predominate in the learning process: the competence of the instruction and the amount of the instruction retained by the learner. At times, because of the instructor's familiarity with a job, he over-estimates the quality of his instruction. Points that appear simple and obvious to the instructor are vague and baffling to the learner.

The situation is somewhat like the story of the young boy in Poughkeepsie, New York, who was asked for directions to the IBM plant. He knew the exact route to the plant, but his directions went like this: "You turn left at the next traffic light, then drive down the road about two miles, and turn right three blocks before you get to the cemetery." These directions appeared clear and easy to follow to him, but how was a stranger in the city to know when he was three blocks from the cemetery? A supervisor's instructions, on the other hand, might be letter perfect with each detail carefully and adequately covered. He may feel any person of normal intelligence ought to be able to follow them. If this is the case, let him recall what happened the last time he stopped at a gas station and asked for directions. Chances are the attendant was able to give perfect directions. "Turn around and go back to the third stoplight and turn left. Drive five blocks to a big A & P super market and turn left again. Drive north on route No. 92 until you come to an underpass. Go to your right in front of the underpass and you will be on the turnpike." These directions are simple enough, but Mr. Supervisor soon realizes that about the only thing he remembers is to turn left at the third stoplight, or was it turn right?—so he stops at the next gas station and asks directions again.

The trouble was that Mr. Supervisor had not had an opportunity to try out his performance. The attendant had not asked him to repeat the instructions, and he was too embarrassed to admit that he had not followed such simple directions. To make the personalized safety training complete, the supervisor makes sure the worker has retained all of the key job points and key safety points by asking the worker to give them back to him. This part of the job-instruction process must be done with patience and tact so that the worker will not become embarrassed or confused. The supervisor must avoid showing annoyance even after repeating a part of the job several times. He keeps repeating until he is sure the worker has got it.

The follow-up

After a thorough try-out of the job performance, the supervisor is ready to put the employee on his own. The job-hazard analysis has made it easier for him to include safety instruction in his job instruction. The employee has been taught to do the job the safe way, the right way. But putting the employee on his own does not mean the training job is ended. Following the preliminary job instruction, some checking back or follow-up is necessary for these specific reasons.

1. To make sure the job is being done the right way, free from any short cuts that may reduce quality, increase cost, or lead to injury of the employee.
2. To cover any safety details that may have been missed in the original instruction such as plant safety rules and hazards in the work area, and to review safety booklets and instructions.
3. To make sure that changes in the operation or the surrounding area have not created new hazards for the employee.
4. To check the new employee's adjustment to his surroundings. Is he happy, free from pressure, fears, or distractions that might lead to an accident, reduce quality, and increase cost?
5. To call changes in the job or the work area to the employee's attention.
6. To make sure the worker has not developed any physical limitations that make it difficult for him to do the job in a safe way.
7. To *make sure the employee fully understands the "why"* of the job method and the safety rules which apply to the job.

The foregoing long list of reasons for a follow-up on safety and job instruction might imply an additional burden for the supervisor. Actually, the follow-up can be made a part of the supervisor's regular job. It can be included with other duties and can work as a valuable aid in achieving quality production at low cost and with freedom from accidents. Two cases illustrate the great need for good job instruction including personalized safety training and an adequate follow-up.

In a metal-working plant, a press operator was instructed by his supervisor on the use of two push-button controls to operate a blanking press. At the time of the instruction, the part being blanked rested securely in the die without being held by the operator. However, two weeks following the original instruction, the engineering department changed the design so that an extension was welded on the part before the blanking operation was performed. This extension made it necessary for the operator to hold the part in the die. Thus, only one hand was free to trip the press. By "astute application of his imagination and creative ability," the worker solved the problem by operating one push button with his head and the other with his free hand. After about three hours of this novel head-and-hand operation, the operator decided it would be easier on his head to "use his head" and tie down one of the push-button controls. The new technique worked well until the operator got his hand in the die zone and lost a finger. Follow-up would have prevented this weird chain of events.

In a chemical plant, a conscientious worker was instructed to dip steel plates in a water tank—to an acid tank—to a water tank—to a cyanide bath—and again to a water tank. The supervisor made a careful check to make sure the process was carried out in the proper order. He failed, however, to explain the important reason for the water dip between the cyanide and acid baths. The end result was a tragic accident. Several weeks later the operator got behind the production line, and to save time, he omitted the one important water dip. Hydrocyanic acid fumes were formed by the combination of cyanide and acid. The operator and two co-workers almost lost their lives. If the supervisor had spent just a few extra minutes explaining the reason for the water dip between the acid and the cyanide and the consequences if the dip were missed, the accident would have been avoided. Telling "How" is not enough. Workers must also know "Why."

Finally, in the follow-up, supervisors can take the opportunity to praise workers for their progress, to give encouragement, to stress specific phases of safety, and to get suggestions from the worker for improving the operation.

Conclusions

Industrial safety training is often thought of in terms of meetings, posters, safety booklets, films, special classroom sessions, and some safety contacts by safety specialists and supervisors. The intent of these various training techniques is to develop safety awareness. It is presumed that by exposure to these various training techniques employees will learn to sense the existence of unsafe practices and unsafe conditions and will avoid them voluntarily. However, carefully conducted tests reveal that employees may be lectured on safety, shown excellent safety films, attend safety conferences, and be supplied with the best safety booklets available, yet they fail to apply these safety messages to the actual work situation. Obviously, there are weaknesses in these so-called mass educational methods. Such education, which, of necessity, must be of a general nature, leaves interpretation and application of specific items up to the individual. Unfortunately, the necessary transfer from the general to the specific does not occur. Hence, there is a great need for personalized safety training which permits the conversion of safety generalities into specific safe practices that apply to a specific job and to the individual doing the job.

There is no restriction on the use of personalized safety training. The approach is applicable to all industry. It can be used with equal success in large and small companies, in utilities and mines, railroads and airlines, manufacturing plants and logging camps, offices and retail stores. Personalized safety training helps improve the worker's attitude about his job. The approach stresses work habits required for safe job performance. It spot-lights hazards and unsafe movements and positions. It substitutes safe acts for unsafe acts. Employees learn *what* the hazards are and *how* to avoid them.

Teaching employees to work safely on a personalized basis leads to improved production performance and fewer accidents. Companies using a personalized-safety-training approach are reporting highly satisfactory results. One large company credited a 65 per cent reduction in total injury rates to its personalized-safety-training program. A utility company in the East, after one year of personalized safety training, achieved a frequency rate of three disabling injuries per million manhours as compared to thirty-three in the previous year. In addition to the good reduction in injury rates and the elimination of pain and suffering, supervisors point to other gains. Often preparation of the job-hazard analysis leads to job-methods improvement, to the elimination of bottlenecks, and to improved plant layouts. A general manager became an enthusiastic supporter of personalized safety training when an increased production rate and a reduction of spoilage occurred with a 50 per cent reduction in his total injury experience. Other gains include an improved supervisor-employee relationship and a greater employee interest in safety activities. Personalized safety training is just one more practical and fruitful approach to good employee relations.

These gains, of course, must be considered in the light of the total situation. It may not properly be concluded that all the gains were due to personalized safety training. Certainly, there were other factors operating which might well have had some influence. No safety program can be successful if it is built on a single function like training or good housekeeping. Results are always much more satisfactory when an effective job is being done in all areas—the development of safe working conditions, the enforcement of safety rules, the promotion of employee safety participation, and persônalized safety training. The climate for success is right when the training process embraces all the elements that contribute to the successful control of accidents.

SELECTED REFERENCES

Fugal, G. Roy, "Reducing Industrial Accidents," *Harvard Business Review,* July, 1951.

Griffin, Glenn F., "Instructing for Safety," *Supervisors Safety Manual,* National Safety Council, Chicago, 1956.

CHAPTER 5

Promoting employee safety participation

The problem is to impress indelibly on the mind of the individual that there is a standard, safe way to carry on most activities. Once he has learned the safe way and follows it, the battle is won. To adopt a standard way of performing a task, we must first develop a desire to adopt it. It is one of education's first aims to develop socially desirable attitudes.

HENRY T. HEALD
The Ford Foundation

Faulty safety attitude, inattention, lack of interest, worry, and impulsiveness are the triggers that set off many accidents. An employee might work in an environment filled with hazards without getting hurt just as long as his attitude about safety remains good and he makes it a matter of habit to remain alert. On the other hand, a worker who has a faulty safety attitude might soon become another injury statistic even in the safest environment. Thus, another key to the success of the safety program is to develop in each worker a "safety awareness" which replaces a faulty attitude about safety. This might mean changing an employee's attitude about safety and his responses to various accident-producing situations. This is a problem in communication.

Safety communication

When safety communication is discussed, there is a tendency to conclude that the employee doesn't know what's what about accident prevention and, therefore, he should be told. But good safety communication is more than a process of conveying information to the employee either orally or in writing. It is not so much what has been said, but rather how people interpret what they have been told. A person absorbs information about things he has an interest in and he interprets information on the basis of his own estimate of the situation.

Therefore, an understanding and appreciation of the communication process will help supervisors deal more effectively with the human factors involved in accident prevention. Just telling the employee what's what about safety is not the answer. Good safety communication must be regarded as a process which changes attitudes and influences behavior by the "whole meanings" that are conveyed by words, actions, expressions, personalities, and moods. Thus, a first requirement is a proper climate for the communication.

It is easy to assume, in talking to people, that the words we use are all that matters. But most of the time the listener reacts to many things besides the spoken or written word. The effectiveness of a safety talk or a safety instruction is dependent upon many factors. For example, it would be a waste of time to start a safety talk with the comment, "The Personnel Department told me to give you this five-minute safety message." Immediately, the supervisor conveys to his audience that the safety message is not his idea. This is something he was told to do and the sooner he gets it over, the better. Likewise, a safety discussion in an untidy, crowded, and hazardous shop would be a verbal exercise; only minimal results could be expected. In a communication situation, the worker responds to what he thinks about the supervisor and about his place of employment. Therefore, past supervisory actions, the implied attitude of supervisors toward safety, the manner in which supervisors follow safety rules, and working conditions all operate singly or in combination to affect the meaning of and the response to a safety message. It is, of course, impossible for a supervisor to take into consideration every angle of good communication every time he talks to a worker or to a group of workers. If, however, supervisors become a little more communication conscious and regard some of their safety problems as problems in communication, they may find that workers will become a little more cooperative about safety.

A supervisor, in planning his communication, can take into consideration several basic factors that underlie employee attitudes. There is a need in all people for a sense of importance, for a sense of belonging, to gain recognition, to participate, and to acquire knowledge. Supervisors are aware of these needs, but they may not be aware of how much these needs influence employees' actions. People, because of their need for a sense of importance, like to have the boss greet them. They like to talk about knowing important people. Conversely, they dislike orders that seem arbitrary and comments that are disrespectful of their individuality, dignity, and feelings. A need for a sense of belonging motivates employees to form social clubs and promote recreational activities, to join unions. Likewise, the need for recognition accounts for the club pin in the coat lapel, the request for a dignified job title, and even the show-off tactics resorted to by some to attract attention. Finally, people like to know what's going on around them. They want the whole story. They want to have a part in the various activities which are related to their jobs.

By being sensitive to some of these basic human needs, the supervisor can do a better job of planning a safety talk, giving a safety instruction, and selling safety. Most supervisors have encountered difficulty getting employees to wear safety glasses or to stop running in the plant. Under such circumstances, it is easy to conclude that the employees are either stubborn or stupid since the safety glasses and the rule about running are for their own protection and well-being. Again, taking into account the full process of effective communication, the supervisor may be overlooking two basic human failings—people resent criticism and resist change. Supervisors must realize that employees are responding to the safety instruction in terms of the meaning the total situation has for them. They are letting their own feelings, not what they hear, determine their attitude and their actions.

Resentment of criticism

It is human nature to resent criticism. When the next-door neighbor asks, "What do you think of my lawn?" he doesn't expect an honest answer. He just wants to be told the lawn looks good. He wants to fortify his decision not to cut the grass. Hence, when he is told,

"Your lawn is filled with crab-grass, and it needs mowing," he goes on the defensive. He starts making excuses like "The next-door neighbor's yard is filled with crab-grass" and "I want to repair the lawn mower before I use it again." This natural resentment of criticism is just as strong in the factory as it is at home. Even the slightest comment made by a supervisor to an employee may be taken as criticism even though the supervisor had no intention of being critical. Hence, in giving safety instructions, pointing out a hazard, or explaining a new safety device, it is well to avoid a comment, tone of voice, or inference that is likely to be interpreted by the employee as criticism. This does not mean, of course, that constructive criticism should be avoided when there is provocation for such criticism. However, communication should not be taken too much for granted. Little will be accomplished if the net effect of the communication tends to arouse emotions or create resentments. An adult employee might resent, for a number of reasons, being told not to run in the plant. He might regard such a simple and obvious instruction as a reflection on his intelligence. The old-timer might think to himself that anyone with an ounce of good sense would know better than to run in the plant, so "Why are they telling me not to run?" Individual resentment might run even higher when employees are told for the first time to wear safety glasses. Some employees will resent being thought not to have demonstrated good judgment by asking for the safety glasses before being told to wear them. Others will feel that having worked for so long a time without wearing safety glasses, they are being imposed upon by being told to wear them now. There is no pat answer to how these and similar situations should be handled. In some cases, individual discussions may be the answer. In other cases, group discussions will be more effective. Hence, each supervisor must appraise the problem in light of existing conditions: his knowledge of the work group and the proper time, place, and method for the communication. His own attitude, his sincerity, and the example he sets will do much to produce a satisfactory response.

Resistance to change

As previously stated, a supervisor who is communication conscious realizes that an individual's response may not always be to the actual situation, but to an evaluation of what is seen in the situation. Consider, for example, the loud protest and emotional upset of window washers when it was announced that a New York City law would require them to wear safety belts. They didn't protest because the installation of window hooks would cost building owners thousands of dollars. They didn't protest because the belts were heavy and created an inconvenience for them. Their response was fired with emotion. The fact that the safety belts were for their personal protection was of secondary importance. Even the high fatality rate among window washers meant little. What the window washers saw in the belts was a threat to their security. A safety belt for window washers would take the danger out of the job. Therefore, it was assumed, less skilled people could do the work. The response of the window washers was based on their evaluation of what they saw in the situation for themselves. Their emotional response and their behavior stemmed from a natural tendency to resist a change or to resist something new. This is a characteristic of human nature supervisors must cope with daily. The trait is not new. It is found everywhere. In 1872, an editor of a large daily newspaper let the world know that he too could exercise the human right to resist the new. This editorial appeared in a morning paper:

> A man about 46 years of age, giving the name of Joshua Coppersmith, has been arrested in New York for attempting to extort funds from ignorant and superstitious people by exhibiting a device which he says will convey the human voice any distance over metallic wires, so that it will be heard by the listener at the other end. He called the instrument a "telephone" which is obviously intended to imitate the word telegraph and win the confidence of those who know of the success of the latter instrument. Well-informed people know that it is impossible to transmit the human voice over wires.[1]

Ambitions, motives, interests, and feelings are not so easily recognized that a supervisor can always know what goes on in the minds of workers. What a worker thinks, how he reacts might change from hour to hour depending upon the constantly changing environment which surrounds him. Life would be pretty uninteresting if this were not the case. But the important point is to recognize that any attempt to satisfy even the basic human needs presents many complex problems. Problems, incidentally, that usually cannot be solved by the pat formulas, the panaceas, and the pseudo-psychologies that are sometimes presented as the key to every problem in the gamut of human relations.

Workers do not always respond the way a supervisor might expect. For example, painting a work area light, attractive colors, installing modern equipment, and installing air conditioning should usually promote a favorable employee response. But not always. A man who

[1] Used by Alan Mogensen, Work Simplification Conference, Lake Placid, N.Y.

is worrying about how he is going to make the payments on the new washer and the car without missing a payment on his home might regard a large expenditure made by his employer to renovate the plant as a threat to his chances of getting an increase in pay. Instead of being pleased about the plant being air conditioned, he complains about a draft on the back of his neck, which he claims was created by the new air conditioner!

Whole volumes could be written on the subject of the necessity to everyone of maintaining a feeling of personal worth and the responses which result when the feeling of worth is placed in jeopardy. At Alan Mogensen's Work Simplification Conference in 1948 and again at General Electric's Advanced Management Course in 1956, Dr. Lillian Gilbreth told a story of a methods improvement her late husband, Frank B. Gilbreth, had made at a factory where an ironing operation was part of a production job. The story is another evidence of the role played by the emotional resistance to change.

Mr. Gilbreth had an unquenched enthusiasm for analyzing job methods and making improvements. Hence, as he walked through the factory he was quick to notice the unproductive and exhausting method being used by a robust middle-aged woman to iron large linen sheets. To iron each sheet she had to pick up and set down a heavy iron several times. Obviously, the job was one of the more exhausting tasks in the shop—just hard, hot work. Mr. Gilbreth set out to improve the job, to make it easier. After the regular work day, he, with the assistance of a mechanic, rearranged the work place and rigged a combination of overhead pulleys which made it possible to attach a counterweight to the heavy iron. The new set-up lightened the task of lifting the iron. The Gilbreths were sure the factory worker would be pleased to find her job so much easier to do. Now she would not be so tired at the end of the day. But to the contrary, the ironer was not pleased at all. As a matter of fact, within an hour after arriving at work the following morning, the robust ironer was visibly upset as evidenced by tears and complaints. Why? Before the job change, she had had great pride in her job because she was the only woman in the factory with the strength and stamina to do the job for a full day. The one factor which distinguished her in the work group was gone. Her feeling of personal worth had evaporated. Now she was just another worker and no longer distinguished by an ability to do a job no one else could do. Her resistance to a change had expanded to explosive proportions.

In 1881 when typing lessons were announced for women, a vigorous protest was made on the grounds that the female constitution would break down under the strain. Fulton's steamboat, Chrysler's first streamlined cars, short skirts, long skirts, mass production, automation have all been resisted because they represented a change. Everyone becomes satisfied with things as they are and resists change because he is not sure how the change may affect him.

This excursion into the background of the resistance to change and the resentment of criticism has been taken because it may indicate to supervisors and others how powerful a factor they have to deal with in these two common but sometimes ignored human traits. Resistance to change and the resentment of criticism are real although, at times, the behavior which results might not appear logical. Hence, when a safety instruction suggests a change, reflects on past conduct of the work group, or fails to satisfy one of the basic human needs, it is likely the employee will not respond to what he hears. Rather, his feelings, what he sees in the situation for himself, will govern his reactions. A safety message or safety instruction must be planned and presented so the response will be favorable. Here are a few pointers:

1. Resistance to change increases with the magnitude of the change and it is inversely proportional to the time required to make the change. Therefore, make big changes in little steps and announce the change well in advance so it will not come as a surprise. A small chemical plant took six months to install a 100 per cent eye-protection program. Because employees had been doing the same job for several years without safety glasses, it was a foregone conclusion that resistance would be high. It would have been natural for employees to think they were being imposed upon by being told to do something which in their minds was unnecessary. Careful planning made the eye-protection program click.

2. Make sure safety instructions are understood. Tell the whole story. Give reasons. Get employees to give their point of view, and don't ignore employee suggestions.

3. Create interest in the safety program by recognizing the safety efforts of employees and by giving employees a definite part in the program. This approach brings double benefits. It contributes to the satisfaction of the employees and it makes it easier for the supervisor to gain the cooperation of everyone in the work group.

Employee safety committees

Employee participation in the accident-prevention program is a factor in the development and retention of worker safety awareness.

A person does not learn to play golf or swim by reading a book or listening to a lecture on the sport. It takes actual practice to reach even a moderate degree of competence. It is a basic principle that people learn "by doing" and their interest is increased when they are taking an actual part in the activity. So it is in safety; employee participation in the accident-prevention program stimulates interest and enthusiasm for the various safety activities. Where safety participation is properly promoted, it becomes an *X* factor which produces outstanding results in the control of accidents and the improvement of employee attitude toward the supervisor and the company. Therefore, supervisors can help themselves by evaluating the various methods for promoting employee safety participation and then using a method which will produce maximum results for them.

When the need for employee participation in the safety program became apparent, more than thirty years ago, one of the first approaches was to organize employee safety committees. Such committees are still a part of many successful safety programs. It is not surprising, therefore, that in most discussions on safety organization, employee safety committees are recommended. Proponents claim these committees enlist safety activity at all levels of the organization, promote employee self-education in safety, and generate greater employee interest in plant safety activities. There is no doubt that in many plants and businesses the safety committee has been a worthwhile part of the accident-prevention program. However, supervisors should not be content to accept employee safety committees as a necessary part of the safety program just because of past successes. Industry has gone far in the reduction of accidents, but there is still far to go in many places. Change well might be a part of future progress.

Some companies, in planning for the future, have substituted for their employee safety committees new techniques for promoting employee safety participation. However, a change was not made just for the sake of change alone. Management philosophies, organization structure, and supervisor-employee relationships have changed considerably since organization of the first safety committees. Top management, in viewing these changes, recognized the need for a plant safety set-up that would be consistent with current management concepts and organization structures. A study of employee safety committees revealed certain limitations. In some cases, the existence of the employee safety committee was actually limiting employee participation to a few employees, and supervisors were ducking their safety responsibility by referring most accident-prevention matters to the committee. Because of the committee, the line of communication on safety matters was more often between the committee and other employees than between supervisors and workers. Then too, management reasoned that it was not necessary to organize committees to discuss and handle production, quality control, spoilage, and cost matters—so why was it necessary to have a committee to handle safety problems? After all, the same supervisory skills required to solve production problems could logically be applied to safety problems. And finally, a review of the minutes of several employee safety committees provided convincing evidence of the shortcomings of the employee-committee set-up. These were the shortcomings discovered:

1. In many plants it was discovered that only a small percentage of the total work force had ever served on the employee safety committee. Often, appointment was made on an annual basis. At the end of the year, for the sake of convenience, the same people were re-appointed.

2. Meetings of the committee were frequently canceled for a variety of reasons—poor attendance, conference room being used by the sales department, too many members away on vacation, behind schedule in production, etc.

3. Members of the committee were irregular in attendance.

4. Items appearing in the safety-committee reports included: coat hanging on fire extinguisher in Building A, no lids on trash cans, basement needs cleaning, barricade needs painting. Obviously, the committees were spending a lot of unproductive time discussing housekeeping items which could have been corrected long before the meeting was held.

5. Frequently, when items appeared in the minutes which would require a large expenditure, they would appear for several months, then would be dropped without any action having been taken. Less costly items like a sign for an acid tank would appear in the minutes several times before action was finally taken.

6. Rather than initiate corrective action immediately, committee members would avoid reporting unsafe conditions until a safety-committee meeting was held. This would give them something to talk about at the meeting.

Where employee safety committees are promoting full employee participation in safety, enlisting employee safety interest, and helping supervisors to win greater acceptance of their leadership, the committee set-up, of course, should be retained. However, if safety-committee activities have become routine and non-productive, it is time for a change. Where the change is made, supervisors can take a personal interest in the matter. Various methods for promoting employee participation can be evaluated and the present safety-committee organization[2] converted to a useful function.

Union-management safety committees

Any discussion of safety committees is likely to initiate a question concerning the practicality of union-management safety committees. Many of the shortcomings of employee safety committees would apply also to union-management safety committes. But, in addition, there are other reasons why such safety committees are not an appropriate solution to the industrial safety problem. Where such committees are used, responsibility for establishing safety policy, making safety appraisals, and administering the safety program is divided between management and the union. Therefore, when management is trying hard to fix responsibility for safety, it may be found that union-management safety committees provide an easy way for supervisors to duck their responsibility for safety and that responsibility is avoided by the committee too. Hence, in view of the modern concept that supervisors must have full responsibility for safety, it would appear advisable not to use union-management safety committees. Although such safety committees appear inadvisable, this does not mean the safety activities of a union are limited. Some unions have recognized the inherent weaknesses of union-management safety committees and have agreed to disband them. However, these unions are still taking an active part in and giving full support to the plant safety program. They promote safety in their union meetings, in their publications, and in other contacts with their members. They encourage the full use of personal protective equipment. They recognize the need for sound safety rules, and they do not impede or harass management when the need for disciplinary action arises. Although it would be basically unsound for management to share its responsibility for safety (and undoubtedly a union would not want to share the cost of accidents), management does need the full cooperation of everyone in its efforts to make the safety program fully successful.

If any further confirmation is required of the assertion in this chapter that there are certain limitations inherent in safety committees, it may

[2] The type of employee safety committee which has been discussed consists, in general, of a group of workmen selected from several sections of a plant with a supervisor as chairman and the plant safety engineer as secretary of the committee. Most of the employees on the committee do not report to the supervisor who is chairman. Membership is usually on a rotating basis.

be found in an authoritative and thoughtful analysis of committees made by David T. Mould, Safety Director, General Motors Corporation. In examining the character and function of union-management safety committees, Mr. Mould draws on years of industrial safety experience with a variety of safety programs in a vast number of operations. General Motors has an outstanding safety record; but, like many companies, they are trying hard to improve the record each year. Even in their plants with excellent safety records, they are doing everything they can to make the record better.

Hence, there is no doubt that if the use of safety committees would assure greater safety progress, the corporation would advocate them. The following is an excerpt from Mr. Mould's address, "Management's Responsibility for Safety," presented before the National Safety Congress, Chicago, Illinois, October, 1948.

One advantage of having a large number of plants and of operating these plants on a decentralized basis is that over the years we have had an opportunity to gain experience in the operation of various types of safety programs. Some of our plants have made use of safety committees—both unionized plants and plants which were not unionized.

This experience has proved to our satisfaction that the methods we use to provide an opportunity for our employees to cooperate actively in the safety program are more effective than the committee method.

Further, we believe it is fundamentally wrong for management to evade even in part the obligations and duties it must assume for the safety of employees by sharing them with others. It is quite proper to enlist the cooperation of all employees—union and non-union alike. But it is not sound to try to shift to the employees or to the union, through so-called *joint* committees, responsibilities which are inherently management's.

In connection with placing responsibilities where they belong, here is an important point which is perhaps too frequently overlooked. Under the terms of union agreements, the union has the right at all times to challenge management actions pertaining to matters covered by the agreement. That is as it should be. The union must be in a position to exercise its proper function—representing the interests of employees, through all the steps of the grievance procedure if necessary, when an employee feels that he has been unfairly treated. This right of the union should not be prejudiced in any way.

In our judgment, much of the confusion in this whole area of labor-management cooperation on safety has resulted from a failure to distinguish between this basic right of *challenge,* which should always be retained unimpaired by the union, and those requirements for joint *agreement,* which are so frequently advocated by proponents of the joint committee approach as the answer to all safety problems.

In our judgment you simply cannot start out with the premise that safety is a management responsibility—and that the union should retain the right of challenge—then turn right around and require joint agreements on safety policies, joint determination of safety rules and joint determination of disciplinary measures. Such concepts are mutually exclusive. Where you have management responsibility for safety, you cannot have a requirement for joint agreement. Where you do have a requirement for joint agreement, you simply do not have management responsibility for safety.

In General Motors, management is responsible for establishing safety policies, and is responsible for working out reasonable safety rules and regulations.

For example, there is no provision that union agreement must be obtained to a rule requiring the employees on grinding operations to wear approved eye protection. On the other hand, safety policies and safety rules and regulations are not adopted arbitrarily. They reflect the experience of the men who are most familiar with the operations concerned. And this, of course, includes the employees who work on these jobs. To gain employee acceptance and respect they must be reasonable. They cannot be arbitrary or capricious. But when it comes to the final determination as to what the rule is to be, that responsibility rests with management.

When there has been an infraction of a safety rule, it is management's responsibility to take the steps necessary to maintain discipline. This again is not a matter for joint agreement. In our judgment, joint establishment of discipline would be grossly unfair to the employee and equally unfair to the union which represents him. In other words it is not right to ask the union to don black robes, and agree on the verdict, then have them make a quick change and appear in the court room as attorney for the defense.

If any employee in General Motors feels that he has been unjustly treated, he has full opportunity to take the matter up directly with his foreman or to resort to the provisions of the grievance procedure under the union contracts. The union in turn has full power to represent him in carrying his grievance through the various steps of the grievance procedure up to and including the impartial umpire. In General Motors the impartial umpire has full discretion in questions of discipline.

In a case involving discipline the burden of proof rests with management. If the impartial umpire decides that we have failed to sustain the burden of proof, he has the power to reinstate the employee and grant him full back pay.

Think this through for a minute. Had the union been a party to the establishment of a safety rule, had it been a party to the joint determination of the penalty to be imposed for the infraction of that rule, how then could it, in good faith, represent that employee in protesting the disciplinary action taken? When a union becomes a party to disciplinary action, it then surrenders, by that very agreement, its right to challenge.

Not only individual employees in General Motors have an opportunity to offer suggestions, advice, recommendations and cooperation on the improvement of safety. The union, as such, has a similar opportunity. Union representatives may take up safety matters directly with supervision in the plant, or they may bring their suggestions, advice and complaints to management in the regular Shop Committee meetings. Our records show that, week in and week out, unions do bring up safety matters for discussion in our plants. Union suggestions, recommendations or complaints submitted in these meetings are taken seriously by management. Immediate action is taken where the facts warrant it.

In view of this discussion on employee safety committees and union-management safety committees, the value of management safety-policy committees, advisory safety committees, special technical safety committees like an electrical or a chemical safety committee, and safety-inspection committees might also be questioned. If production, cost, quality, and other supervisory responsibilities are handled by committees, then it is reasonable to conclude that these various safety committees are worthwhile. However, if all other subjects are handled by management at regular staff meetings of supervisory personnel, it would appear advisable and practical to handle safety in the same manner. It is recognized that even under favorable circumstances, committees have definite limitations. Such group action takes more time and is more expensive than individual action. There is no one person responsible for results. Undesirable courses of action are sometimes approved because of friendships involved or the popularity of one member of the committee. Individual initiative is stifled. And finally, members are not always qualified to discuss the wide variety of subjects and problems referred to the committee. Assuming employee safety committees are disbanded, how then may employees participate in the safety program?

Supervisor safety contacts

If there is any basis for the success of employee-safety-participation programs, it is in the emphasis placed upon the safety relationship between the supervisor and employees. A supervisor's contacts with employees on safety matters must be frequent to keep alive the employee's interest in safety. But there is much evidence which indicates that these safety contacts are minimized unless some formalized program or pattern exists for making such contacts a part of the supervisor's job. It is, of course, understandable that these contacts might be put off, especially when the safety record is good. For example, the manager of a Midwest plant was a little surprised following a plant survey which was made to determine the frequency of supervisor-employee safety contacts. Here is what he discovered:

Case 1. Male employee, Age 39—First-shift freight-handler.

Remarks. This man was unfavorably impressed with the safety talk in the employment office. He said, "The girl who regularly makes talks had a sore throat. Her substitute gave a brief talk mostly on insurance. There was little said about safety." His foreman did not give him any safety instructions. The foreman promised to discuss safety in the management informative meeting to be held in six weeks.

Case 2. Female employee, Age 22—Second-shift assembler.
Remarks. This girl recalled several things she was told about safety in the employment office. Her foreman did not discuss safety with her, but another girl on the same job told her one thing about safety she remembered. This was to hold her left hand so it would be clear if the sharp steel wedge slipped when it was pushed into the assembly. In spite of this precaution, she had injured her hand.

Case 3. Male employee, Age 32—First-shift heat-treat-oven operator.
Remarks. This man remembered safety being part of the employment-office talk. He had read a small part of the employee safety booklet. He received job instruction from the day-shift operator. He was told not to smoke. He received no further instruction in safety. He had been with the company four years.

Perhaps a similar check in many plants and businesses would reveal that these case histories are typical. If so, the matter of supervisor-employee safety contacts takes on added significance. Many companies with outstanding safety records have found that personal safety talks between the supervisor and the employee are an important part of the entire safety program. These daily safety contacts help to create safety awareness. They make it easy for the supervisor to make personal contacts with employees, and provide the employees with an opportunity to make safety suggestions and to bring up any problems they might have on their minds. In turn, the supervisor is able to determine each employee's attitude about safety and to take action where necessary.

To keep these safety contacts on a continuing basis, some companies make it a practice to have each supervisor talk about safety with each of his employees individually at least once each week or on some other regularly scheduled basis. This safety-discussion program can be carried out on a formal basis with a record being maintained of each employee contact. The form used for recording purposes in the General Motors Central Foundry is shown in Exhibit 5–1. Of course, the program can be conducted without the record system. However, some occasional check-up seems important to keep the program from lagging.

Employee safety meetings

Supervisors must persuade individual employees that, to a large extent, their safety depends upon their own actions, their individual alertness, and their ability to avoid hazards and unsafe practices which might lead to accidents. The development of adequate safety aware-

CENTRAL FOUNDRY DIVISION
GENERAL MOTORS CORPORATION

Plant__________

RECORD OF SAFETY TALKS WITH EMPLOYEES

Dept.__________ Shift_____ Week__________

Is the Safety of Your People Worth Ten Minutes of Your Time Each Day?

NAME	CLOCK NO.	DAY OF MONTH																														
		1	2	3	4	5	6	7	8	9	10	11	12	13	14	15	16	17	18	19	20	21	22	23	24	25	26	27	28	29	30	31

I have talked about safety to each employee listed for five minutes on the day checked.

SIGNED__________

Exhibit 5–1. A supervisor in the General Motors Central Foundry is required to talk to at least two employees daily regarding safety policies or safety practices. A record of each contact is maintained by placing a check mark in the appropriate date. column opposite the name of the employee contacted. (Courtesy of the General Motors Corporation.)

ness is a long step toward a successful safety program and the control of accidents. Personalized job safety training teaches the employee the hazards of his particular job and the way to avoid them. But, safety training cannot stop after the initial job training; it must be conducted on a continuing basis. In addition to supervisor safety contacts with individual employees, many companies have found that meetings between a supervisor and a group of employees are an effective means of promoting employee participation in safety and maintaining safety awareness. Recent studies tend to indicate some hidden strength in group meetings that may have been overlooked. Supervisors have reported reductions in their accident rates following a series of group meetings. These meetings were effective because of the mass appeal involved. Enthusiasm for safety was aroused by the catalytic reaction between employees promoted by the mere fact that they were meeting in a group for a single purpose.

Frequency of safety meetings. The difference between a successful and an unsuccessful supervisory-conducted safety meeting is the degree of sincerity and personal interest in safety demonstrated by the supervisor. A good public speaker, a fancy meeting room, elaborate props are not needed to make a safety meeting click. A short meeting held right on the job or in a corner of the plant with packing cases and nail kegs for chairs can produce highly favorable results. The main ingredients are something worthwhile to talk about and a supervisor who is conscientious and sincere about keeping his work group free from accidents.

Working conditions and the magnitude of the accident problem should determine the frequency of safety meetings held by supervisors. In general, the meetings should be held on company time and no less frequently than once each month. Some informal schedule for holding meetings needs to be established. A requirement to hold one or two meetings each month with the actual dates selected at the discretion of the supervisor provides a practical approach. The important point is to establish some pattern so employees will expect and look forward to the next meeting. Supervisors, by all means, should avoid the practice, which has been followed in a few cases, of holding a safety meeting only after a bad accident. This is worse than no meetings at all. When meetings are held, all employees need to be included. This will pose a problem on a continuous production line, but usually with a little ingenuity a solution can be found. Staggering the attendance at the meetings so only one-third or one-half of the group has to be away from the job might be the answer, or, if practical, stopping the line for fifteen to twenty minutes. Workers who are stationed at scattered locations can be called together shortly after the beginning of a shift or just before quitting time. The utility companies solved the problem of where to meet by holding what they call tail-gate meetings. Supervisors get their men together back of the line trucks for short safety meetings in some cases as often as once

Exhibit 5–2. Tool-box meetings to discuss job safety are held without fail on Monday morning for fifteen minutes at every du Pont construction project across the United States. (Courtesy of E. I. du Pont de Nemours and Company.)

a week. Construction companies take a similar approach. They hold "tool-box" safety meetings.

Subject material for safety meetings. Safety meetings held by a supervisor for his own work group provide excellent opportunities to demonstrate the supervisor's personal interest in safety and to emphasize company safety policies. Each meeting should be held with a definite objective in mind—to explain a new safety rule or procedure, to review a recent accident, to discuss the company and department accident record, to establish a key safety point. Planning should precede the meeting. What does the supervisor want to say? What is the best way to cover the subject? Will charts, models, gimmicks, posters help make the meeting a success? What key question should be used to get the work group to participate? The matter of getting employees to speak up is important to the success of the meeting. There will be greater acceptance of the safety program when workers know they have an opportunity to express their personal opinions and if they feel their suggestions will be considered.

Selection of good subject material which will be of direct interest to those attending the meeting is of vital importance. The supervisor in the larger plants can look to the plant safety engineer for help in preparing discussion topics. In plants without a safety man, assistance may be obtained from the personnel supervisor or a staff assistant. But, regardless of the source of material, the topic should have a pretty close relation to the work being done, the work area, and to the workers. Generalities should be avoided. The safety meeting will have served a useful purpose if the material covered can be applied to the worker's job or if the interest and enthusiasm aroused by the meeting motivates employees to give safety their personal attention all of the time.

Being sensitive to the desires and needs of employees, the principles of communication, and the two human failings resistance to change and resentment of criticism will always help the supervisor conduct a good safety meeting. For example, the introduction of a personalized safety-training program might mean something new for a lot of people. Workers might resent being retrained to do an old job. They may wonder just what is meant by personalized safety training. One supervisor anticipated resistance to this new training technique, so he called a safety meeting to describe the program to his work group. He realized his initial remarks would do a lot to minimize his problems. Here is what he said:[3]

You have a well-fed look, even if you are having a late lunch today. I'll bet you haven't missed many meals in your lifetime. Well, speaking of missing, you haven't missed your mouth either, at least not since you can remember, because you've become an expert in the use of this tool. [He holds up a table fork.] Oh sure, an occasional spot of gravy on a nice new tie or on your best suit, but you're such an expert that you can perform amazing feats with this fork and never give it a second thought. You can look at someone across the table from you and unerringly guide a forkful of food to your mouth—you can read the newspaper at breakfast and completely consume your bacon and eggs without a conscious thought

[3] A safety talk by R. F. Bowen, General Foreman, General Electric Company, Louisville, Ky.

of what you are doing—you can even close your eyes and never miss. How you handle it doesn't matter—you can use the firm grip shovel method, the conventional method or the left-hand pile on delivery backwards method, but there's never a doubt that your aim will be true.

Let's examine this fork a little closer: the handle for gripping, the perfect balance, these tines curved to exactly cradle your food with the least chance of spillage, the points for picking up pieces of meat or vegetables. Even the sides can be used for cutting the more tender pieces. Wait a minute, what did I say back there? The points—say, they look pretty dangerous. They could gouge your eyes or scratch your nose or puncture you in any number of places if you weren't skilled in its use.

Were you always so skilled? You've watched a baby make his first attempt to use a fork. I'm sure you agree that your skill has been acquired. Mother has trained you well.

How did she accomplish this training? She gave you a little spoon which she taught you to hold, helped you to fill it and helped you to guide it to your mouth. After many, many guided efforts, she let you try it alone—the result? Well, think back to that child—food in his hair, all over his face, down his front, all over the floor—but Mother was patient. Back she went to filling and guiding and again you were put on your own until gradually you got more food in you than on you. Then came the training with the fork. The points were duller than these, but a hazard still existed and Mother was alert to it as she taught you how to use it efficiently and safely. The same routine was followed in helping you and guiding you, and, with practice three times a day through the years, you developed this amazing skill in using a tool as hazardous as this fork.

That was safety training! The same kind of training that each of us must have to work safely. Rules, posters, signs, campaigns, guards and all the other gimmicks that make up a safety program are useless without the individual safety training of each employee *on the job*. Patient teaching of the fundamentals, careful guiding in your first efforts, daily practice in the safe routines required to do the job are the only answers to becoming skilled in working safety. That's why, in the next few weeks, I plan to make a safety analysis of every job in our section. I need your help. You may know of some job hazards I would miss. After the analysis is complete, I will review it with each of you. If, in the past, you have acquired some unsafe work habits we will work out that problem together. I'm sure I can anticipate your cooperation because we will all benefit by this program.

It is a well-known fact that people respond more favorably to a new device or a change of any kind if they have had some opportunity to express their own feelings and to interchange ideas. A safety meeting is likely to produce good results if there has been some advanced planning, if the supervisor knows beforehand what he wants to say and how he plans to say it. In the above example, there is little doubt that the meeting produced the desired results. The approach very likely promoted employee interest and employee acceptance of personalized safety training.

Safety key points instead of details

Personalized job safety training is detailed. Specific hazards of each job are identified. Workers are taught specific safe work habits. Beyond job training, a lot of safety education has involved the teaching of a multitude of general safety details. A survey of safety booklets in use today will lead one to conclude that an attempt is being made to describe, ahead of time, every hazardous situation that could possibly develop. As a result, the number of general safety details found in employee safety booklets has become so voluminous that it is not possible for an employee to remember even a small portion of the safety material he receives. Then too, some of the subject matter is dry and uninteresting. What, for example, could be less interesting to read than a safety booklet with fifty separate instructions each starting with either a "Do" or a "Don't"? In contrast, a copy-writer in the advertising department takes one or two key points about a product and in all of his copy features these points in short, catchy phrases. Finally, the product becomes associated with a slogan like "The Pause That Refreshes" and "L.S.M.F.T." It is reasonable to conclude that the same approach could be used successfully in safety booklets and posters, in safety meetings, and in supervisor-employee safety contacts. Thus, instead of general safety details, basic safety key points would be used as subject matter. Instead of having hundreds of details to remember, each person would have available certain safety key points that could be used to evaluate a situation from a safety point of view. This approach recognizes the individual responsibility each worker has for his own safety. Because a supervisor cannot anticipate every situation which might lead to an accident, each worker would be taught to evaluate new situations in terms of what he must do to avoid an accident. A set of safety key points would be used as guides. Then the goal for each supervisor would be to stress these key points over and over until their application to any given situation would become a matter of habit. Here are some suggested safety key points that might be included in a supervisor's safety talk and stressed in safety posters and in booklets:

1. *Make it a habit to pause a moment to size up the situation before acting.* Little children are taught to count to ten and look both ways before crossing a street. This, in a sense, helps to create a habit of pausing before acting. But with children the approach may backfire unless carefully explained. Take for example the little girl who said, "Daddy, when I stop to count to ten, I have to run across the street to keep from getting hit." It is important to emphasize the purpose of the pause. The extra second is used to appraise the situation; this will reveal the hazard that otherwise might be missed. The pause is the caution light. The United States Steel Corporation uses an award-winning sound motion picture[4] in its plant and community accident-prevention campaign which is somewhat in line with this approach. Because people sometimes seem to do things which are against their better judgment, the film stresses that knowing how to prevent accidents is not enough. In addition, each person must have a built-in sense of caution, like the yellow flag used at auto race tracks. This built-in caution flag protects against four factors that block out safety awareness. These factors, Improvising, Impatience, Impulsiveness, and Impunity, are pin-pointed in the film by dramatic examples. By pausing before acting, the influence of these four factors can be minimized.

2. *Always assume that the situation may have changed.* The tendency is to take the opposite point of view and assume that conditions have not changed. Hence, people land hard on the floor when a chair is moved from behind them, husbands trip over tea tables when the furniture is rearranged, and at least once in a lifetime almost everyone tries to walk through a closed door. These apparently foolish accidents could not have occurred if the victims had not had their safety awareness blocked by the false assurance that the situation was still the same. The possibility of change had not crossed their minds. They fell into the "I didn't know the gun was loaded" category. Thus, the key point here is, "Keep your guard up and check for change."

3. *Make it a habit to evaluate personal feelings, undue mental stresses, and a weakened physical condition in terms of possible causes of accidents.* Unfortunately, most people do not have control over their daily work schedule. For example, the machine operator is compelled by his need for a day's pay, his loyalty to the company, or the force of habit to report for work in spite of the worries which might burden him, a weakened physical condition, or a hang-over. But just knowing that these sub-normal conditions might lead to an accident will help. The employee can alert himself to stay on guard against mental lapses throughout the day. The supervisor, noticing an unusual change in the attitude of the employee or the weakened physical condition, might take steps to at least minimize the risk involved. A safety contact, a word of encouragement, an expression

[4] *Knowing Is Not Enough,* a sound motion picture produced for the United States Steel Corporation, Pittsburgh, Pa.

of interest or concern could be the *X* factor that prevents an accident.

4. Avoid the point of no return. The swimmer who goes so far out into the lake that he is unable to swim back has gone beyond the point of no return. A motorist passes the point of no return when, because of existing conditions and his speed, he no longer has personal control of his car. The number of auto accidents, especially rear-end collisions, attests how often motorists pass the point of no return. If each person were to make an appraisal of his daily working and living habits, it would come somewhat as a surprise the number of times a life is placed in jeopardy because there is no return. Therefore, for the sake of safety, it must become a matter of habit to avoid situations in which all personal control has been relinquished. Closely related to the case in point is the phrase, "Always be prepared for the unexpected."

5. Look for a second line of defense. The backfield in a football team is a second line of defense. When the opposing ball carrier cracks through the line, a backfield man is expected to stop the play. A similar approach in daily living can provide an extra factor of safety. A handrail on the stairs is a second line of defense. The rail is not actually needed to get down the stairs safely, but it is there in case of a trip or fall. Older people use the rail religiously because they have some doubts about their first line of defense, their equilibrium and sure-footedness. Using a set of blocks in addition to a jack when working under a car, using a net under a bridge, and using safety belts, life lines, and the steel toe cap in a safety shoe are other examples of a second line of defense. In most cases these secondary defenses do not actually stop the accident, but they do stop or minimize injuries. Often a second line of defense is nothing more than an appraisal of what can be done if an accident should occur. For example, a carpenter before he starts to work on a pitched roof can decide what he will grab in case he slips. If nothing is available, a rope or other means of stopping a fall can usually be provided. In New York City two elevator-installation men were saved from death because whenever they worked at a height they habitually made a note of what to grab for in case of a fall. Without safety belts or nets they were working twenty-one floors up at the top of a building installing elevator cables. They had hung five cables in the elevator shaft and were in the process of installing the sixth when somehow the cable gave way. Both men plunged head first down the shaft. Their pre-determined second line of defense was the cables which had been secured previously. At the seventeenth floor one man caught a cable and swung himself swiftly sideways and to safety on the flooring at that level. The second man got his legs wrapped around a cable and slowed his fall. But he was still going down head first. Somehow he managed to grab a second cable with his hands and partially righted himself. He landed heavily on his side at the bottom of the shaft, saved by a pre-determined second line of defense. There is usually a second line of defense available in any situation. The point is to make it a habit to use it.

Undoubtedly, these five key points are not new to supervisors, but it is a good bet most employees have not been taught to use key points to evaluate a situation in terms of their personal safety. Of course, even without teaching, most of the key points are used, but by stressing them at every opportunity it can become a firm habit for everyone in the work group to apply the principles more often. However, for such stressing of key points to be effective, employees must get the big picture. It is not enough, for example, to have employees memorize "Pause before You Act." The principle must be dramatized with examples which show how the key points are applied to an actual situation. Discussion of actual accidents can be used to demonstrate how use of one or more of the key points would have prevented the accident or minimized the injury. Employees can be asked to suggest other principles of safety which apply to their work, and to cite examples which show how they have applied the key points. Thus, by planned discussion, by repetition, and by examples, the key points will take on a broad, clear meaning.

The safety-observer program

Inasmuch as the supervisor is responsible for safety in his department, all action on safety should be channeled through him. In keeping with this concept, supervisor-employee safety contacts on an individual basis and in group meetings have been suggested as desirable methods of promoting employee participation in the safety program. In addition, employees can also be encouraged to submit safety suggestions through the formal suggestion system if there is one. This latter activity is one that produces a good employee response when well promoted in the plant newspaper, in posters and bulletins, and by the tactful urging of supervisors.

It is a well-known fact that most people desire some form of recognition. Receiving an award for a safety suggestion would, for example, be a form of individual recognition, but this recognition would be fleeting and affect only a few people. Another good method for providing employees with individual recognition for their safety efforts and personal identification with the safety program is the appointment by supervisors of employee safety observers, safety representatives, or safety aids. Of course, it is a specific duty of supervisors to develop safe working conditions and to promote safe practices. However, where the operation is scattered, covers a wide area, or contains a large number of employees, it would be difficult for the supervisor to accomplish this alone. Teamwork and cooperation of employees are necessary. A safety-observer program can be used to help promote safety teamwork. An observer program is another method for promoting employee safety participation. Many companies are reporting a great deal of success in using this approach. Paul R. Thomson, Manager, Employee and Plant Community Relations, General Electric's Industry Control Department, Roanoke, Virginia, is enthusiastic about the use of an employee safety-observer program to promote employee participation in safety activities and to provide employees with satisfactory recognition. Mr. Thomson's interesting account of the Industry Control Department participation program follows:

Our Employee Participation Program is based upon having each supervisor select an employee to act as safety observer for one month. Each month, approximately 90 different employees are given the opportunity and the responsibility of participating in our department Safety Program.

Shortly after an appointment is made, the newly-selected safety observer is invited to attend a safety workshop conducted by the sub-section safety specialist. The employee safety observer's workshop agenda is composed of three sections:

1. A general description of the department's Safety Program, problems and responsibilities.
2. The responsibilities of the safety observer in the overall Safety Program.
3. A general question and discussion period.

Teamwork and participation of all employees, at all levels, is stressed, and due credit is given to the fact that our lowest frequency rates have been obtained since full participation has been extended to all members of the team. It is also emphasized that safety is a matter of concern at all levels and that the overall program involves oral and written communications, plus meetings and actual inspections of hazards and conditions by multiple levels of management.

The second portion of the workshop involves the safety observer's part in the overall Safety Program. Each safety representative is impressed with his responsibility and opportunity in the area of safe practices and procedures. Many examples of outstanding contributions by employee representatives are cited. Considerable time is also spent identifying safety hazards and the proper procedure for eliminating them.

The balance of the workshop is devoted to full discussion of the questions of the representatives.

At the end of the workshop, each member is presented with the safety observer's button and given a voucher to pay for the time spent at the workshop.

Soon after he attends the safety workshop, the representative and his supervisor make a careful safety inspection of the area. If this inspection discloses the existence of any hazards, it is the supervisor's responsibility to have these conditions corrected as soon as possible. Should any question arise, or further assistance be needed, the safety specialist is always available to give assistance.

During the balance of the month, the safety observer continues to work with his supervisor in maintaining a safe working area. The Foreman impresses upon him that he is a permanent member of the safety team and urges him to use the Suggestion System to call attention to safety hazards in any area.

Each safety observer, upon completion of his one-month assignment, is presented with a "Certificate of Participation" by his supervisor and the safety specialist. It is surprising to note how many of these "Safety Participation Certificates" have been framed and hung in a conspicuous place in employees' homes.

The spontaneous cooperation of these safety observers cannot be purchased; it can only be obtained on the basis of their feeling that they, too, are making a contribution and are full participating members of the safety organization.

Speaking of cooperation, I would like to cite some examples of incidents which describe the reaction of our employee safety observers to this program.

Let's call the first case "Cooperation and Recognition." Not long ago, an employee turned in a grievance to his supervisor concerning what he considered to be an unsafe condition. Simultaneously, he questioned the employee safety observer who was an ardent union member, and who in turn asked the supervisor to contact the safety specialist and together they looked over the job. The results of their inspection indicated that the job was safe to run and the employee was advised accordingly. Almost before the ink was dry on the grievance, it was cancelled by the initiating shop steward and a happy atmosphere again prevailed. Incidentally, this program provides an excellent meeting ground and a middle-of-the-road between your supervisors and your employee safety observers, and your shop stewards.

The second case might be called "The Conversion of the Unsafe Worker." We had one particular battery truck operator, of a type not uncommon in industry, who was known to his fellow workers as "Cowboy." He was fortunate enough never to become involved in major incidents, but he had had many close ones. One of our foremen exercised a great deal of courage and appointed him as a safety observer for the month. Much to the amazement of all concerned, he did an excellent job as a safety observer. But more important, his conduct since being an observer has been excellent and we have received six safety suggestions from him since he became a member of the safety team.

Let's call the next case, "Pride of Participation." We had a girl assembly worker who was appointed safety observer. Upon sustaining a minor cut on her finger, she refused to wear her safety observer badge when she went to the Works Hospital for treatment. She felt it was "extremely unbecoming" for the safety observer to have to make a visit to the hospital.

These are just a few of the many cases we could discuss to more fully emphasize the interest and desire of an employee to work safely and to be a contributor to the success of the operation.

Safety representative, safety aid, and safety observer are titles that are used interchangeably. Some companies now using an observer program instead of safety committees have continued to call their observers safety committeemen.

A safety-observer program, like any other activity, can fail if certain basic principles of organization and administration are not followed. As a first requirement, supervisors should need and use the assistance a safety observer provides. The observer should have something to do. Duties of an observer include the following:

1. Make a weekly safety appraisal of the area in which he works. It is advisable to ask the observer to make a written report of this appraisal.
2. Call the supervisor's attention to unsafe conditions and unsafe acts on a daily basis.
3. Help get new and transferred employees started in the safe way by seeing that all necessary safety equipment is available and showing the new employee the location of the dispensary, fire-fighting equipment, fire exits, stretchers, etc.
4. Help the supervisor arrange group meetings.
5. Arrange safety displays, posters, etc.

To help the observer make the weekly safety appraisal, use of a hazard check list is suggested. Printed check lists can be obtained from several sources, but in general it would be better to tailor-make the check list to cover the hazards and working conditions peculiar to the observer's department. A sample check list for a machine shop is shown in Exhibit 5–3. A 5-by-8 card has been used to make it easier for the observer to fill out the check list as he walks through his department. Many supervisors make it a practice to accompany the observer on the first appraisal trip. During the trip, the supervisor can take the opportunity to explain the various types of unsafe conditions which might develop and to explain the function of various safety devices. As soon as practical after the appraisal, the supervisor should correct any unsafe conditions discovered. This will help convince the observer that his recommendations are helpful. Following subsequent appraisals, the supervisor may want to take a few moments to discuss the appraisal report with the observer. In particular, observers should be given an explanation if the hazards noted in the report are not to be corrected.

HAZARD CHECK LIST

Safety-Appraisal Report

Name ______________________ Date ____________

Supervisor ____________________ Section ____________

HOUSEKEEPING — State whether or not aisles are clear, stock properly piled, floors free from slipping and tripping hazards, and work area orderly.

____
____
____
____
____
____
____
____

MACHINE HAZARDS — State what guards are found not in use and where guards should be provided This should include gears, sprockets, chains, bolts, shafting, etc

____
____
____
____
____
____
____
____

FIRE HAZARDS — *(a)* Are all fire-fighting appliances and fire exits ready for immediate use? *(b)* Are flammable materials properly handled and stored?

____
____
____
____
____
____
____
____

(over)

(FRONT)

Exhibit 5–3. A hazard check list that might be used by safety observers in their weekly department safety appraisals. Note that the check list becomes the safety-appraisal report when filled out.

PROTECTIVE EQUIPMENT – Are goggles, respirators, safety caps, and other equipment being worn as required? Jewelry and rings are a source of danger around moving machinery.

ELECTRICAL EQUIPMENT – Note condition of switches, outlets, light cords, and ground wires

TOOLS – *(a)* Are the proper tools being used for each job? *(b)* Are handles missing from files; chisels mushroomed; hammers, wrenches, and screw drivers defective?

GENERAL CONDITIONS – *(a)* Are boards with nails left on floor? *(b)* Are ladders, stairs, guards, and other equipment in need of repair?

SET A GOOD SAFETY EXAMPLE YOURSELF

(BACK)

Exhibit 5–3. *(continued)*

Of course, hazards develop in a work area daily. Thus, in addition to a hazard check list which is used for the weekly appraisal report, observers might also be supplied with hazard memos. These memos are used by the observer any time he sees an unsafe condition or practice that requires the supervisor's attention. At the time of the appointment, the observer might be supplied with a pad of such memos. A sample memo is shown in Exhibit 5–4.

Of course, the observer could make a verbal report to the supervisor of unsafe conditions. However, use of the memos tends to

SAFETY OBSERVER'S HAZARD MEMO

DATE__________

THE FOLLOWING UNSAFE CONDITION REQUIRES ATTENTION:

DESCRIPTION OF HAZARD__________

LOCATION OF HAZARD__________

DATE CORRECTED SAFETY OBSERVER

Exhibit 5–4. During the work day a safety observer might note a hazard requiring the supervisor's attention. He uses a hazard memo to put his observation in writing. (Courtesy of the General Electric Company.)

formalize the observer program by providing some tangible evidence of the observer's activities. Also, possession of the memos identifies an employee as a safety observer.

Observer appointments should be for a short duration so there will be wide participation of the work group in the program. One month is about the shortest period practical, three months the longest. No employee should be reappointed as an observer until all employees have had an opportunity to serve. Depending upon the size of a department, the area to be covered, and the hazards inherent in the operation, a supervisor may appoint one or more observers to serve in a single period. A large maintenance department might need as many as four observers because of scattered operations and the high hazard content of many maintenance jobs. Conversely, just one observer in a light-assembly operation might have little to do.

An employee safety-observer program is a good way to promote employee participation in safety. The program promotes cooperative effort and interest in safety because employees gain recognition for their safety activities and they have a definite and a personal part in a joint effort to prevent accidents.

Stated briefly, the benefits of an employee safety-observer program are:

1. It promotes a better working relationship between management and employees.
2. It provides a uniform and thorough means of teaching safety throughout the whole organization.
3. It promotes a full realization of hazards and the broad problems of industrial safety and, therefore, fosters safety awareness at all levels.
4. It recognizes and emphasizes the supervisory and employee team responsibility in developing good safety practices.
5. It provides an atmosphere of mutual understanding and a unity of purpose, thus becoming an excellent working tool in a sound employee-relations program.
6. It establishes safety as an integral part of a business operation.

But, no matter how well the observer program works, the primary responsibility for safety must remain with the supervisor. Therefore, nothing should be said or done which would even imply that the safety observer has assumed some of the supervisor's safety responsibilities. The basic function of the observer program is one of assistance and promotion of employee safety interest through participation. Supervisor-employee safety contacts, safety meetings conducted by each supervisor with his own work group, and a safety-observer program make an ideal employee-safety-participation package. To be sure, the need for one or all of these employee-safety-participation functions would depend upon the nature and the scope of the safety problem. At some locations, supervisor-employee safety contacts and an occasional group safety meeting might be adequate. At other locations, an observer program, frequent group meetings, and daily safety contacts might be required because of the nature of the work. This is a matter which must be decided on the basis of the indicated need of each plant, company, or establishment.

CHAPTER

6

Enforcing safety rules

We believe strongly in the philosophy of preventive safety rather than after-the-fact correction. We place great stress upon safety violations rather than upon injuries as such. We are tough toward wilful violators, as we are more interested in eliminating the chance for injury by working safely without violations of good practice than in setting records. Where we are reasonable but firm on violations, a safety consciousness is gradually developed among the entire work force.

EMILE F. du PONT
E. I. du Pont de Nemours
and Company

At 30 seconds past 4:00 P.M. a mad rush for the plant gate would start—each worker intent on getting a seat on the bus. A large woman in the group who always elbowed and shoved was called the "bulldozer." Needless to say, she got on the bus first. Day after day this California Gold Rush scene was repeated. Time would be lost because of the commotion and disorder. Tempers would flare. Then it happened! A starter, a brusque Irishman, was placed at the corner by the bus company. His first official act was to make the mob line up. Now, instead of elbows, there was friendly needling—"Get to the end of the line." The occasional unruly individual who tried to ignore the rule was straightened out with dispatch. The first violation was usually the last. Even the "bulldozer" liked the new order of things. Significantly, in about three months, the starter left. He was not replaced. But even to this day, people at the plant gate continue to get in line. The starter's leadership and insistence had substituted order for confusion, teamwork for misdirected effort. Everyone had been convinced that the discipline imposed by the starter was constructive—it was good for them. Why go back to the old order of things?

The need for safety rules

The bus story parallels the results a supervisor may expect if he promotes a decent respect for existing plant rules. Once a work group realizes that the intention is to work according to accepted standards, there will be little temptation to try to get away with something. Plant rules, including safety rules, will be recognized as necessary to good job performance, orderliness, and security. Supervisors who believe in accident prevention rather than after-the-fact correction naturally place great stress on the need for motivating employees to work safely—to follow safety rules. These supervisors have discovered that whenever safety rules are ignored, other rules are usually ignored, too. Conversely, they are aware that by insisting upon respect for safety rules, respect for rules in other areas is generated.

Unfortunately, though, during World War II, because of the stresses of war production and the labor shortage, it became fashionable in many areas to ignore safety rules. Many rule books were rewritten. Management went to great lengths to explain that safety rules really weren't rules at all but just the application of good "common sense." The slogan that became popular was, "Safety by Education, Not Legislation." Of course, the educational approach is good. It does lead to observance of safety rules by a large majority of the work group. But, unfortunately, it is the small minority which creates the problem. There will generally be a few individuals who will insist upon violating safety rules. Thus, where education has failed, supervision must be prepared and willing to take the proper disciplinary action. To compromise or temporize with an established safety rule can lead to eventual failure of the safety program. Because good discipline means order and a decent respect for the rights of others, most employees will endorse any just action taken by supervisors to maintain acceptable standards of performance. Likewise, they will resent being told to observe certain safety rules and then seeing the rules ignored by other employees, supervisors, or even plant visitors.

In a recent survey, over 2000 supervisors were asked to list three existing safety rules not being followed in their operations. Surprisingly, a large majority of the group were able to prepare such a list. There was general admittance that many existing safety rules were not being enforced. Thus, on the basis of the results of the survey, it is logical to ask, "Are safety rules necessary?" To this question, the same supervisors who admit they have ignored the violation of certain safety rules answer a resounding, "Yes!"

It is not surprising that the contradictory "Yes!" answer was received. Supervisors and employees have been pre-conditioned to accept rules and regulations as necessary at home, at school, and in their community. They have been subject to long lists of rules all of their lives. Visualize, for example, a basketball game without rules. In any sport, rules are necessary to let the players know how the game will be played. Likewise, in sports, penalties correct those who make a mistake. At the plant level, rules are a part of training. Experienced supervisors have found that if employees conduct themselves according to certain set patterns, work will be done more safely, more efficiently, and in more pleasant surroundings. Hence, there are many strong arguments for establishing safety rules and then seeing that they are followed.

Reasons safety rules are not followed

Rules at fault. About 1920, a germ-conscious plant manager had several signs put up in his plant which read "Employees Are Expected Not to Expectorate in the Bubbler." The signs are still up. Employees have learned not to spit in the drinking fountain. Now there is no need for the rule, so keeping the signs up may serve only to offend employees' sensibilities.

A simple check of existing rules would help to eliminate such a situation. If rules tend to arouse resentment, if there is no intention of enforcing them, if they are difficult to follow, then something should be done. Hence, it is a good plan to make a periodic check of existing safety rules. The reason a rule is not being followed may rest with the rule itself.

These check questions might serve as useful guides:

1. IS THERE A REAL NEED FOR THE SAFETY RULE? DOES THE EMPLOYEE UNDERSTAND THE NEED, OR DOES HE THINK IT WAS SOMETHING DREAMED UP BY THE FRONT OFFICE WITHOUT ADEQUATE CONSIDERATION OF HIS PERSONAL FEELINGS? During World War II, because of the shortage of male help, many companies began to hire women for the first time. As a safety measure, an attractive safety cap with a visor was designed for women working on machines with revolving, exposed spindles. On drill presses, for example, the hazard of being scalped was obvious. Nevertheless, supervisors had a tough time getting women to wear the caps. In one company, real trouble developed when management decided to extend the safety-cap rule to every woman in the plant. Assemblers and women inspectors were quick to point out that there was no need for such a rule on their jobs. Resentment ran high—the caps were hiding fancy hairdos. Finally, to forestall a threatened sit-down strike, the plant-wide rule was withdrawn. One aspect of this story is significant. On jobs where there was a hazard, where there was a need for the caps, the women did not resent strict enforcement of the safety-cap rule. They were willing to concede that the rule was necessary. Of course, it was still a problem to keep the caps properly in place. Women could not resist the temptation to push the visor back to uncover an attractive hairdo even though they were willing to agree that such protection was needed.

2. HAVE EXISTING SAFETY RULES KEPT PACE WITH CHANGES IN CONDITIONS? FOR EXAMPLE, ARE THERE RULES WHICH WERE MADE SOME TIME AGO TO PROTECT EMPLOYEES AGAINST AN UNSAFE CONDITION THAT HAS NOW BEEN CORRECTED? In seeking an answer to this question, supervisors will want to review existing signs in their areas. The results of such a review might be surprising. One supervisor reported finding a sign saying "For Fire Use Only" over an air hose. Somewhere along the line, a fire extinguisher which hung under the sign had been removed, but the sign had not. Also, he found a "Danger, Do Not Enter" sign over a main entrance. The sign had been put up during a construction period. The construction was completed, but no one bothered to take down the sign. Similar reviews may reveal "No

Smoking" signs in areas where smoking is permitted, "Danger" signs where there is no danger. Failure to remove such meaningless signs detracts from the effectiveness of warning signs which are needed. Therefore, the need for keeping safety rules up to date and eliminating outmoded rules is obvious.

3. DOES OBSERVANCE OF AN EXISTING RULE CREATE AN INCONVENIENCE OR AN ANNOYANCE FOR THE EMPLOYEE THAT MAKES IT ALMOST HUMAN NATURE FOR HIM TO VIOLATE THE RULE? Undoubtedly, many supervisors have seen employees walking over conveyors which are posted with signs that state "Do Not Walk Over Conveyor." As a matter of fact, they may have been guilty of the violation themselves. Perhaps the questions which should be asked are these: "Why are certain safety rules almost always ignored?" "Why do people walk through doors marked 'Do Not Enter,'—take short cuts through areaways marked with big, easy-to-see signs 'This Is No Thoroughfare'?" Usually such rules are ignored because it is just contrary to human nature to follow them. To avoid walking over a conveyor might mean a walk of a few hundred feet around the conveyor. It is human nature to take the short cut. Besides, no one has ever been stopped in the past. Where possible, a solid effort should be made to make it convenient to observe all safety rules. Making the conveyor safe to walk on or erecting a stile might work out much better than the warning sign. Posting a supposedly mandatory rule, then completely ignoring violations encourages employees to disregard the authority of their leaders. It encourages employees to try to get away with violations of other rules in other areas. Thus, the practical solution is this: Make safety rules so it is convenient for individuals to follow them. Don't try to defy human nature.

4. ARE THERE TOO MANY SAFETY RULES? The term *safety rules* can be used rather loosely. Safe practices and job instructions are, at times, classified as safety rules. Thus, the volume of "safety rules" becomes so large everyone is confused. Few of the rules are remembered. One manufacturing company recognized the need for a clear distinction between safety rules and safe practices and procedures. A review was made of all existing so-called safety rules. Needless rules were tossed out. Necessary rules were stated in clear, easy-to-understand language. The final list was printed in a small booklet which was given to each employee. A reason for each rule was given, and employees were told that disciplinary action would be taken for non-conformance. A supervisor reviewing the following set of rules should agree that this clear-cut approach to the establishment of safety rules makes sense.

THE ABC COMPANY
GENERAL SAFETY RULES

Every organization or group of people requires a set of rules for the proper regulation, safety, and protection of the individuals who make up the group. The safety regulations which are listed below have been formulated not as restrictive measures, but as guides to workers and supervisors in their cooperative efforts to prevent accidents. One of the important points to keep in mind about your job is the necessity for working safely and following the safety rules which apply to each operation. Years of experience indicate that it is foolhardy to make a safety rule unless the intention is to enforce it. Experience also indicates that certain safe rules have a substantial impact on the safety of an individual or the entire workforce. A single violation might place the safety of many employees in jeopardy. Where this is the case, it becomes basically unsound to follow the usual three-warning-notices procedure.

For These Reasons, It Has Been Mutually Agreed That an Intentional Violation of the Following Safety Rules Will Result in *Immediate Disciplinary Action* Ranging from a Temporary Lay-Off to Discharge, Depending upon the Circumstances. The Warning-Notice Procedure Will Not Apply. This Action Is Necessary to Emphasize the Importance of the SAFETY RULES Which Follow and to Safeguard Our Well-Being and Our Jobs.

1. No Smoking. Smoking in the manufacturing, warehousing, and shipping areas is strictly forbidden. This rule is necessary because materials in these areas are highly flammable. A match or cigarette carelessly thrown away could start a fire that would endanger many lives and everyone's job. For your pleasure and relaxation, smoking is permitted in the cafeteria.

2. Horseplay Prohibited. Fooling or "horseplay" is dangerous and a poor excuse for fun. Horseplay as applied to your job includes running, tripping others intentionally, throwing things, directing compressed air at another person, and any act which may startle or distract other employees. Horseplay has resulted in serious injury and even death. Horseplay will not be tolerated on company property.

3. Personal Protective Equipment Must Be Worn. Personal protective equipment such as safety glasses and respirators are provided on certain jobs because of an indicated need. Refusal to wear such equipment will lead to discharge.

4. Observe All Safety Tags. Red and yellow safety tags are placed on electric switches, valves, and other controls to protect personnel and equipment. Unauthorized removal of such tags, misuse of such tags, or operation of a control that has a tag attached is a serious offense.

5. Use Safety Devices and Guards. Employees are paid to use the safety devices and guards installed on the machines and equipment they operate. Use of such equipment makes each job a lot safer and in most cases easier. For his personal protection, an employee is not permitted to make a safety device or a guard inoperative or to remove it. Also, equipment must not be operated if the safety device is not functioning properly. Report the condition to your foreman.

The Regular Warning-Notice Procedure Will Be Followed for Infraction of Any of the Following Safety Rules. However, This Fact Should In No Way Minimize the Importance of These Rules and the Need of Following Them.

1. Maintain Good Housekeeping. Each employee is required to keep his machine or bench clean at all times. All paper, rags, scrap, and rubbish must be placed in containers provided for waste disposal in each department. There is a very practical reason for good housekeeping. It is easier to work when you know where everything is and you don't have to struggle over clutter in the aisles and work place. It is also safer to work in an orderly plant.

2. Get First-Aid Promptly. Prompt first-aid attention should be obtained for any injury no matter how slight. There are two reasons for this rule. The treatment received may prevent complications, such as an infection, from developing. Also, your report will enable your supervisor to make a prompt investigation of the accident and to take steps to prevent a similar accident. At times, the investigation your supervisor makes might reveal a hazardous condition that could lead to a more serious injury if not promptly corrected.

3. Wear Proper Clothing. When working around machines with exposed spindles and revolving parts, do not wear loose-fitting clothing or dangling neckties. Finger rings must not be worn. Women must wear suitable head coverings to keep their hair from becoming tangled in moving parts. Because of the heavy material handled in the plant, safety shoes are required. An employee coming to work with open-toe shoes, slippers, or cloth shoes will not be permitted to work until he changes to safety shoes. This step is necessary for your personal well-being.

4. Running. Running in the plant or on plant property is an extremely unsafe practice. Because of the hazards involved, it is expected that all employee will exercise good common sense and not run—even in case of fire, walk to the nearest exit.

5. Do Not Operate Unless Authorized. Equipment such as cranes, elevators, industrial trucks are marked "Do Not Operate Unless Authorized." To operate this equipment in a safe manner, specific training and skill are required. Failure to observe a "Do Not Operate" rule could be dangerous to you and to your fellow employees.

You will be required to observe the above safety rules so your actions will not lead to injury to yourself and other employees or to damage to company property. From your point of view, as well as ours, we cannot afford to overlook a safety violation. You should really want it this way because some one else's safety violation could cause your injury.

John Jones
Plant Manager

Of course, the formulation of written safety rules is only the first step. The important thing is to acquaint employees with the need for following the rules. The safety rules must be sufficiently publicized to make them part of the "working knowledge of every employee." Bulletin-board notices, items in the plant newspapers, payroll inserts, letters to employees' homes, and verbal explanations of the rules by supervisors are among the various means of acquainting employees with company safety rules. Taking prompt corrective action also serves as an effective device for making safety rules known to employees.

In this connection, some discussion is in order of the need for taking corrective action after the first violation of certain safety rules rather than after the usual three-warning-notice procedure. For example, when an employee is found smoking in an explosive powder room posted with a large "No Smoking" sign there seems to be something unrealistic about giving him a warning notice and sending him back to his job. Under such circumstances, the supervisor is in effect saying, "We gave you one chance to blow up the plant, and under our warning-notice procedure we will give you two more chances. If after the third try you haven't succeeded in blowing up the plant, we will fire you." Where a safety violation places the safety of the work group in jeopardy, involves gross insubordination, or is likely to result in a serious injury to the violator, it would seem basically wrong for management, by its action, to minimize the gravity of the violation. Resorting to the warning-notice procedure in a case like the one described above would de-emphasize the importance of the "No Smoking" rule. Management's action must indicate beyond any doubt that certain safety violations cannot be tolerated. Firmness in securing conformity with such safety rules is wholly consistent with the wishes of most employees. What supervisors should do is use past experience and information contained in the records as a basis for designating those safety-rule violations which should be followed by immediate disciplinary action. The rules selected would vary from plant to plant, but in all likelihood those selected by the ABC Company would be chosen with, perhaps, one or two deletions or additions. For example, some companies might decide that "unauthorized use of certain equipment" was an offense giving just and sufficient cause for immediate disciplinary action. In another company, "running" in the plant might warrant correction following the first offense rather than a warning notice.

Now for the fifth and final question.

5. ARE EXISTING SAFETY RULES SO BROAD OR GENERAL IN NATURE THAT THEY HAVE NO REAL MEANING TO EMPLOYEES? Meaningless rules in some cases have been the product of management's attempt to anticipate every safety situation that might arise and write a rule to cover it. This, of course, is not possible, but in an attempt to bridge the gap, a few catch-all safety rules have been tossed into safety rule books. Such rules are not constructive. They are without meaning. They are misunderstood. They undoubtedly are regarded as so much double talk by many employees. This is an example: "Any offense that is detrimental to the safety of the employee, fellow employees, or company property shall be considered a safety violation." Obviously, such a rule covers a lot of ground, but such a blanket rule tends only to confuse the issue. Hence, an important aim in formulating safety rules is clarity. Rules should tell employees what to do and how to do it and why the rule is necessary. Safety rules must be

specific. There should be no doubt regarding their meaning, and, of course, they must be uniformly applied.

Thus, in summary, in evaluating the need for and the effectiveness of existing rules, these five check questions might be asked:

1. Is there a real need for the safety rule? Does the employee understand the need, or does he think it was something dreamed up by the front office without adequate consideration of his personal feelings?
2. Have existing safety rules kept pace with changes in conditions? For example, are there rules which were made some time ago to protect employees against an unsafe condition that has now been corrected?
3. Does observance of an existing rule create an inconvenience or an annoyance for the employee that makes it almost human nature for him to violate the rule?
4. Are there too many safety rules?
5. Are existing safety rules so broad or general in nature that they have no real meaning to employees?

Employees at fault. A lack of knowledge, a physical limitation, poor judgment, and faulty attitude may be the basis for an employee's failure to conform with existing safety rules. A chipper in a foundry was discovered wearing the frames of his safety goggles with the lenses removed. This act could easily be interpreted as a stupid violation of a necessary regulation. Immediate disciplinary action might have been taken rather than a search made for the real reason for the employee's act. Fortunately, the supervisor chose the latter course of action. The chipper explained, in broken English, that he had removed the lens to prevent blindness. Somewhere along the line, the chipper had been told that the thickness of safety-glass lenses would cause a lot of eye trouble. In his mind, this misrepresentation was confirmed because after wearing the safety glasses for a few days, he got a headache. Mention of the headache provided a lead. The supervisor asked the chipper to see an eye doctor. This step revealed the source of the trouble. The chipper needed corrective glasses. A pair of prescription safety glasses eliminated the probability of repeated violations of this particular rule. In this case, misjudgment and a lack of knowledge led to a violation of a safety rule. Thus, in making a final decision regarding proper corrective action, the supervisor should make allowances for these human shortcomings. However, the supervisor's goal is conformity with existing work standards. To ignore or excuse a deliberate attempt to deceive would be as much wrong as to fail to give the mitigating circumstances full consideration. Quite often poor judgment, rather than an intention to violate the safety rule, can be the reason for the violation. An employee will take a guard off a portable grinder to get the work out a little faster or to make the grinder easier to handle. An understanding of the need for the guard would lead the operator to keep it in place for his own protection and the protection of others in the area.

In another case, a supervisor may discover that an employee is not following safety rules because of a faulty attitude. The employee may be indifferent to safe practices because he has not been convinced his method for doing the job is unsafe. He may be a show-off type who gets a certain amount of satisfaction from his willful disregard of rules. He may be dissatisfied with his job. A safety violation might be his way of expressing this dissatisfaction. Where faulty attitude is the root of the safety violation, there is no pat solution. The problem must be handled on an individual basis. The so-called appeals to the employee's pride, fear of injury, loss of pay, sense of leadership, desire for recognition, distaste for ridicule, and so forth may be valuable leads to a solution. On the other hand, these appeals might be an over-simplification of the problem. Success in the development of a healthy employee attitude toward safety rules is the product of a combination of factors. Recognition that safety is truly the supervisor's responsibility is the key. This recognition must be fortified by a sincere desire to prevent accidents and a continuous and conscientious safety effort. Where employees are not following safety rules because of faulty attitude, the gamut of supervisory abilities must be applied to the problem. The most potent factor in such situations is the force of example—the example set by the supervisor.

Supervisors at fault. Finally, where safety rules are being ignored, the fault may rest with the supervisor. For example, a factory foreman was asked how he planned to make a new eye-protection program work. He replied, "I will do my best to sell them on wearing safety glasses." In response he was asked, "What would you do if some of your employees refused?" "Oh, I would just sell them some more like I do my kids." Of course, *just selling* may not be the answer. It is true that about 90 per cent of the work group will go along with most rules. But, more selling might not be the practical solution to the problem. Corrective action is usually necessary to bring the 10 per cent into line. Taking corrective action will be consistent with good human-relations practices because most employees feel supervisors ought to have reasonable control over the work group. They have less respect for the supervisor who shuns taking corrective action. Where infractions are ignored, frustration is generated because no one in the work group is exactly sure where he stands. There is a feeling that the supervisor may someday reverse himself and start enforcing the rules he has previously ignored. On the other hand, if all rules are enforced, there is a feeling of security engendered. Everyone knows what the supervisor will do. There is little temptation to try to get away with something. It becomes popular to work by the rules. Thus, when a supervisor lets it be known that he intends to enforce safety rules, he sets a pattern that will have the endorsement of most people. As Professor Fritz J. Roethlisberger pointed out following the now-famous Hawthorne Works Studies, "Employees like to know what is expected of them and where they stand in relation to their bosses' expectations."

Closely associated with success in the enforcement of safety rules is the observance of safety rules by members of supervision. Where supervisors fail to follow safety rules, it is impractical to expect employees to conform. If machine-shop employees are expected to roll their shirt sleeves and take off finger rings and neckties, then supervisors must set the example by following such rules themselves. Likewise, a supervisor's failure to fully explain a safety rule and a lack of follow-up may lead to frequent violations.

In summation, where safety rules are not being followed, the fault may rest with the *rule,* with the *employee,* or with the *supervisor.*

From the foregoing discussion, four basic principles which govern the establishment and maintenance of sound safety rules emerge:

1. Safety rules should be few in number and easily understood—no rule should be made unless the intention is to enforce it.
2. Supervisors and all members of management must always set a good example by following safety rules themselves.
3. Prompt corrective action must be taken for failure to comply with safety rules—the emphasis being on education of the group, not punishment of the individual.
4. Safety rules should not be made which require conduct contrary to human nature or infringe on the basic rights of individuals.

Taking disciplinary action

Most supervisors have read or heard statements like these—"The term 'maintaining discipline' is not liked by workers"; "Instead of 'discipline' let us discuss the '*esprit de corps*' of the plant"; "I never use the word 'discipline' in my work as a foreman"; "Discipline is for school children and not for grown men and women." A check usually reveals that the origin of such statements is either misunderstanding, double talk, or a distorted view on human relations. Experience shows beyond a doubt that discipline is necessary for attainment of a pleasant, safe place to work, efficient production, and orderliness. Of course, the type of discipline under discussion does not mean the same as punishment. It is rather the positive constructive action supervisors take to achieve conformance with existing rules. It is training and correction which in the end becomes self-discipline.

Common-sense reasoning will convince most employees that a safety rule should be followed. But, there might always be the small minority who insist upon ignoring the rules. Experience indicates that with such people disciplinary action must be taken. *If corrective action is not taken, the rule soon ceases to exist.* Selling and education are important. However, there is no such thing as a safety program that has been successful through selling and education alone. In the final analysis, action must be taken to get at the 5 per cent or 10 per cent of the group who fail to conform. If action is not táken, the 10 per cent ignoring the rules will become 20 per cent, the 20 per cent will become 40 per cent, and the rule will soon become meaningless.

Thus, supervisors must believe in the establishment of fair and easily understood safety rules and in consistent enforcement. This does not mean, of course, that management should rely on punitive action instead of taking the positive steps of safety education, development of safe working conditions, and employee safety participation.

The following questions will serve as a guide to supervisors who find it necessary to take disciplinary action.

DISCIPLINARY-ACTION GUIDE

I. Is the Action I Am About to Take Based on a Careful Review of *All* the Facts?

A. Did I get the employee's side of the story in a private interview so there would be no embarrassment?
B. Did I check the employee's past record?
C. Have I found out what has been done in similar cases in my plant?
D. Have I shown any discrimination toward an individual or group?
E. Does the corrective action fit the violation?
F. Will the corrective action help prevent a recurrence?

G. Will the corrective measure create a desire on the part of the employee and the group to do what is right?
H. Have I checked the decision with my immediate supervisor?

II. Have I Initiated the Corrective Measure in the Proper Manner?

III. Am I Prepared to Explain to the Employee Why the Action Is Necessary?

A. Can I explain the effect of the violation on the company, fellow employees, and himself?
B. Will I be able to tell the employee how he can prevent a similar offense in the future?
C. Am I prepared to deal with any resentment the employee might show?

IV. Have I made the Necessary Follow-up?

A. Has the measure had the desired effect on the employee?
B. Is the employee convinced that the action was for his best interest?
C. Will the action have the desired effect on other employees in the department?

It is, of course, important to ask, "What effect will the disciplinary action have on the individual—on the group?" Likewise, it is equally important to ask, "What effect will failure to take disciplinary action have on the individual—on the group?" For example, an employee ties down one button of a two-hand press control. The violation is discovered by a supervisor. No action is taken.

What will other press operators think? They know that by tying down the control, the operator was beating the rate.

Will failure to act promote disrespect for safety rules?

Will failure to act indicate to employees that the supervisor is not sincerely interested in their safety?

Supervisors, in the fulfillment of their safety responsibilities, have a duty to strive for consistency in setting realistic safety standards for the work group and dealing effectively with departures from such standards. Usually taking corrective action produces these desirable results:

1. Prevents recurrence of the same violation.
2. Calls attention to the safety rule that has been violated and impresses employees that safety is part of their jobs.
3. Emphasizes that safety violations cannot be tolerated.
4. Shows that supervision has authority to back up instructions given.
5. Builds respect for supervisors if the rule is fair and impartially and uniformly applied and the discipline is consistent and commensurate with the violation.

The negative impact of failure to take disciplinary action when there is justification for such action should not be overlooked. Firmness and fairness in securing compliance with existing rules are wholly consistent with good management practices. Supervisors who are firm and fair have the warm approval and stout support of their work groups. Nevertheless, it is not uncommon to search for an excuse for not taking corrective action. For example, there are some who feel disciplinary action should not be taken when the violator of a safety rule is injured. The point is made that the injury is a sufficient deterrent to a repeat violation. It is argued that the injury is equivalent to the corrective action that otherwise might have been taken. That this is not the case requires little emphasizing among experienced supervisors. Even in the case of a serious injury that is the result of a safety violation, the impact of the injury on the safety attitude of the injured employee and the work group is fleeting. The initial shock wears off quickly, and the rule is again disregarded. Thus, if supervisors have been consistent in taking corrective action for a safety violation where no injury is involved, to maintain this consistency, corrective action should be taken also where there is an injury. It is an established fact that a lack of consistency is more productive of discontent and grievances than unusual strictness. Of course, in deciding the extent of the disciplinary action, some amount of leniency might be in order depending upon the extent of the injury. But to ignore a violation because an employee was injured would be basically wrong and unfair to the work group. Likewise, it would be equally wrong and unjust to discipline an employee just because he was injured. In the matter of taking disciplinary action, it is not the injury but the intent on the part of the employee to do wrong which deserves primary consideration.

Where a safety program is not producing the desired results because employees are not following safety rules, one of three steps can be taken. The violation can be ignored. This choice has been made in some cases because the wrong application of discipline in the past caused so much trouble that management decided the only solution was not to take any action. As a second choice, safety standards can be lowered to the point where everybody conforms. Of course, the standards will be so low that few accidents will be prevented and in the long run, production will suffer. Finally, supervisors can take a stand and insist that employees live up to the rules. There are three choices, but *taking action* is the only right choice if supervisors intend to do all they can to protect employees from accidental injury.

SELECTED REFERENCES

Company Rules—Aids to Teamwork, Studies in Personnel Policy, No. 95, The National Industrial Conference Board, New York.

Constructive Discipline in Industry, Special Research Report No. 3, American Management Association, New York, 1946.

PART III

DEVELOPING SAFE WORKING CONDITIONS

CHAPTER

7

Human factors in machine and equipment safety

Human engineering is defined as "the application of the principles, laws, and quantitative relationships which govern man's response to external stress to the analysis and design of machines and other engineering structures, so that the operator of such equipment will not be stressed beyond his proper limit or the machine forced to operate at less than its full capacity in order for the operator to stay within acceptable limits of human capabilities.

THEODORE F. HATCH
University of Pittsburgh

It is often stated that a high percentage of industrial accidents are due to unsafe acts, and reams of data and reports are available which classify accidents as having resulted from poor work practices, lack of judgment, inattention, recklessness, and even downright stupidity. Thus, the conclusion is made that all that needs to be done is to eliminate these unsafe acts and accidents will stop. Literal acceptance of this conclusion has not helped safety. Too often it leads to complacency concerning the development of safe working conditions. Actually, a high percentage of accidents result from a combination of unsafe acts and unsafe conditions, seldom solely from an unsafe act or an unsafe condition. Evidence exists which indicates that many so-called operator errors leading to accidents have been touched off by faulty design or construction, poor housekeeping, operating practices that created hazards, or lack of standardization and identification which so confuses the operator that he is literally trapped into making mistakes. Thus, potential accidents have been built into machines and equipment by failure to human engineer the work place.

For example, reaching into the die zone of a slide- or dial-fed power press has been classified as an unsafe act. But is it always? Visualize a power-press operator blanking or forming a thousand parts each day. His work method takes on a set pattern—place part on slide feed, push in slide, step on foot treadle, pull out slide; again and again this rhythmical pattern is repeated. Each movement of the operator signals the next step in the operation. Everything goes fine until something happens to interrupt the operating sequence. A part fails to seat properly under the punch. Instinctively, the pressman reaches into the danger zone to correct the error and to save a die. Simultaneously, he trips the press. Inattention, recklessness, unsafe act—no—the operator could have no more controlled the motion of his hand toward the danger zone than a blink of his eye. The fault was the inadequacy of the press guard, *an unsafe condition.* When the human element is factored into the power-press operation, it becomes apparent that although a feeding device is used, it is still necessary to provide a barrier or cage guard so the operator cannot reach over or around the feeding device into the danger zone.

Man-machine relationships

A principal objective of the supervisor and safety engineer in the development of safe working conditions is the elimination of bottlenecks, stresses and strains, and psychological booby-traps that interfere with the free flow of work. It is an accepted concept that the less an operator has to fear from his job or his machine, the more attention he can give to his work.

Exhibit 7–1. The development of safe working conditions involves no secret formula—it simply combines good sense and the ability to anticipate the hazards that may arise on a given job. The above picture shows the various steps that are taken to "human engineer" an operation. Following is a key to the numerals:

1, 2 Stop buttons at work points
3 A gear guard
4 Chain-drive guard
5 Shield for revolving knife
6 Guard for counter-drive
7 Non-skid platform
8, 9, 10, 11 Stub shaft guards
12 Guard at roll-feed pinch point

Also note the excellent housekeeping and that all wiring is in metallic conduit. (Courtesy of the General Electric Company.)

In the development of safe working conditions, attention is given to many things, including machine design and machine guarding, personal protective equipment, plant layout, manufacturing methods, lighting, heating, ventilation, removal of dusts and fumes, and the reduction of noise. Adequate consideration of each of these areas will lead to a proper climate for accident prevention, increased productivity, and worker satisfaction.

Ross A. McFarland, Associate Professor of Industrial Hygiene, Harvard School of Public Health, has this to say in reference to the need for developing safe working conditions:[1]

Exhibit 7–2. It is not difficult to see that poor housekeeping, poor lighting, inadequate machine guards, and congestion interfere with the free flow of work and lead to numerous accidents. There is a direct relationship between good production, good housekeeping, and safety that cannot be ignored.

The "human-engineering" approach to the solution of the accident problem is to build machines and working areas around the operator, rather than place him in a setting without regard to his requirements and capacities. Unless this is done, it is hardly fair to attribute so many accidents to human failure as is usually the case.

If this point of view is carried out in practice, fewer accidents should result, training costs should be reduced, and extensive redesign of equipment after it is put into use should be eliminated.

All possible faults in equipment and in the working area, as well as the

[1] R. A. McFarland, "Human Engineering Aspects of Safety," *Mechanical Engineering,* May, 1954, pp 407–410.

capacities of the operator, should be subjected to advance analysis. If defects are present, it is only a matter of time before some operator "fails" and has an accident.

Obviously the development of safe working conditions involves procedures that may go beyond the occasional safety appraisal or search for such obvious hazards as an oil spot on the floor or a pallet in the aisle or an unguarded pinch point on a new lathe. Man-machine relationships have improved considerably with increased mechanization and automation. Nevertheless, with the decrease in manual labor has come specialization, increased machine speeds, and monotonous repetition of a single task, which create work relationships involving several physiological and psychological stresses and strains. Unless this scheme of things is recognized and dealt with effectively, many real problems in the field of accident prevention may be ignored. Fortunately, leaders in the field like Dr. McFarland, Mr. Theodore F. Hatch,[2] Professor of Industrial Health Engineering, Graduate School of Public Health, University of Pittsburgh, and others are making contributions to the literature on human engineering which provides valuable guides to the industrial supervisor, safety engineer, and industrial hygienist.

Engineering source material

In the development of safe working conditions, supervisors have the ability and services available to cope with most problems. Within their grasp are many basic accident-prevention principles and safety and health standards to help them make competent safety appraisals at the plant level. In addition, for solution of technical problems, supervisors may call upon qualified safety engineers and industrial hygienists in their own company or other companies. Many outside organizations including the National Safety Council, the American Standards Association, state safety and health departments, the United States Bureau of Mines, the Bureau of Labor Standards, the engineering departments of insurance companies, and other agencies are also ready to render valuable assistance on safety and health matters.

Volumes of detailed material are available on how to guard a lathe, a drill press, a bread slicer, a paper cutter, and hundreds of other machines. Reams of information can be obtained regarding removal of free silica, carbon tetrachloride, and other toxic dusts and fumes. Likewise, specifications on lighting, ventilation, layout, and other

[2] T. F. Hatch, "Proposed Program in 'Ergonomics,' Human Engineering," *Mechanical Engineering*, May, 1955, pp. 394–395.

aspects of plant safety are well documented. In the development of safe working conditions, the help available and the reference material provide valuable aids for the supervisor and safety engineer. Because of the wide range of problems involved, it is understandable that no one person could always have the answer to all safety and health problems. It should be expected, however, that supervisors and safety engineers would know where to go for help. Likewise, they should be expected to recognize most health and safety problems. These check questions might well be asked when considering the safety of any operation:

1. What factors in the operation create an unsafe condition? Are there unguarded pinch points, inadequate clearances, flying particles, dusts or fumes, flammable materials, irritating chemicals, unusually high or low temperatures, conditions likely to cause a trip, slip, or fall, high noise levels, crowded work space, poor or distracting lights and contrasts, or other hazards which would obstruct normal, safe operation?
2. Can the hazard be eliminated or isolated with a guard, ventilating equipment, etc.?
3. Should the hazard be identified by the use of color, warning signs, or barriers?
4. Should interlocks be used to protect the worker when he forgets or makes the wrong move?
5. Is it necessary to design the machine, the electrical circuit, or the pressure circuit so it will always fail safe?
6. Is there need for standardization?
7. Is there need for emergency controls and are controls easily identified and accessible?
8. Is there a need for explaining the job hazards to the worker and training him on how to avoid the hazards?
9. What unsafe conditions would be created if the proper operating sequence were not followed?

Some of the terms such as "fail safe," "interlocks," and "operating sequence," because of their importance to safe operation, deserve detailed discussion.

Definition of safety-engineering terms

Fail safe. Many safety devices could become real booby-traps if a machine could be operated or a process continued after the safety device had failed. Likewise, if failure of a control circuit would cause a machine to operate unexpectedly, the operator might be exposed to a serious hazard. This condition can be avoided by incorporating "fail-safe" features into the set-up or process. For example, the modern gas furnace has a "fail-safe" feature. If the pilot light is extinguished, a thermally operated valve in the gas line is closed. Likewise, electronic safety devices including photoelectric cells that produce a curtain of light in front of a danger zone such as a press die can be so arranged that any failure of the light curtain or the electronic circuit will make it impossible to operate the press until the condition is corrected. Electrical controls can be wired so an accidental ground will blow a fuse or open a circuit-breaker rather than complete a control circuit that would cause the machine to operate. Exhaust fans or paint spray booths can be installed so a failure of the electrical circuit will simultaneously close the air-pressure line to the paint spray guns. Foot switches used to keep a worker away from some danger spot can be designed so failure of any part of the switch will open the circuit. Thus, the term "fail safe" has important implications in safety work. Understanding the use of the term will be helpful in any analysis that might be required concerning the safety of a machine or device. The lead questions are, "What will happen in case of a failure?", "Will the worker be protected?"

Safety interlocks. Safety interlocks might be described as devices, design features, or attachments that remember when the worker forgets. The simple electrical disconnect on the door to a modern automatic clothes dryer is a good example of a safety interlock. Opening the door activates a spring-type switch which opens the control circuit to the revolving drying drum. Thus the drum is stopped and a hazard is eliminated. Similar interlocks are installed on the control cabinets to resistance welders, so even if the operator forgets to open the primary disconnect, power will be removed when the cabinet door is opened. Standard electrical switches, the type found in many homes, are designed so the switch box must be closed before the circuit can be closed. The interlock protects the worker when he forgets to follow the proper operating sequence.

Limit switches. Over-travel of a hoist hook or the hook block of a crane could create a serious hazard. To keep cables from snapping when the hook block hits against the lifting beam, a limit switch is installed directly under the lifting beam. When the hook block reaches maximum travel, it trips the limit switch, which automatically removes power. This is one example of the use of a limit switch to provide an extra factor of safety in a common industrial situation. Without such a safety device, a moment's inattention on the part of the crane operator could lead to a costly accident. Elevators, conveyors, planer tables, motorized doors, and much other equipment have been made safer by the use of limit switches which automatically stop the upward, downward, or horizontal movement of the equipment within safe bounds.

Dead-man controls. Occasionally in examining the safety features of a machine or of equipment, the need is indicated for providing some

Exhibit 7–3. Rubber mill equipped with emergency stop bars. Note that the upper bar runs the full length of the mill. It can be reached by either hand. The lower bar is arranged with foot pedals which can be depressed by either foot. The mill can be stopped either by pulling down the upper bar or by depressing one of the foot pedals. (Courtesy of the General Electric Company.)

safeguard in case an operator should faint or become unconscious. The obvious solution is a control that will automatically stop the equipment when the operator's hand or foot is removed. Such a device is usually called a dead-man's control.

Emergency controls. Generally, the function of an emergency control is to limit the seriousness of an accident. However, where the element of time is a factor, an emergency stop may actually prevent an accident. Such would be the case if a worker realized a jam was about to occur on a conveyor while he was several yards away from the control switch. An emergency stop cord which runs the full length of the conveyor could be pulled to avert the jam. A rubber mill with large horizontal in-running rolls provides an excellent example of the use of emergency controls to limit the seriousness of an accident. Since the possibility is recognized that both hands of the mill operator might become caught in the rolls, emergency stops which actuate a dynamic braking device and can be operated by either hand or either foot are standard equipment on most rubber mills (see Exhibit 7–3). Speed and ease of operation should be the determining factors in the location of such emergency stops. Consideration must be given to the type of accident that is likely to occur, and the controls must be designed and located so the accident will not prevent operation of the control.

Location of controls

A common error is to locate a switch which controls the operation of a fan, mixer, pump, or other tools and equipment in a room separated from the apparatus. This error leads to an accident when the equipment is started inadvertently by one worker while another unseen worker is exposed to a pinch point or other hazards of the equipment. Thus, an effort should be made to locate the control on or as near to the equipment as possible. Also, by following this rule, the type of accident will be avoided which occurs when the worker attempts to clean or repair equipment in motion rather than undergo the inconvenience of walking to the control.

In the location of controls the manner in which the controls are to be used, the sequence of operation, and the frequency of use must be considered. For example, these factors dictate the location of two-hand controls on a power press. The controls must be located so they are reached easily by the operator—in general, not higher than eye level or lower than waist level and not wider apart than the distance from elbow to elbow when both arms are extended. On a positive-type clutch press the distance from the controls to the danger zone must be sufficient to prevent the operator's hands from reaching the danger zone before the ram completes the down stroke. The controls must be so located or protected by barriers that the operator cannot trip the press by means of one hand and elbow or in some other way while one hand is free. Also, the controls must be designed and located to prevent wedging or tying down one of the controls. These same principles apply to the location of two-hand controls on almost any type of equipment where the use of such controls would be practical.

Proper operating sequence

On some operations an accident might result if a worker failed to follow the established operating sequence. A simple example would be pouring water into acid instead of acid into water. In the development of safe working conditions, the supervisor should look for opportunities to suggest design changes, re-arrangement of equipment, or other steps that might be taken to assure proper sequence of operation. The American Standards Association code for the design of a three-prong electric plug is a good example of the steps that may be taken to maintain a safe sequence of operation. Users of portable electrical tools with a two-prong plug and a pig-tail ground clip are instructed to connect the ground clip first, then to insert the plug into the outlet. However, it is not uncommon to insert the plug first and then make the ground connection. As a matter of actual practice, the ground connection is often omitted. By substituting an A.S.A. type three-prong plug and using a three-pole adapter on the two-pole outlet, the proper sequence will always be followed. This is true because the A.S.A. type of plug has been designed with the grounding prong longer than the two current-carrying prongs. Thus, contact with ground is always made first.

At times, a sequence-of-operation problem may not be solved easily. Under such circumstances, lacking a solution, the supervisor may consider substitution of equipment or materials, use of personal protective equipment, or other steps to minimize the hazard when the proper sequence is not followed. This would be the case in the plating room, where the operator's good judgment, attention, and training are the only guarantee that water will not be poured into acid. A rubber apron, gloves, and goggles minimize the hazard if a mistake is made.

Standardization

Standardization, meaning conformance with a pre-established pattern, has an important bearing in the development of safe working conditions and safe work habits. Workers use the five primary senses, sight, smell, taste, touch, and hearing, to perceive objects, signals, and changes in the work environment. Each perception is relayed through the nervous system to the brain, where the information is noted and evaluated. In making the evaluation the worker is guided by past training and experience. Where the perception is consistent with the worker's previous experience, a correct evaluation is made in a split second. On the other hand, a new situation, and in particular one which is inconsistent with previously established patterns, may confuse the worker or at least slow up his reaction time.

Standardization of methods, the use of colors, the design of tools, and the location of controls will eliminate this confusion and make it easier for workers to evaluate any given situation quickly and accurately. But, by way of comparison, where machine controls are located helter-skelter and where there is little consistency as to information imparted to workers by colors or signals, there is always the likelihood that the inconsistency will confuse workers. The end result might be an accident.

A survey made in the machine section of a manufacturing plant points up the need of standardization safety-wise and production-wise. Controls on forty power presses were found at six different locations. On some presses the control was on the right side of the press frame, in others on the left, and at varying heights from the floor. Other presses had the controls at the front of the press. Some of the controls had been painted blue, some red, and many controls were the same color as the press. To add further to the confusion, the push-button controls on a few of the presses had the stop button at the top; the others had the stop button at the bottom. Some of the controls had both the stop and go buttons in black plastic. Others had a red-plastic stop button and a black go button. The need for standardization was obvious. Pre-planning would have eliminated a lot of confusion and at no additional cost.

The use of color, if not carefully standardized, can result in some peculiar incongruities. Perhaps the classic example is the use of red for exit signs although that color usually denotes danger or stop. A uniform system of applying color to warn of various industrial hazards, to indicate first-aid and fire-protection equipment, to stimulate good housekeeping, and to guide the movement of workers has been formulated by the American Standards Association. Where the code is followed, workers soon learn to associate a particular color with a specific device or condition or with the location of a hazard. The color safety code in Table 7–1 is used by many plants.

Normal behavior patterns

Several years ago an industrial truck or jitney was manufactured with the steering mechanism arranged so a steering wheel, which was operated by the left hand, was turned to the right or clockwise to turn left and vice versa. This was just the reverse of the normal method for steering an automobile or any other vehicle. Thus, anyone placed on these industrial trucks was faced with the problem of opposing the strong and dependable habit of turning the steering wheel to the right for a right turn. Broken bones, damaged equipment, and wrecked trucks soon affirmed the dangers of trying to reverse a normal behavior pattern. Supervisors in their reviews of existing working conditions must be constantly on the alert for a set-up, a new tool, or a new device that requires movements of the worker which are contrary to normal behavior patterns.

TABLE 7–1. SAFETY COLOR CODE FOR MARKING PHYSICAL HAZARDS AND THE IDENTIFICATION OF CERTAIN EQUIPMENT

RED—shall be the basic color for the identification of:

1. Fire-protection equipment and apparatus
   (*a*) Fire-alarm boxes
   (*b*) Fire-blanket boxes
   (*c*) Fire-hose locations
   (*d*) Sprinkler piping, etc.
2. Danger
   (*a*) Safety cans and other containers for flammable liquids
   (*b*) Red lights at barricades
3. Stop
   (*a*) Red lights at barricades
   (*b*) Stop buttons

ORANGE—shall be used as a basic color for designating dangerous parts of machines or equipment. Suggested applications are:

1. Inside of transmission guards for gears, pulleys, chains, etc.
2. Safety starting buttons
3. Exposed parts (edges only) of pulleys, gears, power jams, etc.

YELLOW—shall be the basic color for designating caution. Suggested applications are:

1. To mark aisles and direct the flow of traffic
2. Construction equipment such as bulldozers, tractors, etc.
3. Caution signs
4. Handrails, guardrails, barricades
5. Markings for low beams, pipes, projections, etc.

GREEN—shall be used as the basic color for designating "Safety" and the location of first-aid equipment. Suggested applications are:

1. Safety bulletin boards
2. First-aid kits
3. Stretchers
4. Personal-protective-equipment supply cabinets

BLUE—shall be the basic color for designating machine and equipment controls such as:

1. Electrical controls
2. Valves
3. Brakes
4. Disconnects

PURPLE—shall be the basic color for designating radiation hazards. Suggested applications are:

1. Radiation warning signs
2. Containers of radioactive material
3. Signal lights to indicate radiation machines are in operation

BLACK OR WHITE—or a combination of black and white shall be the basic color of housekeeping markings. Suggested applications are:

1. Stairways (risers)
2. Location of refuse cans
3. White corners for rooms and passageways
4. Food-dispensing equipment

Source: Material in Table 7–1 has been adapted from the *American Standard Safety Color Code for Marking Physical Hazards and the Identification of Certain Equipment,* Z53.1—1953.

Perhaps the key question is this. Are there any previously acquired habits or natural body movements of workers which must be opposed in order to do the job? First consideration should be the elimination of such unsafe conditions, but if they cannot be eliminated, then job training must be intensified so old habits will be discarded.

Conditions listed below are contrary to what a person generally expects therefore, they constitute a hazard:

Doors that are below the standard door height of 6 feet 6 inches.
Different floor levels at each side of a door.
Steps of varying heights in the same stairs.
Passing on the right instead of on the left.
Low-hanging pipes, etc., in an aisle.
Pipe rail or fence that is not securely anchored to floor.
Hot-water faucet on right side of sink.
Change in any established sequence.
Large objects that are very light or small objects that are very heavy.
Moving to the left to turn right or to the right to turn left.
A great change in the coefficient of friction underfoot.

Sudden changes in force required to operate a lever, push a cart, etc.
Obstacles in main aisles.
Uninsulated and unmarked electrical conductors.
Hazardous materials in unlabeled containers (like gasoline in a water bucket).

The above list provides the supervisor with leads to things to look for in the work environment, conditions that are the subtle causes of many accidents. By the elimination of these abnormal conditions, the worker is made free to devote his full attention to his job. He can follow his natural instincts and his acquired habits with safety.

Environmental conditions—ranges of comfort and safety

A worker will be capable of performing with maximum efficiency and safety if working conditions are adjusted to his physical and mental limitations. It is known that poor light can be irritating and can cause eye fatigue, that excessive noise may disrupt normal conversation and may lead to hearing impairment, that fumes and dusts may constitute a health hazard, and that high or low temperatures can impair efficiency. A great deal of research remains to be done in order to set accurate limits on the various factors of environment at the work place. Nevertheless, Table 7–2 will provide some valuable guides for determining whether or not conditions are within the range of worker comfort and safety.

The ranges of comfort and safety indicated for the various factors in Table 7–2 are merely bench marks or guides for the supervisor. Where existing environmental conditions fall outside the recommended range for safety and comfort, the supervisor should check the matter with the safety engineer or other qualified people.

Conclusions

In recent years much progress has been made in the development of safe working conditions. The establishment of a large number of standards of comfort and safety has helped management relate plant equipment and plant layout to the physical and mental needs of the worker. The use of safety interlocks, fail-safe devices, machine guards, and personal protective equipment has helped to protect the worker in spite of distractions of the job or the unsafe work habits he may have acquired. Nevertheless, the opportunity for continued progress is still great. Conditions that could be easily corrected may go un-

TABLE 7–2. RANGES OF COMFORT AND SAFETY IN THE WORK ENVIRONMENT

CONDITION	RANGE		COMMENTS
Air contaminants	*Gases* (maximum allowable concentrations) Sulphur dioxide—10 ppm* Carbon tetrachloride—25 ppm Benzol—35 ppm Turpentine—100 ppm Naphtha (coal tar)—200 ppm Carbon dioxide—5000 ppm *Toxic Dusts and Fumes* Cadmium—0.1 mg/cu m* Lead—0.15 mg/cu m Mercury—0.1 mg/cu m Zinc oxide—15 mg/cu m *Mineral Dusts* Silica—5 mppcf* Portland cement—50 mppcf Mica—20 mppcf Talc—20 mppcf		Only a few of the air contaminants common to industry are listed here. Complete lists can be obtained from industrial hygienists, state health departments, etc. Supervisors should always check the toxic properties of any new material introduced into the operation. Adequate controls are necessary to preserve the health and efficiency of the worker.
Aisles	One-way traffic—2 feet wider than widest vehicle loaded. Two-way traffic—3 feet wider than twice the width of the widest truck loaded. Ramps should not exceed a grade of 10 to 12 per cent.		It is important to avoid sharp inclines, narrow passageways, and low ceilings.
Electrical current	*Current in Milliamperes*	*Effect on Body*	Current, voltage, and resistance are all factors that determine the effects of electricity on the human body. Any voltage above 35 in the 30 to 300 cycle range should be considered hazardous.
	Less than 1	No sensation	
	1 to 8	Shock—not painful	
	8 to 15	Painful shock	
	15 to 20	Loss of muscular control	
	20 to 50	Severe loss of muscular control	
	50 to 100	Possible heart failure	
	100 and up	High possibility of being fatal	
Illumination	Depends upon task involved—30 foot-candles recommended for reading, 650 foot-candles for precision die-making.		Glare, shadows, color contrasts and reflections are factors affecting comfort and safety.

TABLE 7–2. *(Continued)*

CONDITION	RANGE	COMMENTS
Manual lifting	Weights within safe limits for continuous or repetitive lifting for average-sized workers Male—50 pounds plus Female—25 pounds plus	All workers should be instructed in the proper lifting techniques. Safe limits vary with size of the worker and nature of the task.
Noise	For 300 to 10,000 cycles, the hearing-damage-risk noise level is about 90 decibels. 120 decibels produces discomfort—130 decibels produces pain—at 0 decibels sound is barely audible.	Reduce to permit conversation at least 3 feet from ear with no extra effort.
Stairs	Preferred slope—30 to 35 degrees from horizontal. Never less than 20 degrees or more than 50 degrees. Treads should be not less than 9½ inches.	It is a good practice to make stairs of the same size, tread, and riser throughout a plant.
Temperature	Maximum limits (can be endured for short periods) Hot-dry exposures—105F Warm-moist exposures—90F	Hot-dry exposures common to steel, glass, and tin plants. Warm-moist exposures common in laundries, dye shops, and some mines. Optimum temperature ranges from 60F to 80F with a relative humidity of 45 per cent, depending upon the task.
Ventilation	20 cfm* of fresh air	Must be increased where toxic or explosive fumes are present.

*ppm = parts per million
mg/cu m = milligrams per cubic meter
mppcf = million particles per cubic foot
cfm = cubic feet per minute

Data in this table have been adapted from papers by Ross A. McFarland, *Mechanical Engineering,* May, 1954; T. F. Hatch, *Mechanical Engineering,* May, 1955; W. B. Kouwenhoven, *Electrical Engineering,* March, 1949; and National Safety Council, Safe Practices Pamphlets.

noticed because they have come to be regarded as an accepted part of the work environment, such as a banging door, the squeak of an unoiled machine, the screech of escaping air, foul odors, oily floors, crowded work areas, dark, unpainted interiors, cluttered aisles, drafts, poor lighting, unguarded pinch points. Yet with the development of an awareness of the adverse effects of such conditions, prompt correction can be made usually with relative ease.

Today, with the amount of information available on the physical and mental limitations of the worker, supervisors and safety engineers are prepared to make a human-engineering approach to the solution of the accident problem. Basic principles for the development of safe working conditions can be applied to a particular machine, to equipment, or to plant layout, and practical decisions for making the work place safer and more comfortable can be made. By giving constant attention to how a worker is likely to react rather than to how the supervisor would like to have him react, the relationship between man, the machines he operates, and his work environment will be improved. This improved relationship will make work easier and safer.

To help supervisors appraise working conditions in their own areas, safety subjects common to most plant operations including noise control, fire prevention, electrical safety, radiation hazards, and other general subjects will be reviewed in this book. However, any attempt to cover the wide range of material available on the development of safe working conditions would not be possible or practical in one book.

Hence, supervisors and safety engineers are urged to make full use of the many excellent publications and source material available. A partial listing is contained in the selected references which follow:

SELECTED REFERENCES

Accident Prevention Manual for Industrial Operations, National Safety Council, Chicago.

American Safety Standards, American Standards Association, 70 East 45th Street, New York 17, New York. (A partial listing.)

Building Exits Code—A9.1–1951.

Industrial Lighting—A11–1942.

Safety Code for Floor and Wall Openings, Railings, and Toe Boards—A12–1932.

Scheme for the Identification of Piping Systems—A13–1928 (Reaffirmed 1947).

Safety Code for Wood Ladders—A14–1948.

Safety Code for the Use, Care, and Protection of Abrasive Wheels—B71–1947.

Safety Code for the Protection of Industrial Workers in Foundries—B8–1932.

Safety Code for Power Presses and Foot and Hand Presses—B11.1–1948.

Safety Code for Mechanical Power-Transmission Apparatus—B15–1927.

Safety Code for Compressed Air Machinery and Equipment—B19–1938.

Safety Code for Conveyors, Cableways, and Related Equipment—B20.1–1947.

Safety Code for Forging and Hot Metal Stamping—B24.1—1952.
Safety Code for Mills and Calenders in the Rubber Industry—B28.1—1949.
Safety Code for Cranes, Derricks, and Hoists—B30.2—1943.
Code for Pressure Piping—B31.1—1951.
Safety Code for Industrial Power Trucks—B56.1—1950.
National Electrical Code—C1—1951.
Machine Tool Electrical Standards—C74—1942.
Safety Code for Woodworking Machinery—O1.1—1944.
Safety Code for Paper and Pulp Mills—P1—1936.
Safety in Electric and Gas Welding and Cutting Operations—Z49.1—1950.
Safety Color Code for Marking Physical Hazards and the Identification of Certain Equipment—Z53.1—1945.
Safety Code for Industrial Use of X-Rays—Z54.1—1946.

Annual Safety Equipment Issue, March issue, *National Safety News*, National Safety Council, Chicago.

Brandt, A. D., *Industrial Health Engineering*, John Wiley and Sons, New York, 1947.

DeReamer, C. R., and H. E. Vann, "Factoring the Human Equation into Electric Testing," *Electrical Engineering*, March, 1956.

Heinrich, H. W., *Industrial Accident Prevention*, third edition, McGraw-Hill Book Co., New York, 1950, Chapters 7, 8, and 9.

Human Conditioning in the Factory, Thomas K. Meakin for the Human Conditioning Group, New York, 1954.

McFarland, Ross A., "Human Engineering Aspects of Safety," *Mechanical Engineering*, May, 1954, pp. 407–410.

McFarland, Ross A., "Human Factors in Industrial Safety," *The Journal of The American Society of Safety Engineers*, August, 1957.

Noise Control, The Acoustical Society of America, New York.

Simonds, R. H., and J. V. Grimaldi, *Safety Management*, Richard D. Irwin, Inc., Homewood, Ill., 1956, Sections I and VI.

CHAPTER 8

Safeguarding machines and equipment

Even though industry has progressed far in the field of accident prevention, there still is a large area which can be improved only through diligent application of the basic principles of machine guarding. Therefore, even though these principles are merely ideas about safety that have their roots in ancient times, it would seem that conditions call for their constant repetition and re-examination to inspire their use with renewed vigor and dedication.

WALTER E. MONTGOMERY

Robertson, Hall and Henshaw, Ltd.

Occasionally the complaint is made that supervisors will resist the use of machine guards and other safety devices because of the cost involved or because they feel such devices will interfere with production. If ever there was such an attitude, it is disappearing fast. Examples of improved production following the installation of a well-designed guard are numerous. This is understandable. When a machine operator must divide his attention between the immediate task and an unprotected machine hazard, it is no wonder that production and quality suffer. Picture, for example, a worker at a grinding wheel without the usual transparent shield. To avoid flying particles, he squints and looks away as he grinds. Under such conditions, the operator's attention is divided between avoiding the hazard and the job. Thus, the chances for an accident are increased, rate of production is decreased, and quality usually suffers.

Supervisors agree that the unsafe condition of machines and equipment has an important influence on an operator's work habits, production performance, and even on his mental attitude. This being the case, supervisors should be able to increase their effectiveness by broadening their knowledge of various machine guarding principles.

A good knowledge of the basic principles of machine guarding has a two-fold effect on supervisory performance. Such knowledge helps supervisors recognize various machine hazards that otherwise might be ignored. Likewise, supervisors are prepared to make the proper selection of a machine guard or a safety device once the hazard has been pin-pointed.

Principles of machine guarding

Industrial machines, excluding the many special machines that are now available, may be classified as follows:

1. Forming, punching, and shearing machines, including power and hand presses, forging hammers, power brakes, and shears.
2. Milling, drilling, and grinding machines, including drill presses, boring mills, lathes, shapers, and grinders.
3. Sawing, ripping, and planing machines, including circular and band saws, jointers, and planers.

These machines have the following sources of hazards:

1. Unguarded points of operation, such as the punch and die of a power press, the cutting edge of a power shear, and the circular blade of a power saw.

2. Unguarded belts, chain drives, and gears, such as the belt drive on a drill press and the gears of a lathe.

3. Unguarded spindles, shafts, and flywheels, such as the spindle of a drill press and the flywheel of a power brake.

The basic objective of machine safeguarding is to prevent personnel from coming in contact with any revolving or moving machine part such as belts, chains, pulleys, gears, flywheels, shafts, and spindles and any working part of the machine which creates a shearing or crushing action, creates a pinch point, or may entangle the worker. There are several safeguarding methods available. A machine can be designed and constructed so all hazard points are covered or out of reach. Automatic and semi-automatic feeds and ejection devices can be used so the worker is not required to reach into the point-of-operation, and barriers, enclosures, and various protective devices can be attached to the machine.

Fortunately, two factors are likely to accelerate safe machine design. One is the automatic production line which is part of the coming age of automation. The other is competition. Many machine safety features are becoming definite sales features. The know-how is available for really making new machines safe, but the big concern of safety engineers and supervisors is the thousands of machines presently in operation. Safety might not have been factored into the original design. Operations with these machines are the ones that need the most attention. Enclosing hazardous belts, pulleys, gears, and other power-transmission parts can be done with little difficulty. Protecting the operator at the point of operation is usually more complicated. The nature of the work or the per-unit cost of automatic and semi-automatic feeds may make it impractical to substitute automatic or semi-automatic feeding for hand feeding. This being the case, some other satisfactory method of safeguarding the operator at the point of operation must be selected. Hence, an understanding of the various safeguarding methods available would be most helpful to supervisors and safety engineers.

Fixed-barrier guards

A fixed-barrier guard provides positive operator protection. This safeguarding method prevents access to the danger zone but permits the feeding and removal of stock. Such barriers may be attached to the machine or made an integral part of the tool or die. Particular attention must be given to the construction of the fixed barrier. A

Exhibit 8–1. A power shear with a barrier guard for the hold-down fingers and blade. Opening between lower edge of guard and shear table is held to a maximum of 3/8 inch.

common error is to make openings in the barrier so large that the operator can reach a pinch or shear point through the guard. To eliminate this possibility, openings in the barrier or between the barrier and any part of the machine must not be greater than those shown in Table 8–1.

TABLE 8–1. SAFE OPENINGS

Distance of Opening to Danger Point	Maximum Width of Opening
0 to 1 1/2 inches	1/4 inch
1 1/2 to 2 1/2 inches	3/8 inch
2 1/2 to 3 1/2 inches	1/2 inch
3 1/2 to 5 1/2 inches	5/8 inch
5 1/2 to 6 1/2 inches	3/4 inch
6 1/2 to 7 1/2 inches	7/8 inch
7 1/2 to 8 1/2 inches	1 1/4 inches

Reference to Table 8–1 may suggest several safeguarding possibilities. For example, a barrier with a 1 1/4-inch opening 4 inches from a nip point is unsafe. Moving the guard 3 1/2 inches so the barrier is 7 1/2

Exhibit 8–2. Milling machine with a barrier guard for the cutter. The guard is transparent to permit a view of the work. It is also hinged to permit access to the work. The guard could be further improved by an interlock which would prevent operation of the machine when the guard was up.

inches from the nip point makes the barrier an effective safeguard. These opportunities for repositioning a presently ineffective barrier should not be overlooked. In addition to the matter of safe openings, the basic requirements for design and construction of barriers and enclosures are:

1. Enclosures and barriers should be simple in design and sturdy in construction. The guard should be easy to install and to adjust, and it should be firmly attached to the machine by means of cap screws, bolts, or, where practical, welding.
2. Where possible, enclosure and barrier construction should be such that there is no interference with the repairing, oiling, or adjusting of the machine.
3. The enclosure or barrier itself should not create a hazard such as a pinch or shear point with any moving part.
4. Where state or local laws exist, the enclosure or barrier design and construction should comply with these laws.
5. Openings in enclosures or barriers should be such that it is not

possible to place any part of the hand through the guard and reach a shear or pinch point. (See Table 8–1.)

6. Any hinged or movable section of a barrier or any barrier which is hinged, pivoted, or easily removed by hand should be interlocked so the machine cannot be operated while the operator has access to the danger zone.

Limited openings or adequate clearances

Two relatively simple methods for eliminating pinch points are to limit openings between moving parts to ¼ inch and to provide sufficient clearances between moving parts, or a stationary and a moving part, so a shear or pinch point is not created. A traveling crane, the location of a large planer, the position of a barrier guard on a press provide examples of installations where the matter of adequate clearance must be considered. Workers have been trapped between building columns and a crane bridge, between the moving table of a planer and another machine, and between the top of a press barrier guard and a protruding section of a press ram. Each of these hazards could have been avoided if the matter of adequate clearance had been considered.

An accident on a kick press brings the limited-stroke principle into sharp focus. The press involved was set for a 2-inch stroke. A finger amputation occurred when the operator failed to remove his fingers from between the punch and anvil as he kicked the foot pedal. The accident investigation revealed that unsuccessful attempts had been made to guard the operation. A barrier guard was considered impractical and two-hand controls could not be used because the operator had to hold the part. The hazard was eliminated by adjusting the length of the press stroke to ¼ inch. This opening allowed sufficient room for the stock but not enough clearance for a finger to get under the punch.

Two-hand and remote controls

The three methods for machine safeguarding which have been discussed, safe machine design, use of barrier guards, and limited openings, may be classified as methods for providing positive protection. Each method *prevents* the worker from placing his hands or any other part of his body within the danger zone. But certain production methods require access to the point of operation. Resistance-welder, riveter, paper-cutter, lathe, drill-press, and power-press operators are frequently required to feed their machines by hand. This means reaching into or near the point of operation while motion of the working tool is stopped but power is on. The problem here is to be sure the operator's hands are out of the danger zone during the intermittent operation of the machine. A two-hand machine control might be the practical solution. Such devices are so designed as to require the simultaneous use of both hands to put the machine into motion. This means, of course, that the controls must be located so the operator's hands are in a safe position during operation of the machine; also, the two-hand controls must be designed and located so the operator is unable to tie down or wedge one control or use one hand and arm to operate both controls. These controls allow free access to the point of operation. Production-wise this is an advantage. Safety-wise there is a disadvantage because a mechanical or electrical failure might cause the machine to operate while the operator has his hands in the danger zone (see page 143).

A remote control and a two-hand control operate on the same principle. In the case of the two-hand control, the movement of the operator's hands is controlled during motion of the machine. In the case of the remote control, the movement of the person himself is controlled. For example, a remote control may be operated from a one-hand push button or a foot pedal which is located at a safe distance, that is, out of reach of the danger zone.

Interlocked movable barriers and electronic control devices

Still another method for safeguarding the point of operation is to install devices which automatically prevent operation of the machine until the operator has removed his hands from the danger zone. For example, interlocked movable barriers are used on table-top high-voltage-test enclosures, wire-cut-off machines, and power presses. Such devices are hinged or pivoted so the barrier can be raised to allow access to the point of operation. When such barriers are raised or opened, an interlock prevents operation of the machine, or energizing of the circuit in the case of the electrical-test enclosure.

The use of electronic control devices also may be considered practical when a sufficiently wide light beam or electrical or magnetic field can be provided across the plane of entry into the point of operation. Protection is provided for the operator since any interference with the light beam or field actuates electrical relays which stop the motion of the machine. Therefore, while the operator is feeding the machine or has his hands or any other part of his body in the danger zone, the machine cannot be operated. Two points about electronic controls require emphasis. (1) Such controls cannot be used on machines that cannot be stopped at any point of the operating cycle. For example, on a power press with a positive-type clutch, the ram cannot be stopped once it starts its cycle. Therefore, an electronic control should not be used on this type of machine. (2) Also, it is important to install electronic controls in such a way that any failure of the relays and the light, sound waves, or electromagnetic fields will make the machine inoperative.

Pull-out and sweep devices

Finally, another method for safeguarding various machines at the point of operation is to use pull-out devices or sweep devices, which either pull or sweep the operator's hands out of the danger zone during travel of a machine part. The pull-out devices employ cables extending from a ram connection to the rear of the operator and over pulleys to the operator's wrists. A cable is attached to a thumb-and-wrist harness on each hand of the operator. The stroke of the machine pulls the operator's hands out of the danger zone. Such devices must be carefully supervised and readjusted each time an operator is changed or a machine set-up is changed.

Sweep devices employ the principle of a single or double arm which sweeps across the point of operation just ahead of the closing of a nip or shear point. Such devices are activated by the motion of a ram or other machine parts. The sweep arm or rod moves across the danger zone at each stroke of the machine. Sweep devices should be used only on small machines. Adequate protection may not be provided if a long sweep is required to cover the danger zone because of the possibility that the operator may place his hands in a pinch point after the arm has swept past. Also, the operator might be able to reach around the sweep arm into the point of operation.

Basic safeguarding methods summarized

The goal for supervisors and safety engineers is the selection of a machine-safeguarding method which provides adequate operator protection without interfering with production. Much can be accomplished if an effort is made to match the safeguarding method to the man on the machine and the method of machine operation. Consideration of such factors as the type of exposure, the length of the production run, the basic design of the machine, the limitations and the advantages of the various safeguarding methods, and the physical and mental characteristics of the operator will help assure adequate protection of personnel with no reduction in efficiency.

Supervisors and safety engineers will profit by their knowledge and clear understanding of the four basic safeguarding methods available. These methods may be summarized as follows:

A. Safeguarding methods which prevent access to the point of operation and other danger points, including:
   1. Machine design and construction which encloses or places all danger points out of reach of personnel.
   2. Limited openings (¼ inch) at nip points. (*Note:* This principle does not apply to the inrunning side of feed rolls, etc.)
   3. Adequate clearance so a nipping, shearing, or crushing point is not created.
   4. Fixed-barrier guards or enclosures which isolate the points of hazard.

B. Safeguarding methods which allow access to the point of operation but control the operator's movements during travel, rotation, or other motion of the machine, including:
   1. Two-hand controls.
   2. Remote controls.

C. Safeguarding methods which prevent operation of the machine until the operator has removed his hands or any other part of his body from the danger zone, including:
   1. Electronic machine controls.
   2. Movable-interlocked-barrier devices.

D. Safeguarding methods which automatically move or sweep the operator's hands out of the danger zone when the machine starts, including:
   1. Hand-pull-out devices.
   2. Hand-sweep devices.

At present, machine accidents are accounting for more than 30 per cent of all permanent partial disabilities and about 9 per cent of all permanent total disabilities and fatalities. An analysis of these serious work injuries should not omit the fact that many of these accidents are occurring on machines which have supposedly been safeguarded. Improper selection of the safeguarding method, faulty adjustment of the guard or safety device, lack of adequate supervision, machine failures, and poor machine maintenance are some of the factors which have led to these accidents. Machine safety requires more than the selection and application of a safeguarding method. Adequate follow-up on a continuing basis is required. Supervisors and safety engineers must be alert to the fact that positive operator protection is provided only when the machine operator is not required to place his hands or any other part of his body within the point of operation, and a bar-

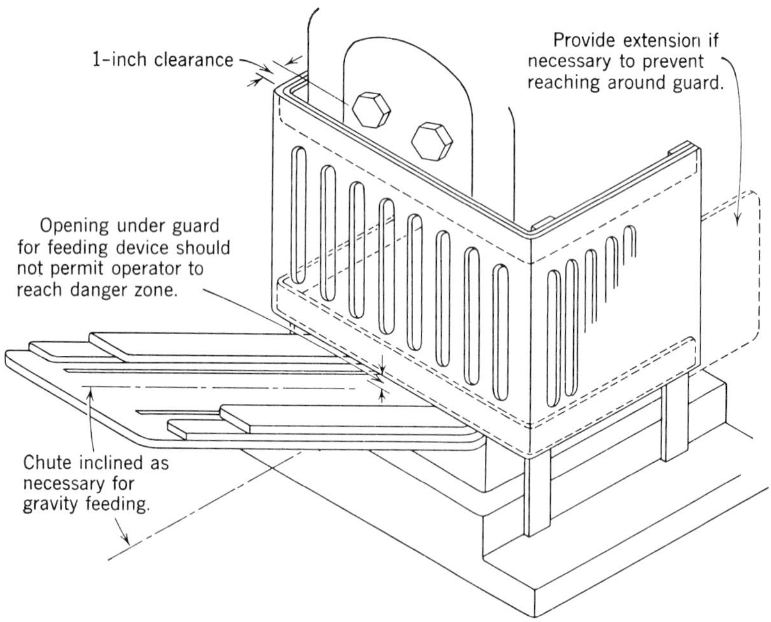

Exhibit 8–3. Chute feed. One of the most widely used semi-automatic methods of feeding consists of the horizontal or inclined chute into which each piece is placed by hand. The piece then slides or is pushed into the lower die. A pick or other means for removing pieces of stock that may jam in the die should be provided. Parts are ejected by air. Note clearance between top edge of guard and protruding bolt heads on ram. It is not necessary or possible for the operator to place his hands in the danger zone. This is positive protection. (Courtesy of Liberty Mutual Insurance Company.)

rier, enclosure, or limited opening actually prevents access to the point of operation. For example, a chute feed makes it unnecessary to reach into the point of operation. A barrier guard prevents access to the point of operation. In combination, the chute feed and the barrier provide positive protection.

Two-hand controls, remote controls, movable-barrier devices and electronic control devices protect the operator against his own lapses during normal operation of the machine, but because of free access to the point of operation, no protection is provided in case of a mechanical or electrical failure. Pull-out devices and sweep devices also allow access to the point of operation. Because these devices operate directly from the moving part of the machine, the operator is protected in case of a machine failure. Nevertheless, such devices have limitations. In the case of both devices, it is difficult to determine by a visual inspection if the devices are properly adjusted. Where the pull-out devices are used, the operator might fail to hook the cables to his wrists unless he is closely supervised, and on machines with a sweep device, the operator might be able to reach around the device into a nip point. Obviously, the limitations of these various devices require careful consideration.

Power presses—point-of-operation guarding

A really tough problem is to devise suitable point-of-operation guards for lathes, milling machines, boring mills, and drill presses. Of course, guards have been devised for these operations, but they usually serve as splash guards for the coolant or as protection against flying chips. There is no positive protection provided for the machine operator against contact with cutting tools, revolving spindles, or chucks.

A careful study of the various safeguarding methods which have been used to protect power-press operators might provide valuable leads in the solution of safeguarding problems involving the above machines and equipment.

Some companies have adopted a realistic policy which prohibits the press operator from placing his hands or any other part of his body between the punch and die or in a pinch area. This rigid policy has been adopted because, in spite of press guards and safety devices, occasionally something would go wrong and a serious press accident would occur. It was reasonable to conclude that these accidents could be stopped if no part of the body was ever placed in the danger zone. This same policy might be applied to other machine-tool operations.

To keep hands out of the point of operation requires a lot of ingenuity and inventiveness. Machine loading and unloading devices, hand tools, automatic and semi-automatic feeds, parts-ejection apparatus, barrier guards, and other devices are required. But such a policy has considerable merit. When it is put into effect, press-room injuries and amputations are stopped. The significant point for supervisors is that all of this effort toward greater safety has, in many cases, brought about an increase in production and a decrease in spoilage in addition to an excellent press-room safety record. Steps taken to keep hands out of the danger zone have lead to press set-ups which permit continuous runs instead of intermittent press operation, to the use of mechanical parts ejection instead of removing parts from the die by hand, to the use of coil feeds instead of piece-by-piece press feeding, and other changes which in the end lead to better profits. This same safeguarding effort would likely be equally productive when applied to other machines.

As previously stated, preventing the operator from putting any part of his body in the danger zone is the essence of accident prevention in press operations or in any machine operation for that matter. There is general agreement that press safety begins with good die design and good methods planning. This means taking into consideration the various methods of press feeding and then designing the die to facilitate the selected feeding method. Likewise, safe removal of the processed part must not be overlooked. Spring knockouts and other parts-ejection methods can be incorporated in the die. But is is not the intent here to review all the details that must be considered by the die designer or the guard constructor. Rather, key points will be discussed which will help supervisors appraise any given machine-safeguarding problem.

Causes of press accidents

The Power Press and Forging Section of the National Safety Council analyzed 590 power-press accidents. The principal causes of press accidents revealed by this extensive study were these:

1. Press was not guarded or the guard in use was inadequate, having openings which were too large or lacked side barriers.
2. No rod or stick had been provided for removing or re-aligning jammed parts or operator failed to use rod or stick which had been provided.
3. Defective clutch, brake, solenoid, or key caused a repeat action of the ram. Operator was placing hands under the ram.
4. Swing guard was out of adjustment.
5. Two-hand pull-outs were improperly adjusted, defective, or not fastened to operator.
6. Two-hand press controls were out of adjustment or one was tied down.
7. Movable-gate guard was not properly adjusted. Press operated before gate reached bolster plate.

8. Operator failed to use hand tools to feed and remove stock.
9. Operator failed to shut off power and block ram when making adjustments, changing dies, or making repairs.

These are the types of conditions to look for in a safety appraisal of power presses and other machine operations. Knowing the principal causes of machine accidents provides leads regarding the types of machine guards and safety devices required to protect machine operators.

Exhibit 8–4. Die storage rack showing individual die guard attached to each of the dies.

Individual die guards. The big problem in a press room is the numerous die changes which are usually required. Long, continuous runs, especially in a small press, are the exception rather than the rule. Each die change requires an adjustment of the press guard to meet new conditions. To solve this problem, many companies have gone to a grill-type or perforated metal guard individually designed for each die. Hence, the die which goes into the press has its own tailor-made guard. The guard is an integral part of the die and is attached to it, so each die when installed is adequately enclosed to protect the press operator.

Barrier guards. On short runs, an adjustable press barrier guard may be practical because one guard can be used for several dies. This will lower guard costs. Of course, the set-up man and the press-

Exhibit 8–5. A barrier guard for a blanking press. The openings between rods are not wide enough to permit the operator to reach a pinch point. Rods on front barrier are placed vertically to prevent eye strain. If placed horizontally, the travel of the ram in back of the rods would be annoying to the operator. Note, however, that the side barriers have the rods in the horizontal position to permit feeding of strip stock through the guard.

room supervisor must make sure that proper adjustments are made and maintained each time a die change is made. There are two types of barrier guards. The first type may be used where dies vary in size and shape but the nature of the operation allows complete coverage of the die without requiring openings which would permit the operator to reach a pinch point with his finger or hands. The second type may be used when periodic access to the die is required to remove scrap, adjust die pins, or relieve a jam. However, gates, pivoted panels, or slide sections which provide access to the die zone should be interlocked mechanically or electrically so the press cannot be operated when the guard is open. A hand tool or pick should always be used for reaching into the die zone.

Supervisors might wonder about the need for a hand tool to relieve a jam or remove scrap when the press cannot be operated because of the interlock. Placing a hand in the die zone is something akin to Russian Roulette—there is no way of being sure a mechanical or electrical failure, a faulty brake, worn clutch, or broken pitman will not cause the press ram to descend. A crushed tool can be replaced. Little can be done with a hand squeezed between the dies of a press.

Press safety devices. Press *guards,* which include individual die guards, fixed-barrier guards, and adjustable-barrier guards, do not permit access to the point of operation. Press *safety devices,* which include two-hand controls, sweep devices, pull-outs, movable-barrier guards, and electronic controls, do permit access to the point of operation and either prevent operation of the press until the operator's hands are removed from the danger zone or pull or sweep the operator's hands from the danger zone when the ram starts down. There are several types of commercial power-press safety devices on the market that with proper installation, supervision, and maintenance can effectively protect the press operator. However, many experienced safety engineers feel that for maximum safety hand tools should be used in conjunction with any safety device, like two-hand controls, for example, which permits free access to the point of operation. Hand tools may be omitted if the press is equipped with safety blocks which move into place under the ram after each stroke of the press. The action of the safety blocks must be made automatic, by a mechanical linkage between the blocks and the press controls. Exhibits 8–6 and 8–7 illustrate this principle.

Two-hand controls. Two-hand controls and other safety devices have been discussed previously in this chapter. Subsequent discussion will cover additional points which are specifically applicable to power-press operations (see page 135).

Presses equipped with two-hand controls require a single-stroke attachment so only one cycle of the ram will result for each operation of the controls. On friction-clutch-operated presses, the two-hand-controls arrangement should be such that if either hand is removed from a control during the down stroke, the ram will stop. Where two

Exhibit 8–6. A hydraulic press equipped with two-hand controls. Note the positive protection provided by the spring-actuated dual safety blocks which pivot into place under the open ram. These blocks are made of solid steel. They would keep the ram from descending in case of a mechanical or electrical failure of the press. Also, note the hand-feeding method being used by the operator. The holding method does not expose the operator's fingers to a pinch point. (Without the safety blocks, a hand tool should be used for feeding the press.)

or more persons are required to operate a press, separate sets of two-hand controls are required for each person. In place of an extra set of two-hand controls, a foot control may be used, provided the foot control can be located no less than 36 inches, measured horizontally, from any pinch point.

Two-hand controls have these limitations:

1. Because operator has access to point of operation, no protection

Exhibit 8–7. Depressing two-hand controls actuates the mechanical interlocking attachment which moves dual safety blocks from under the ram.

is provided in case of a mechanical or electrical failure of controls or repeat action. This limitation provides a strong argument for use of hand tools or safety blocks.

2. On positive-clutch presses, hands are free the instant ram starts down. Depending upon location of controls, operator might be able to reach into danger zone after tripping press.

3. Two-hand controls cannot be used where operator is required to hold part.

Sweep devices. A sweep device is designed to push or sweep the operator's hands out of the danger zone. The sweep is activated by the motion of the press ram. These are the applications and limitations of sweep devices.

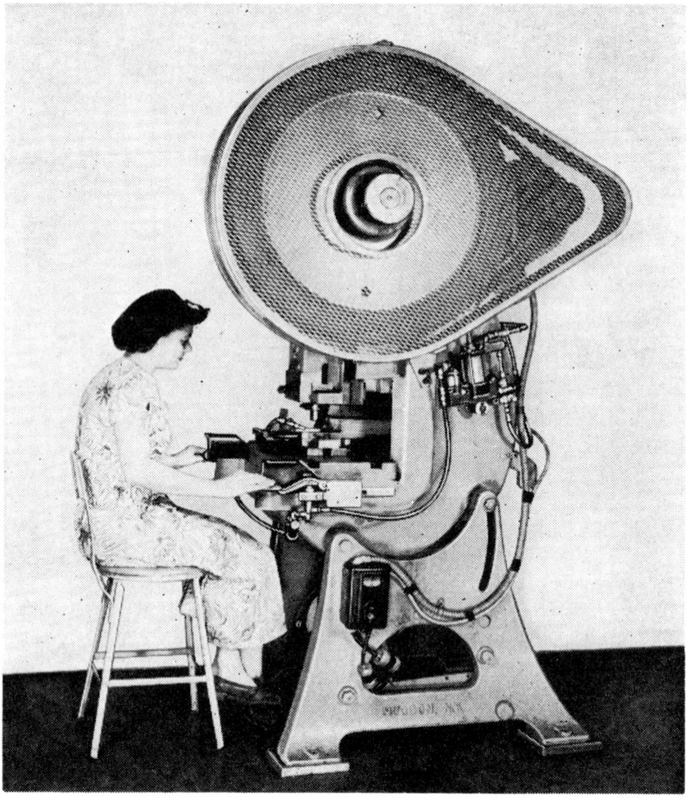

Exhibit 8–8. Two-hand press-control device—both buttons must be pressed simultaneously for the press to operate. (Courtesy of A. Schrader's Son, Division of the Scovill Manufacturing Company.)

Applications:

1. The best use of these devices is on small presses and dies (not over 6 inches wide).
2. The same protection is provided in case of clutch failure as for a regular stroke of the press.
3. The guard is easily adjusted.

Limitations:

1. If device swings in arc and radius of arc is small compared to length of front of die, there is a space which is never guarded at end of stroke.

2. When not properly designed or adjusted and sweep moves quickly, it may be possible to reach into a nip point after sweep passes; or if it moves slowly, the sweep may not clear danger zone in time.

Exhibit 8–9. A sweep device. Pictures show position of sweep arm when the press ram is in the normal open position and when the ram has completed one-half of the down stroke. (Courtesy of the Wiesman Manufacturing Company, Dayton, Ohio.)

3. If die is large and the arm of the operator is struck by the sweep, there is a possibility the elbow will bend and the hand remain in the danger zone.

4. It is easy to reach around device into point of operation.

Electronic safety devices. Photoelectric relays and other electronic controls which operate because of the interruption of a light beam protecting the danger zone have been applied with success to presses with friction clutches or brakes adequate for stopping the press at any point of the ram stroke. It is important to install this equipment in such a way that failure of the light or photoelectric relay will make the press inoperative.

Applications:

1. No moving or mechanical mechanism is in front of operator to interfere with operation.

2. View of operating area is unobstructed.

3. Device is applicable to large presses which are usually difficult to safeguard.

Exhibit 8–10. Photoelectric relays which operate because of the interruption of a light beam protect the danger zone of this press. The lines shown in the above picture indicate the area protected by the beam. The press cannot be operated when any part of the body or other objects obstruct the ray of light. Also, after the ram has started a cycle, interruption of the light beam will stop it.

Limitations:

1. Device is limited in application to presses that can be stopped during ram stroke.

2. Device must be far enough from danger zones so it will stop ram before operator's hand can get under ram.

3. A sufficient number of light beams must be used to cover the open area with a curtain of light.

Pull-out devices. Three types of pull-out devices are available commercially. They all employ cables to pull the operator's hands away from the danger zone if he fails to remove them. The cables are attached to a ram connection. Thus the device provides protection even if there is a repeat action of the press.

Applications:

1. When properly attached and adjusted, device removes hands from danger zone in all cases of ram descent.
2. Use of device does not introduce any additional motions in press operating cycle.
3. Device provides full protection if properly used, adjusted, and supervised.
4. View of operating area is unobstructed.

Limitations:

1. Device is generally limited to nesting or secondary operations.
2. Device is limited to jobs where the operator can remain in the feeding position.
3. Operators may resent being tied to machine and having their movements restricted unless educated in its uses.
4. Operators may fail to hook cables to wrists.
5. Careful adjustment of device is important.
6. Guard must be readjusted or checked every time press set-up or operator is changed.
7. It is difficult to tell by a visual inspection whether or not device is properly adjusted. An actual test of the adjustment must be made.
8. On short-stroke presses, sufficient pull back may not be obtained without proper multiplier.
9. The additional space required in front of the press for installation of the device may obstruct the movement of stock trucks.

Movable-barrier devices. Where movable-gate guards are used, the tripping mechanism of the press is so arranged that the operator actuates a barrier which comes down in front of the die before the press can be tripped. If hands or anything else is in the way, the device is stopped by the object and therefore the press cannot be tripped. However, if the barrier reaches the point where protection is certain, the clutch can be engaged. The tripping may be accomplished by fastening the clutch-tripping mechanism to the barrier so that the barrier actually trips the press by mechanical or other means. The barrier may return to the raised position by action of counterweights, or it may be lifted by mechanical or other means.

Application:

1. Operator has free access to die when gate is up.

Exhibit 8–11. A hand-pull-out device. Cables extend from the operator's wrists through a linkage to the ram of the press. Thus, the downward motion of the ram will pull the operator's hands out of the danger zone. (Courtesy of W. E. Plumb, Safeguard Manufacturing Company, Woodbury, Connecticut.)

2. Press cannot be tripped unless device is protecting the point of operation.
3. In some cases barrier may be re-arranged and used as fixed-barrier guard.

Limitations:

1. Device provides no protection in case of mechanical failure or repeat action of press.
2. Unless properly designed and applied, device may be up before ram has completed down stroke.

Exhibit 8–12. A movable-barrier device—the installation shown is a movable-gate-type device which forms a complete die enclosure prior to movement of the press ram. The pressman is demonstrating that the ram will not come down while his hand is under the transparent gate. (Courtesy of American Allsafe Company, Buffalo, New York.)

Hand tools for manual feeding

In some press rooms the hazards of hand feeding of power presses has been minimized through the use of feeding pliers, tongs, magnetic and suction lifts, and tweezers. These feeding devices are used with two-hand controls, sweep devices, and other press safety devices which leave the die zone open. It might seem unreasonable or impractical to use hand tools in addition to a press safety device, but there is evidence to support the practice. Accidents are still occurring in press rooms where supervisors permit the operator to put his hands into the danger zone. Where hand tools are used in addition to a protective device, accidents have occurred less frequently.

In many cases, hand tools can be used without increasing the cost of the operation. A manufacturing specialist using methods time standards, for example, has this to say concerning the economy of feeding small punch presses with hand tools.[1]

> The pliers method for loading small presses requires the same time to get and release the part as is necessary to get and release the part with the fingers. The motions are the same. The learning period with the pliers might be slightly longer than with the fingers, but after the learning period, the rate for the two methods will be about the same.

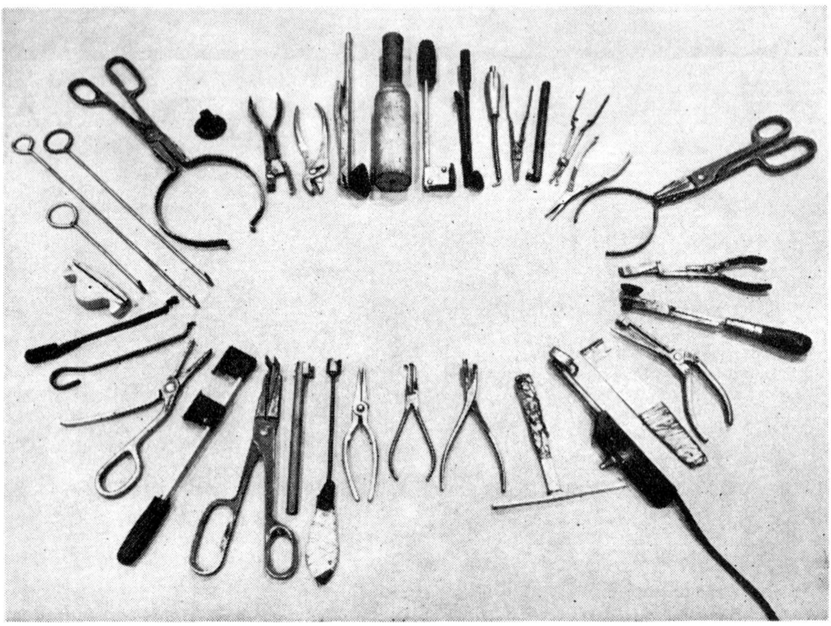

Exhibit 8–13. An assortment of hand tools, each tool designed for a specific purpose.

Actually, in some cases, the use of hand tools will save time. For example, the feeding of larger presses may require an 18″ to 24″ reach to load the die. This requires the operator to move his body and his arms each time he loads and unloads the press. By feeding the press with 12″ pliers instead of the hands, the long reach and the body movement are eliminated. This will result in a slight saving of time with each loading and unloading of the die. Closing and opening the pliers takes the same amount of time as closing and opening the hand.

---

[1] J. L. Laymon, Manufacturing Specialist, General Electric Company.

Loading small presses with a magnetic lift instead of fingers saves time too. It takes less time to apply the magnet to the part and release than to close the fingers on the part and release. The transport to and from the die is the same for the two methods.

Hand tools should never be used in place of press safety devices but in conjunction with them. Likewise, supervisors must always be alert to take corrective action whenever operators fail to use the hand tools provided. To assure continual use of hand tools, proper design and construction of such devices are essential. An attempt to use a standard pair of pliers or other standard hand tools will produce unsatisfactory results. The hand tool must fit the job. These are the factors to be considered:

1. Design the hand tool to give maximum comfort to the operator; use light-weight material, have good balance, and shape handles for gripping ease.
2. Equip pliers with a spring which keeps the jaw in an open position and requires only closing pressure by the operator.
3. To prevent damage to dies and injury to employees from flying particles, use a soft metal or other material which will not shatter on impact.
4. Design or shape each hand tool to fit the shape and size of the part being fed into the press. Always select the hand tool which facilitates application of good job methods.

Conclusions

Safeguarding of spindles, shafts, gears, belts, pulleys, and flywheels is a relatively easy task. The basic safety objective of preventing personnel from contacting such moving parts can be achieved by installation of simple enclosures, barriers, or rail guards or by safe locations. Nevertheless, there are times when these machine hazards are not guarded because the hazard is considered too minor to require a guard. For example, an operator suggested an enclosure guard for the drive shaft of a power shear. Investigation revealed that the shaft revolved at 30 rpm. The shaft was smooth and without a projecting keyway or attachments. It was located at the rear of the shear well out of reach of the operator. The decision was not to guard the shaft. Subsequent events demonstrated the need for a guard. A girl went behind the shear to pick up sheet-metal scraps. As she bent down, her hair caught on the slow moving, smooth shaft. She lost a handful of hair and part of her scalp. The suggested guard was then installed.

An unguarded belt drive 10 feet from the floor is considered safe because of its location. But what about an overhead belt which extends across a well-traveled aisle? There is a hazard here that might be missed. Belts occasionally break. If there is a sufficient distance between pulleys, the broken belt will lash across the aisle. The danger to personnel can be eliminated by installation of a belt guard. Couplings between motor-generator, motor-pump, and motor-compressor sets are another point of hazard that might be overlooked. Such equipment is frequently located in an out-of-the-way area of the plant. Thus, the suggestion to place a cover guard over the coupling evokes the comment, "If they are dumb enough to get caught, there isn't much you can do about it." A review of accident case histories provides convincing evidence that a coupling guard is needed. These sets operate intermittently from a remote control. Thus, without a guard, there is nothing to prevent an unsuspecting worker from placing his hand on the coupling just a second before the starting control kicks in. The worker is trapped by a condition which deceptively looks safe.

Point-of-operation guarding may be simplified in the future. Increased use of automatic equipment and careful consideration of safety in machine design will eliminate many point-of-operation hazards which at the moment are accepted as a necessary part of the manufacturing process. Nevertheless, current efforts to provide positive point-of-operation guards for machine tools, including milling machines, lathes, shapers, and drill presses, cannot be relaxed.

The choice of any single guard or safety device depends upon consideration of such factors as the nature of the operation, the length of the job run, the cost of the guarding method, and the effect of the guard on production. A positive approach to machine safety is to arrange the operation so it is unnecessary for the operator to put his hands into the point of operation and, where practical, also to install barrier guards which make it impossible to reach into the point of operation.

Of course, the most costly guard or safety device will give little protection if it is not used all of the time. Supervisors must be satisfied that guards provided for their machines are adequate, and that the guards or devices do not produce such an inconvenience that operators will be tempted to remove them or make them inoperative. If the guard has limitations, it is the supervisor's responsibility to insist upon corrections. He can make valuable suggestions for changes or even a complete redesign of the guard. Supervisors and safety engineers who are eager to increase their understanding and knowledge of machine-safeguarding principles and practices have many good references available. The point is to use them.

SELECTED REFERENCES

Accident Prevention Manual for Industrial Operations, National Safety Council, Chicago.

American Standard Safety Code for Mechanical Power Transmission Apparatus, B15.1-1953, American Standards Association, New York.

American Standard Safety Code for Power Presses and Foot and Hand Presses, B11.1-1948, American Standards Association, New York.

Faulkner, L. A., "Don't Overlook Operator Safety in Press Tool Design," *American Machinist,* September, 1952.

Heinrich, H. W., *Industrial Accident Prevention,* third edition, McGraw-Hill Book Co., New York, Chapters 8 and 9.

CHAPTER

9

Reducing industrial noise

Noise is a multi-field problem. It is not going to be solved by any one discipline. We must turn to the fields of medicine, safety engineering, industrial hygiene, physics of sound, communications, psychology, physiology, architecture, structural engineering, law, and many others. Each field must contribute its share to the analysis of noise, its effects on man, its control, and its legal and cultural consequences for management and society.

R. H. BOLT

Massachusetts Institute of Technology
and Bolt, Beranek and Newman, Inc.

The purpose of this chapter is to summarize present knowledge of the noise problem which industry faces and to suggest steps supervisors can take to quiet noisy machines and operations. It is recognized, of course, that the reduction or elimination of industrial noise often presents complex problems requiring professional assistance for solution. However, by being aware that the reduction of noise will improve working conditions and contribute to the well-being of employees, supervisors can frequently take constructive steps to correct a bad situation.

Although the increased use of power and high-speed equipment may have increased noise levels in recent years, the noise problem is not new. "Boiler maker's ear" has been talked about for a long time. But currently, for many reasons the subject of noise has been given considerable attention. Safety engineers are aware that high noise levels may account for some accidents through interference with hearing instructions and warning signals. Industrial physicians and enlightened management recognize the annoying and unpleasant effects of high noise levels. Psychologists and others have reason to believe that loud noise affects the over-all efficiency of the work group. Thus, industry has been devoting more attention to the need for reducing noise to assure workers' safety, comfort, and efficiency.

Awareness of the noise problem becomes acute when reviewed in light of possible financial responsibilities of the employer for occupational deafness. It has been accepted by state workmen's compensation courts that exposure to high noise levels can damage the hearing of some people. New York, in 1948, and Wisconsin, in 1953, handed down decisions under their workmen's compensation laws that employees are entitled to awards for loss of hearing arising from exposures to high noise levels in their employment. These decisions brought on a rush of claims that may indicate the extent of existing potential liability. Employees in one large company in New Jersey, for example, have filed compensation claims totaling more than 5 million dollars, and the number of hearing-loss claims has increased considerably throughout the United States. While there is no doubt that the employer faces financial liability for occupational deafness, as late as 1958 the matter was still confused. Workmen's compensation commissions are searching for a fair answer to many questions. Should compensation be paid if there is no wage loss? How much noise does it take to produce occupational deafness? How much deafness is the result of noise and how much is the natural result of old age (presbycousis)? How can the permanency of the hearing loss be determined? Once these questions are answered and suitable legislation passed, the backlog of hearing-loss claims will be processed. Faced with this financial threat, industry can take steps now to limit its liability. There is no point in taking a "let the sleeping dog lie" attitude about the matter. Undoubtedly, a plant noise survey and the supervisor's attention to the noise problem will arouse employee interest and prompt compensation claims. Yet, if the hearing of a worker has been impaired, there is no reason to believe the employee will not take action simply because management has ignored the condition. Newspaper and magazine articles, the worker's labor union, and his neighbors will enlighten him if management does not. From an employee-relations point of view, it is better for management to face the problem squarely and take action first.

How noise impairs hearing

Sound can be described as rapid pulsations in air pressure produced by a vibrating source. The mechanism of the ear is sensitive to these pulsations. Thus, anything that reduces this sensitivity is likely to have an effect on normal hearing. Contrary to popular belief, the eardrum is not usually damaged by high noise levels. The damage occurs in the inner ear, which is seated deep inside the skull. A sound wave creates a pressure which causes the eardrum to vibrate. This vibration is then passed on to the middle ear, which contains the three bones commonly called the hammer, anvil, and stirrup. From the middle ear, the vibration is carried to the inner ear. At this point, the mechanical vibration is converted into a nerve impulse as it strikes against a delicate structure of hair-like cells. High noise levels create an over-stimulation of these hair-like cells. Over an extended period or even in a short period, at approximately the 120 decibel range, these cells become damaged. Thus, some sound waves are no longer converted into nerve impulses to the brain and there is an impairment of hearing. The question of the level at which this damage occurs is still a matter of controversy. However, attempts are being made to determine the level and amount of noise which can be considered injurious to hearing.

Until definite standards are set, the consensus concerning the effects various ranges of noise have on hearing may provide a helpful guide to supervisors.

1. In general, if the noise level does not exceed 85 decibels, no injury to hearing results.

2. A noise level of 85 to 100 decibels may harm the hearing of highly susceptible people after long exposures.

3. Exposure over extended periods to noise levels in the 100-to-120 decibel range will damage the hearing of most people exposed.

4. Noise levels over 120 decibels may do permanent damage to the hearing of normal people even after short exposures. Sound levels over 120 decibels create immediate discomfort; those over 130 decibels produce pain.

The discussion to this point might create the impression that most hearing loss is the result of exposures to high noise levels. This, of course, is not the case. Childhood diseases, ear injuries, abscesses, and advancing age are just a few of the conditions which might impair hearing.

Noise level

Before discussing steps supervisors can take to control excessive noise, it will be helpful to review some general facts about sound. Two significant properties of sound are its noise level and its frequency. When a plant noise survey is made, the various existing noise levels can be measured with a sound meter, which indicates the level of the noise in decibels. A decibel is not a unit of measure like a volt or a pound. It is the ratio of any sound to the lowest sound pressure level an average person can hear. By experiment, this lowest audible pressure level was determined to be 0.0002 dynes per square centimeter. For comparison, average conversation produces a sound pressure level of 60 to 65 decibels; a circular saw, 100 decibels; a power press, 120 decibels; a jet engine, 130 decibels. Because average conversation produces a 60-decibel recording and a power press produces a 120-decibel recording, it might be assumed that the press is twice as noisy. However, as previously stated, a decibel is a ratio. When the two readings are converted to energy, the power-press noise level produces one thousand times the energy of average conversation. Thus, calculation reveals that an increase of 3 decibels doubles the noise level.

Frequency of sound

The source of sound is always in a state of vibration. The number of these vibrations per second is the frequency of the sound. This too is a property of sound that must be considered in a plant noise survey.

The higher-frequency sounds are more damaging to hearing than the low-frequency ones, and in some cases the frequency of the sound determines the control steps to be taken. Thus, in addition to determining the sound pressure level in decibels, engineers analyze existing plant noise to determine the frequencies of the noise. A sound analyzer or an octave-band frequency analyzer is used to measure frequencies. General data on sound frequency of interest to supervisors is summarized in the following list:

1. The human ear distinguishes frequencies from 20 to 16,000 cycles per second.
2. The frequency range for normal conversation is from 250 to 3000 cycles.
3. Most factory noise ranges in frequency from 600 to 10,000 cycles per second.
4. Noise in the range of 800 to 5000 cycles per second may be more damaging than lower-frequency noise.

Factory noise is composed of a wide variety of sounds at numerous pressure levels and frequencies. Hence, analysis of existing noise is difficult. Fortunately, instruments for doing the job are being improved constantly. While supervisors may not be directly concerned with the use of these instruments, they do have a vital interest in the results of a plant noise survey. When a noise problem is found, there are three possible steps that may be taken. First, various means can be used to reduce the noise level. Second, where reduction of the noise is not practical, isolation of the noise source can be considered. Third, where neither reduction nor isolation of the noise is possible, the use of personal protective equipment such as ear plugs or muffs is suggested. Where sound enclosures, resilient materials, vibration mounts, or sound-absorbing material is suggested as a solution to the noise problem, someone familiar with acoustical engineering should be consulted. But, even though expert help is required, the need for supervisors being familiar with methods for controlling noise is not diminished. Much that may be accomplished could be undone by a lack of understanding.

Reduction of noise at the source

If a sound meter is not available for determining noise levels, there is a simple way to make a noise check. Where workers must raise their voices to carry on a conversation, it is probable that the speech interference is annoying and that perhaps it is affecting employee morale and efficiency. Where the noise level is so high that two people at arm's length cannot hear each other in loud conversation or a shout, supervisors can anticipate that the hearing of some people in the noisy area will eventually be damaged. If these two checks indicate a problem, supervisors can take corrective action themselves. Also, they can call upon the plant safety engineer, the insurance company, or the state health bureau for assistance.

Admittedly, many noise problems will require highly technical solutions, but these technical aspects do not provide supervisors with the excuse for ignoring the matter. There is much that can be done.

Many machines and equipment are noisy because of worn parts, poor maintenance, or lack of lubrication or because they are out of balance. A planned maintenance program and the replacement of worn parts will do much to eliminate unnecessary noise. Likewise, establishment of a regular schedule for the lubrication of all machines will silence many annoying squeaks.

Extensive use of compressed air for cleaning purposes and parts ejection creates excessive noise of the most annoying sort. In many cases these noise sources can be either eliminated or dampened by taking a few relatively simple steps. Often a high-frequency noise is produced by a leaky air valve. Replacement or repair of the valve will solve the problem and result in a savings, too, because compressed-air costs run much higher than is normally assumed. Reduction of air pressures is still another approach. Use of reducing valves will make it possible for supervisors to use lower pressures for air ejection and cleaning where the usual 90-pounds-per-square-inch shop pressure is excessive. Frequently, copper tubing with the end squeezed to a narrow opening is used for air ejection. The narrow opening produces a high-frequency whistle-like sound. Increasing the size and changing the shape of the opening may lower the noise level appreciably. The use of a spring or other mechanical types of ejection instead of air may be an even better answer. Another approach where air is used is to provide automatic shut-offs so the air is available when needed rather than on a continuous-flow basis. Some equipment like air hoists, and other pneumatic devices produces loud hissing or roaring noises at the air exhaust outlet. Use of a muffler or silencer can effect a satisfactory reduction of this nerve-racking noise.

Changes in a process, substitution of equipment, or modification of existing equipment may provide numerous opportunities to eliminate or reduce a noisy process or operation. Of course, these changes or substitutions must be considered in light of the costs involved and the effects the change will have on production. While some suggested changes may be economically impractical, it is not uncommon for a change to result in savings and an improvement in the quality of the work done in addition to the better working conditions produced by the decrease in the noise level. Here are a few examples of the types of changes which might be considered:

1. Grinding instead of chipping.
2. Use of electrical tools in place of pneumatic tools where the pneumatic tools are excessively noisy.
3. Pressing instead of forging.
4. Welding instead of riveting.
5. Compression riveting instead of pneumatic riveting.
6. Mechanical ejection in place of air-blast ejection.
7. Wheels with rubber or composition tires on plant trucks and carts instead of all-metal wheels.
8. Wood or plastic tote boxes instead of metal tote boxes.
9. Use of an undercoating on machinery covers.
10. Wood instead of all-metal work benches.

Prevention of noise at its source provides a promising method of noise reduction. Although a change in equipment or a tool used will not always be possible, supervisors can be on the alert for opportunities (1) to use a quieter tool or quieter equipment, (2) to replace worn, noisy parts, (3) to streamline the machine-lubrication program, and (4) to keep high-speed machines in good quiet balance.

Isolating the noise source

If noise reduction by substitution or modification of existing equipment proves impractical, it may be possible to isolate the noise source or to move employees out of the noisy area. If an enclosure is built around the noisy machine, it should be designed by someone familiar with acoustic principles or it may not be effective. However, in order to obtain full utilization of the enclosures, supervisors will find some basic principles of enclosure design useful guides.

Exhibit 9–1 provides a graphic presentation of the basic principles in sound transmission and absorption. In the selection of materials to be used in the construction of sound-enclosing structures, an understanding of these principles is essential. Light-weight porous materials like fiberboard, cork, foam rubber, cloth, and mineral wool absorb a large fraction of the sound striking against them, but these materials also transmit sound through them with relatively little attenuation (sound reduction). Hard, massive materials, like brick or concrete, reflect a large fraction of the sound waves and prevent transmission of sound to the other side. However, little of the sound is absorbed. Basically, the transmission of sound is proportional to the mass of the wall material. Thus it develops that an ideal structure for enclosing

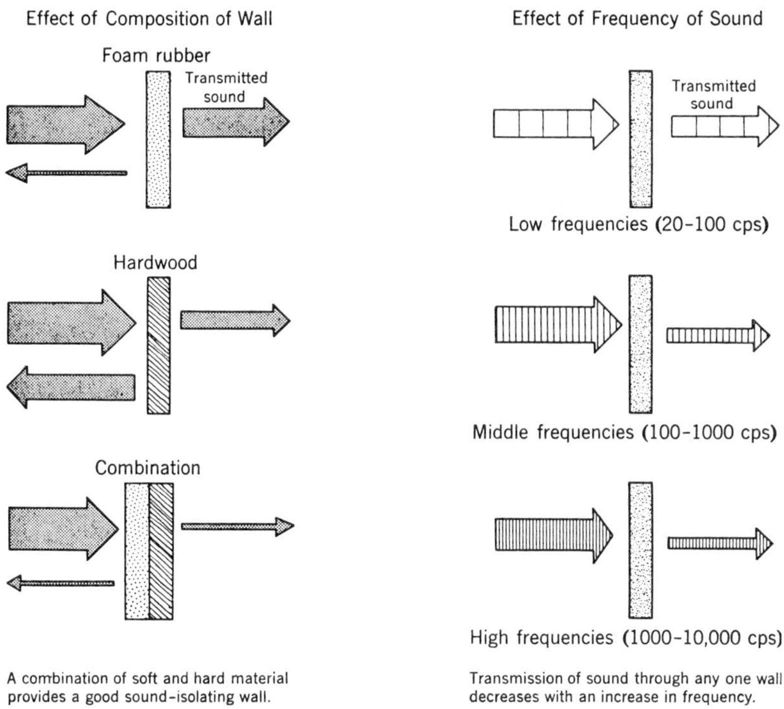

Exhibit 9–1. Basic principles in sound transmission loss. (Courtesy of Bolt, Beranek and Newman, Inc., and *Noise Control*, a publication of the Acoustical Society of America.)

or isolating a noise source would have walls of a heavy, hard material such as steel, brick, or concrete to prevent the transmission of sound to the outside and an inner lining of a soft material such as foam rubber or cork for sound absorption.

Also presented in Exhibit 9–1 is the effect of frequency of sound on its transmission through a wall of fixed weight and thickness. At the middle and high frequencies a smaller fraction of the sound is transmitted to the other side. The sound-transmission characteristics of various materials and the effect the frequency of sound has on transmission are factors to consider in the solution of various noise problems.

Where enclosures are used for isolating sound, it would be well for supervisors to keep in mind that small openings in the enclosure can reduce the effectiveness of the enclosure by a considerable amount. Hence, it is important to keep doors, lids, and hatches in the enclosure closed tightly. In some cases, even the cracks around a door in an enclosure provide a path for escape of a large fraction of the noise.

Another point for supervisors to keep in mind concerns the use of sound-dampening materials. Panels or other structures hung around a noisy machine may improve the situation for persons in the surrounding area, but they do nothing for the machine operator. The noise level will still be about the same for him because his position will be between the sound-absorbing panels and the noise source.

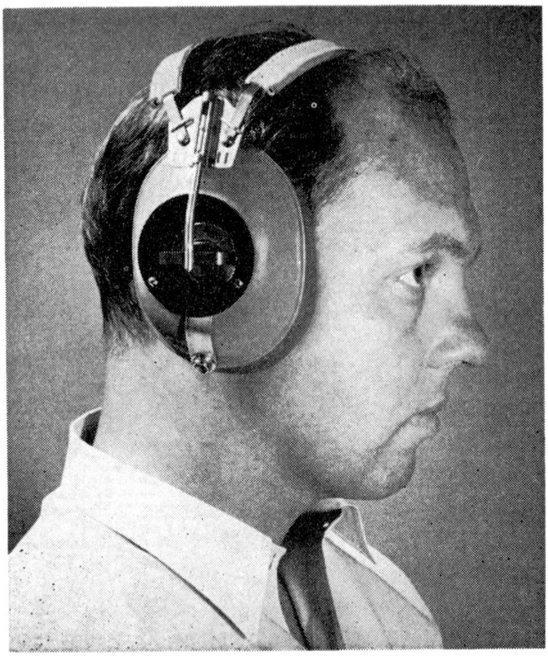

Exhibit 9–2. Ear muffs which are designed to provide worker protection against high noise levels. (Courtesy of the Mine Safety Appliances Company, Pittsburgh, Pennsylvania.)

Personal ear protectors

In some cases, reduction of the noise at the source and isolation of the noise by enclosures or other means will not be possible or economically practical. Under such circumstances, personal ear protection is the answer, especially if the noise level is in the range of 90 decibels and more. Where it is necessary to require employees to wear ear plugs or ear muffs (see Exhibits 9–2 and 9–3), the supervisor is in a strategic position to help promote the ear-protection program. Unfortunately, the task will not be an easy one. Ear plugs are unpleasant to wear and they present many problems regarding fit and proper use. At the outset, it will be difficult to convince employees that the plugs

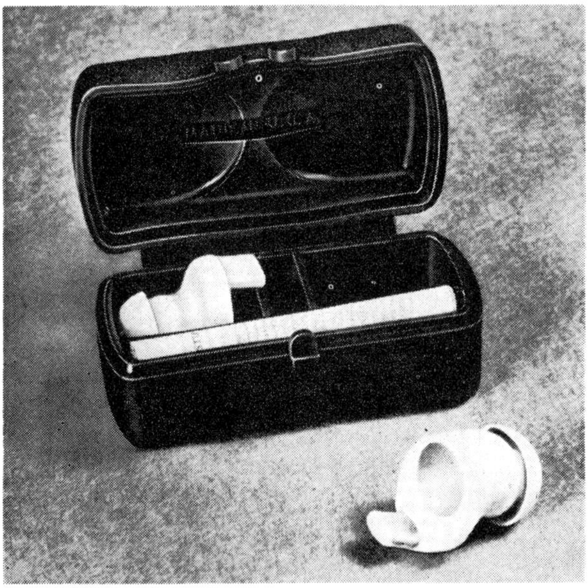

Exhibit 9–3. Ear plugs. These may be made of soft rubber, plastic material, or a moldable material such as wax and cotton which the wearer forms to fit his own ear canals. (Courtesy of the Mine Safety Appliances Company, Pittsburgh, Pennsylvania.)

are needed. Since the loss of hearing is a slow, gradual process, the average employee will have little awareness of the effectiveness of the plug. Unless the noise level is so high that actual discomfort results, many employees will wear the ear plugs for a short period of time, then discard them. Therefore, supervisors must take part in a program to educate employees on the hazards of noise and the proper use of ear plugs. Just handing a set of ear plugs to an employee is not enough. The employee must be told to keep the plugs clean to avoid ear infection. The plugs must fit. In some cases, it may be desirable to have the fitting done by the plant physician. Medical advice should also be sought for selection of the type of ear plugs to be used.

Usually it is better to give employees a choice of many different types of plugs. This will usually permit selection on the basis of comfort for the employee and good fit.

Despite some misconception, wads of dry cotton and swimming ear plugs in the ear canal do not provide protection against excessive noise. However, an impregnated cotton is effective if it is formed to provide a good closure of the ear canal.

One objection to ear plugs made by workers is that they will not be able to talk to one another when they are wearing the plugs. Supervisors can explain that this is not the case. In a noisy area use of ear plugs will actually improve speech reception. The plugs will reduce the sound level of the plant noise and the sound level of the speech the ear receives. By this reduction of the sound level the speech will still be within the normal hearing range and the plant noise will be closer to the normal hearing range. Although the ratio of the noise to the speech level remains the same, at the lower level speech reception is improved.

An actual demonstration of the plugs in a noisy area might help convince employees that the plugs make it easier for them to carry on a conversation.

Conclusions

Factory noise is still accepted as a necessary evil of the job just as thirty to forty years ago unguarded machines were taken for granted. But as a broader understanding of the underlying principles of noise control is gained by engineers and supervisors, this picture will change. Competition for the better employees and the financial liability associated with hearing-loss claims will motivate employers to take steps to reduce high noise levels. It can also be anticipated that manufacturers of factory machines and equipment will give careful consideration to the noise problem in their new designs.

As previously stated, supervisors are in a strategic position to tackle many of the present-day noise problems. Lubrication of machines, a good maintenance program, proper balancing of high-speed equipment, substitution of less noisy tools, use of soft rather than hard material, and finally, good administration of a personalized ear-protection program are all factors in the control of industrial noise worthy of supervisory consideration.

SELECTED REFERENCES

American Industrial Hygiene Association Quarterly, Vol. 17, No. 1, (March, 1956), pp. 17–60.

Bolt, R. H., et al., *Handbook of Acoustic Noise Control,* Wright Air Force Base, Ohio, Air Development Center, 1952.

Campbell, Douglass A., "Design of Noise Control Structures," *Noise Control,* September, 1955.

Hatton, Jack K., "Industrial Noise—Application of Control Measures by the Industrial Safety Engineer," *Noise Control,* September, 1955.

Sataloff, Joseph, *Industrial Deafness,* McGraw-Hill Book Co., New York, 1957.

CHAPTER

10

Fire prevention and fire-fighting methods

The details involved in the prevention and limitation of fire loss are numerous but the fundamental principles on which these details are based are relatively simple. Stated briefly, they are:

Knowledge of the hazardous characteristics of the materials handled as regards their fire and explosion potentials.

Prevention of the start of fire by adequate inspection and maintenance, good housekeeping, the segregation and reduction of combustible materials.

Prompt discovery and extinguishment of fires while they are still small.

Limitation of spread of fire by protected vertical and horizontal openings, enclosure with fire-resistive construction and confinement by adequate fire walls.

MATHEW M. BRAIDECH
National Board of Fire Underwriters

The largest fire loss in the history of American industry occurred August 12, 1953, when the General Motors Hydra-Matic Transmissions plant at Livonia, Michigan, burned to the ground. In a matter of fourteen hours three lives were lost and property estimated to be worth $40 million was damaged. General Motors has one of the best safety records in the country and this plant had been provided with modern fire-fighting equipment. Hence, the catastrophe immediately raised the big question—How could a modern steel and brick building burn with such frightening speed? The answer—There are large quantities of combustible materials in practically every manufacturing plant which, if not properly stored and handled, can become the fuse of a disastrous fire. At Livonia, widespread use of mineral oils for quenching, cooling, and rust-proofing resulted in there being a large amount of flammable liquids in the building. A spark from an acetylene welding torch provided the source of ignition.

The Livonia fire was just one of the over one hundred fires which occur in United States manufacturing plants each day. The others, of course, are less spectacular, but annually, these fires account for $150 million property damage, the loss of thousands of jobs, and the closing of many businesses. Fires are unpredictable. Even the best fire-prevention programs do not stop all fires. But a good fire-prevention program and knowledge of what to do when a fire starts will do much to keep fire losses down.

Fire-prevention terms

The problem of keeping a plant safe from fire is two-fold. Steps must be taken to eliminate the various causes of fire, and trained people and proper equipment must be available to extinguish a fire after it starts. Putting out a fire requires knowledge combined with practice. Hence, supervisors, members of a plant fire brigade, and others will find it helpful to learn a few basic facts about fire. The first thing to learn is that usually it takes three things to start a fire. They are:

Fuel: anything that will burn, like paper, cloth, wood, oil, gasoline.

Heat: sufficiently high temperature to cause the fuel to burst into flame.

Oxygen: enough air to keep the fire burning.

A fire can be put out by eliminating any of the three factors: the fuel, the oxygen, or the heat. A candle will illustrate how the three factors operate together to produce fire. The wick and tallow of the candle are the fuel. A lighted match will supply heat sufficient to raise the wick to the ignition temperature, producing a flame. The candle will then continue to burn until the tallow (fuel) is consumed, or the temperature is reduced by cooling with water or blowing out the flame, or the source of oxygen is eliminated. The last can be demonstrated by placing an inverted water glass over the candle. In seconds the candle goes out because the supply of oxygen in the glass is consumed.

There are three types of fires, based on National Fire Protection Association classifications:

Class A—Fires in ordinary combustible materials such as wood, paper, textiles, and rubbish. To extinguish such fires, the quenching or cooling effects of water or solutions containing large proportions of water are required.

Class B—Fires in flammable liquids such as gasoline, solvents, oil, grease, paint, varnish, and lacquers, where a blanketing or smothering effect is essential to put out the fire.

Class C—Fires in electrical equipment such as motors, generators, and switch-panels. Because of an electrical hazard, a non-conductive extinguishing agent is required.

In many discussions on fire prevention and fire fighting, terms such as flash point, ignition temperature, and explosive limits come up. These terms should be understood. Their definitions follow:

Flash point. A so-called flammable liquid itself does not burn; it is the vapor produced by evaporization of the liquid that burns. Hence, the flash point of a flammable liquid is the lowest temperature at which enough vapor is given off near the surface of the liquid to produce a flammable mixture with air. A flammable mixture is one which contains the proper ratio of vapor and air to support combustion. These ratios vary widely from liquid to liquid, but it should always be assumed that any flammable solvent above its flash point is evolving a flammable vapor-air mixture. Essentially this means that if a solvent is above its flash point, any source of ignition—a burning match, an electrical spark, a friction spark, a static spark, etc.—might produce a fire. Once the fire has started, its heat rapidly volatilizes more solvent until soon the whole mass is aflame. In general, the lower the flash point, the more flammable the material becomes, and the more violent is the resulting fire.

The fact that a solvent's temperature is below its flash point does not mean necessarily that it is safe. If a material—kerosene, for example—with a flash point of 100 F is brought in contact with a source of intense heat—a welding torch, furnace, or open fire—a small part of it could be heated above the flash point, give off vapor, and burst into flame. The heat so produced would heat the rest of the kerosene and the fire would spread. Some of industry's most costly fires have occurred in just such a manner when a container of high-flash solvent has spilled and contacted a suitably intense source of ignition. If a high-flash solvent is sprayed into the air, the resultant mist-air mixture is almost as easily ignited as though it were a true vapor-air mixture.

Most solvent vapors are heavier than air. It is possible for the vapor from a container of solvent to flow along the floor and be ignited at a distance from the source. This distance may vary widely, depending on prevailing ventilation. There have been reports of fires being started and flashing back to the source of vapor which was 50 or more feet away.

TABLE 10–1. COMMON FLAMMABLE LIQUIDS USED IN MANUFACTURING PROCESSES

	Flash Point (degrees F)	Explosive Limits (per cent by volume)	
		Lower	Upper
Acetone	0	2.6	12.8
Amyl acetate	77	1.1	. . .
Amyl alcohol	100	1.2	. . .
Benzene (benzol)	12	1.4	7.1
Butyl acetate-*iso*	64	. . .	. . .
Butyl alcohol (normal)	84	1.4	11.2
Ethyl acetate	24	2.5	9
Ethyl alcohol (ethanol)	55	4.3	19
Ethyl ether	−49	1.9	48
Gasoline	−45	1.4	7.6
Hexane-*n*	−15	1.2	7.5
Isopropyl acetate	43	2.0	12
Kerosene	100	0.7	5
Methyl alcohol (methanol)	52	7.3	36
Methyl ethyl ketone	30	1.8	10
Naptha, petroleum	0	1.1	5.9
Toluene (toluol)	40	1.4	6.7
Xylene (xylol)-o	63	1.0	6.0

Explosive limits. Each flammable liquid has a minimum concentration of vapor in air or oxygen below which a spread of flame does not occur when the vapor is in contact with a source of ignition. There is also a maximum concentration of vapor above which the spread or propagation of flame does not occur. These limits are known as lower and upper explosive limits. They vary widely for different flammable liquids. For example, gasoline vapor in air will explode upon ignition if the percentage of gasoline vapor in the air is not less than 1.4 and not greater than 7.6. The 1.4 per cent is called the lower explosive limit, the 7.6 per cent is called the upper explosive limit, and the spread between 1.4 per cent and 7.6 per cent is the explosive range. Automobile mechanics are referring to the explosive range when they speak of a gasoline mixture in an engine being too lean or too rich. By too lean they mean that the volume of gasoline vapor is below the lower limit; by too rich they mean that it is above the upper limit. In either case, no explosion occurs.

Ignition temperature. This is the temperature at which ignition (production of a flame) and burning will be continued after the source of ignition or the source of heat is removed.

Fire-prevention methods

Modern fire-prevention methods place a great deal of emphasis on the layout of the manufacturing area, the availability of fire-fighting equipment, and the need for keeping the accumulation of combustible materials at a minimum. The goal is that if a fire does start, the loss will be minimized because it will be easy to get at the fire, only small quantities of combustible material will be available, and proper fire-fighting equipment will be on hand. This approach gives more positive results than an attempt to eliminate all sources of ignition. This latter approach is almost impossible as a list of some of the more common causes of industrial fires attests:

COMMON CAUSES OF FIRES

1. Electrical equipment improperly installed, poorly maintained, or worn. Electrical devices or fittings of types unsafe for areas in which flammable vapors or dusts are present. Fires caused by arcing or over-heating.

2. Hot bearings, misaligned or broken machine parts, material choking or jamming in machines, improper adjustments of moving machinery, grinding and sanding operations. Fires caused by heat of friction or frictional sparks.

3. Thoughtless use of matches, thoughtless disposal of lighted cigarettes, especially in vicinity of flammable liquids or easily ignited combustibles.

4. Combustibles too near or in contact with boilers or furnaces, heaters, hot ducts or flues, electric lamps, or hot metal.

5. Faulty gas and oil burners, misuse of torches including gasoline blow torches. Fires caused by burner flames igniting leaking fuel, flammable vapors or dusts, or other combustibles.

6. Abnormally high process temperatures due to faulty operation of processes involving such materials as heated flammable liquids and materials in ovens and dryers.

7. "Sparks" or globules of molten metal from gas cutting and welding torches, and from electric welding torches, when used without adequate precautions against fire.

8. Spontaneous ignition of oily waste or rubbish, accumulated deposits in ducts and flues, and waste materials in storage.

9. Static electricity producing sparks in the absence of adequate grounding, static eliminators, and humidification, igniting vapors and combustible dusts.

10. Molten metal escaping from ruptured furnaces or spilled during handling, including molten glass and tempering salts.

The foregoing list gives an indication of the number and variety of fire-ignition sources that can be found in a manufacturing plant. Of course, by the proper teaming of maintenance programs and the use of equipment of a safer design, it is possible to keep ignition sources at a minimum.

But as previously indicated, a productive approach to fire prevention is the reduction of combustible materials in the plant. Good housekeeping is an important factor. Rubbish and waste under benches and in corners, oil deposits on machines, large accumulations of combustible dusts, flammable packing materials, open containers of flammable solvents, and oil-soaked floors greatly increase the chances for a big fire. Basic rules for keeping down the quantity of combustible material in a plant are easy to follow.

1. Establish a regular schedule for cleaning oil, dust, and other flammable deposits from machines and equipment.

2. Use metal self-closing containers for oily rags and waste.

3. Remove waste paper, rags, and rubbish from the plant daily or more often, if necessary.

4. Keep flammable solvents in safety cans.

5. Exclude paints, solvents, and other highly flammable materials from the plant, except for quantities required for daily production.

6. Use fuller's earth not sawdust on oily floors.

Safety cans

Casual observation might not reveal the basic safety feature of safety cans, mentioned in rule 4. These containers, which can be obtained in 1-quart to 5-gallon sizes, are usually painted a bright red and have a self-closing spout to prevent spillage. However, the principal safety

Exhibit 10–1. A safety can with a cut-away section to show a fire baffle located in the spout. This is a double-wall perforated metal screen with proper size perforations to permit filling and pouring but prevent the propagation of fire within the container. (Courtesy of the Protectoseal Company, Chicago, Illinois.)

feature is an anti-flash screen or flame arrester in the spout. The principle of the flame arrester was developed more than one hundred and forty years ago by Sir Humphrey Davy. The fine-wire-mesh screen of the flame arrester absorbs and dissipates the heat of the fire before it reaches the flammable liquid. It also prevents the entrance of sufficient air into the container to support combustion. Points to check on a safety can include the flame arrester, to make sure it has not been removed, and the metal can and the self-closing lid, for leaks.

Automatically closing covers

Large tanks and containers with automatically closing lids are used in many plants where large quantities of flammable liquids are used for washing and dipping operations. Covers on such tanks close by

Exhibit 10–2. A wash and dip tank with a fusible link in the cover which melts quickly when the contents are ignited, thereby closing the cover and extinguishing the flame before damage from the fire can occur. (Courtesy of the Protectoseal Company, Chicago, Illinois.)

gravity. They are held open by a chain with a fusible link which melts at a low temperature. In case of fire, the link melts, permitting the cover to close by the force of gravity. Thus the fire is quickly smothered by the elimination of the air supply necessary to support combustion. It is not uncommon to find obstructions in these tanks, especially drying racks, that would keep the lid from closing. Obviously such obstructions must be removed so the lid will close should a fire start.

Portable fire extinguishers

Supervisors should be able to identify the different classes of fires and should know the right type of portable or mobile extinguisher to use. However, selection of the right extinguisher is not all that is required. Supervisors and employees must know also how to use the extinguisher. This is especially true when fighting flammable-liquid fires. To be prepared, it is advisable to set up practice sessions for persons who would be expected to use an extinguisher in an emergency. Just a few sessions could mean the difference between a burned-out plant and a small fire. In those cases where people have never used an extinguisher, strange things happen. One man seeing a small fire under a work bench ran for a portable soda-acid extinguisher. He took the extinguisher from a rack and placed it over his shoulder, top down. The soda and acid were mixed and the resulting pressure expelled all the water before he reached the fire. To make matters worse, he slipped in the water and hurt his back. Then, thoroughly soaked and injured, he left the fire fighting to a fellow worker who did know something about extinguishers.

The selection of fire extinguishers must be based on the class of combustible material present in the area. An extinguisher which expels water would be placed in an area in which there are wood, paper, textiles, and other such materials. If flammable liquids are present, a foam, carbon dioxide, or dry-chemical extinguisher is required. Water (except water sprays or fog) on a Class B, flammable-liquid, fire would spatter flaming liquid over a wide area. Water on a Class C, electrical, fire could be dangerous because the electric charge follows the water stream back to the fire fighter. Therefore, a carbon dioxide or dry-chemical extinguisher is required in an area with electrical equipment such as control panels, large motors, transformers, and the like. A chart, Exhibit 10–3, will provide supervisors with information concerning the selection, function, and appearance of the five basic types of portable extinguishers.

Knowledge of a limitation of the carbon tetrachloride fire extinguisher is essential. Exposure to the fumes generated when a carbon tetrachloride fire extinguisher is used may produce harmful results. It is claimed that this liquid in contact with an open flame might generate phosgene gas, which is highly poisonous. Also, fumes from materials saturated with the carbon tetrachloride can be especially harmful to some people. Although a carbon tetrachloride fire extinguisher is effective on Class B and C fires, the disadvantage of the toxic fumes produced should not be overlooked. In order to be on the safe side, a carbon tetrachloride extinguisher should not be used in a confined area such as an elevator, welding booth, crane cab, small room, or basement.

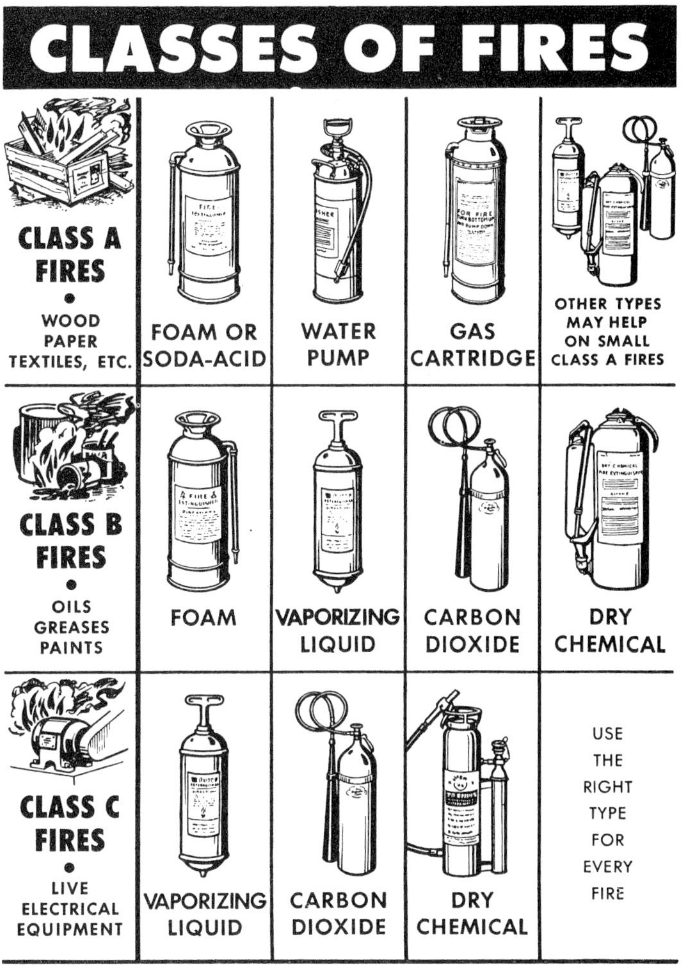

Exhibit 10–3. Safety poster, National Safety Council, Chicago, Illinois.

A portable fire extinguisher is a "first-aid" appliance. It is used to keep small fires from becoming big disasters. In a plant, back-up equipment includes fire hose, the sprinkler system, and the fire wagon. All of this equipment must always be ready for prompt use. This means that extinguishers and other equipment must be located correctly, conspicuously marked for instant location, easy to reach, and proper for the class of fire. Immediately after use, an extinguisher should be recharged. Periodically, equipment should be checked to assure that it is in proper working order.

M6D-50M-2-53

IMPORTANT
CUTTING *and* WELDING
PERMIT

Precautions on reverse side must be followed without fail

Date__________

Building__________

Floor and Dept.__________

Time Started__________Completed__________

Work to be done__________

The location where the above work is to be done has been personally examined, necessary precautions have been taken and permission is granted for this work. This permit expires __________

Signed__________
Title

FILE FOR F.I.A. INSPECTOR'S REVIEW

See Other Side

DANGER

Prevent Fires

DO NOT CUT OR WELD UNTIL THE FOLLOWING CUTTING AND WELDING PRECAUTIONS HAVE BEEN TAKEN AND THIS CARD SIGNED.

Check each item.

1. No cutting or welding to be permitted:
   A. While sprinklers are out of service.
   B. In presence of flammable lint, dust, vapors and liquids or unpurged tanks and equipment previously containing such materials.
   C. In area or on equipment other than that specified in permit.
2. Restrict all operations to fire safe areas.
3. Before cutting or welding operations are started:
   A. Area must be personally examined and approved by Company Official and necessary safeguards arranged for prior to issuing permit.
   B. Sweep clean and wet down floors and surroundings.
   C. Relocate all combustibles 30-40 ft. from operations. Completely protect remainder with asbestos curtains, metal guards or flame-proofed covers (not ordinary tarpaulins).
   D. Cover over tightly any floor or wall openings within 40 ft. of operations.
   E. Assign responsible men to watch for dangerous sparks in area as well as in floors above and below.
   F. Provide ample fire protection equipment—hand hose, extinguishers, water pails, etc.
4. Patrol area including floors above and below for at least ½ hour after work completed.
5. Cutting and welding equipment should be maintained in good repair.

I have taken the required precautions for safe cutting and welding practices as checked above.

Signed__________ Operator

FACTORY INSURANCE ASSOCIATION
CHICAGO HARTFORD SAN FRANCISCO

See Other Side

Exhibit 10–4. Permit for gas and electric cutting and welding.

Fire-prevention check questions

Other key points for supervisors concerning fire prevention are covered in the check questions which follow:

1. Are adequate precautions taken when gas and electric welding or cutting is done in your plant *outside of regular welding areas*? (At many plants a guard with fire-fighting training is required to stand by with fire extinguishers while either welding or cutting is being done by maintenance and construction people.) A "cutting and welding

permit" might be used to keep such situations under control. (See Exhibit 10–4.)

2. When a fire starts it might explode through a building with frightening speed. An oil-soaked floor and oil-covered machines and conveyor lines form a fire trail. *Are there such fire trails in your plant, or could you quickly localize a fire by closing fire doors or blanketing the area with an effective extinguishing agent?*

3. When outside contractors work in your area, are they required to take adequate precautions against fire?

4. Are regular inspections of fire-fighting equipment made to be sure it is ready for emergency use?

5. Have the local Fire Department officials made an inspection of your plant so that in case of fire all fire hazards will be familiar to them?

6. Are regular fire drills held so that in case of fire, evacuation of the plant will be conducted in an orderly manner?

Volunteer firemen

Many companies have well-trained fire-fighting organizations in various sections of the plant and on each work shift with ability to handle a fire or other emergencies. Employees who volunteer for the fire-fighting teams receive specific training on the use of fire equipment and attend regular meetings and fire drills. Training includes all the instructions for handling fires caused by the accumulation of wood and paper, oil, or electrical equipment. Instruction may also include use of gas masks and portable inhalators. Volunteers go into action under the direction of their respective supervisors. They function until relieved by regular firemen. Usually each volunteer is assigned one of the following specific duties: closing fire doors, using portable extinguishers, calling the fire department, directing regular firemen to the fire, shutting off power to machinery, closing gas lines, and finally, seeing that used extinguishers are recharged. Maintenance employees are usually well qualified for volunteer fire brigades. However, other employees should also be provided with the opportunity to serve on the fire brigade.

Summary

Preventing fires and keeping them small requires knowledge of the various classes of fires and the various fire-fighting equipment suitable for each class. Equally important is sufficient practice in the use of fire extinguishers and a volunteer fire-fighting team trained and ready for an emergency. Supervisors have a big part in fire-prevention and fire-fighting functions. Good housekeeping, maintenance of fire-fighting equipment, and the enforcement of rules like "No Smoking" are supervisory responsibilities that have a bearing on the success of the fire-prevention program.

It should be emphasized, of course, that the steps to be taken for a complete fire-prevention program are extensive. Information and assistance that can be obtained from the fire-prevention associations, insurance companies, and manufacturers of fire-prevention and fire-fighting equipment should not be overlooked. Frequently the fire that is stopped by supervisory knowledge and diligence will mean more than just saving a building from destruction. It will mean saving a job—saving a business.

SELECTED REFERENCES

Annual Fire Protection Issue (July issue), *National Safety News,* National Safety Council, Chicago, Illinois.

Fire Extinguishing Appliances, Pamphlet Nos. 10–19, National Board of Fire Underwriters, New York, New York.

Fire Extinguishing Auxiliaries, Pamphlet Nos. 20–27, National Board of Fire Underwriters, New York, New York.

Industrial Fire Brigades, Training Manual, National Fire Protection Association, Boston, Massachusetts, 1954.

Stecher, Gilbert E., "Fire Prevention and Protection Fundamentals," *The Spectator,* Philadelphia, 1953.

Stop Fires—Save Jobs, National Board of Fire Underwriters, New York, New York.

Training Your Fire Brigade to Use First Aid Extinguishers, Walter Kidde and Company, Belleville, New Jersey.

CHAPTER 11

Personal protective equipment

Excellent equipment and devices in a great variety to protect any part of the body are commercially available. But, the existence of such equipment should not deter efforts to eliminate the hazard at the source by engineering design, methods revision, or substitution of non-hazardous materials. It is emphasized that personal protective devices do not eliminate hazards —they are a second line of defense which protects workers from injury providing they are used.

ROBERT D. GIDEL
Bureau of Labor Standards

EYE PROTECTION

In American industry there are thousands of workers who have been convinced that an eye-protection program is good business. A flying object headed straight for a precious eye of theirs has been stopped by the protective lenses of safety glasses. Over fourteen thousand of these fortunate workers have become members of the Wise Owl Club,[1] an organization sponsored by the National Society for the Prevention of Blindness, 1790 Broadway, New York City. A look at the case histories of these Wise Owl Club members reveals that an eye injury can occur almost any place, any time. Here are a few examples:

While the operator was grinding a milling cutter, the stop broke and a flying part hit the left lens of his safety glasses.

Drill broke; a piece shattered the operator's safety glasses.

Heavy chip flew from lathe and hit safety glasses.

Lead pot erupted; molten lead covered the lenses of operator's safety glasses.

Piece flew out of power press and cracked safety glasses.

The serious consequences of an eye injury are ample reasons for an adequate eye-protection program. But aside from this humanitarian consideration, the medical and compensation expense involved in the loss of one eye—$2300 to $14,536, depending upon state compensation laws—makes the eye-protection program economically sound.

There are numerous successful eye-protection programs throughout industry that are administered according to the best concepts of modern management. But, perhaps at this point it would be helpful to review some of the reasons why eye-protection programs have failed. Then, in turn, the essentials of a successful program will be discussed.

Some programs have been planned failures. Here is why:

1. No attempt was made to sell employees on the need for eye protection or to explain the characteristics and benefits of safety glasses.

2. Eye protection was provided in one section of the plant, but not in other sections where similar eye hazards existed. Therefore, em-

[1] Any employee who, at the time of an accident, saved the sight of one or both eyes from damage because he was wearing eye protection can become a member of the Wise Owl Club.

Exhibit 11–1. Safety glasses which saved eye of milling-machine operator. Milling cutter broke and hardened tip hit left lens with the frightening result shown. Upper picture shows what happened when piece of a shattered abrasive wheel hit the safety goggles of a grinder operator. In each case the worker was uninjured.

ployees in the area where eye protection was provided could not understand why they had to wear safety glasses. They concluded that management was being unfair.

3. Supervisors did not wear safety glasses in areas where employees were required to wear eye protection.
4. Safety glasses were not properly fitted and employee complaints were improperly handled.
5. Infractions of rules regarding eye protection were ignored.
6. Long delays occurred between time of employment and arrival of safety glasses.

The experienced supervisor and safety engineer will recognize that the above list is a partial one. Many more reasons for failure of the eye-protection program could be added, but it would be better to review the basic principles of a successful eye-protection program.

Key points about eye-protection programs

It is a good business to provide employees with necessary eye protection in all areas of the plant where eye hazards exist. But before embarking on a program, it might be helpful to review these key points.

Eye protection should be provided because of known eye hazards.

Employees should be educated to recognize these hazards.

The purpose of eye protection and the need for it should be understood by employees.

It would be wrong to temporize with a rule requiring the wearing of eye protection. Once the eye protection is provided, its use should become a condition of employment.

The last key point is of particular importance. Too often an eye is lost because the safety glasses which should have been worn are left in a bench drawer, tool box, or work-apron pocket. Enforcing a rule on safety glasses is not harshness. Basically, it is a demonstration of the supervisor's sincere interest in and concern for the safety of each employee.

When eye protection is required in an entire plant, a specific area of the plant, or for specific jobs, there are certain basic rules that should be followed:

1. Employees who are required to work in areas or to enter areas where eye protection is required should not be permitted access to such areas until the protection has been provided. (This may necessitate providing employees who need correction with a temporary means of protection such as plastic eye shields which can be worn over regular glasses until the prescription safety glasses are ready.)
2. No one, including plant visitors, should be permitted to enter an area where eye protection is required without adequate eye protection. (In plants with a 100-per-cent program, it is a practice for the receptionist to give visitors a pair of safety glasses with the visitor's pass. Inexpensive visitor's safety glasses are now on the market.)
3. Safety glasses preferably should be dispensed from one location and individually fitted by a qualified person.
4. Complaints that plano safety glasses cause headaches and nausea

are not uncommon. In some cases, the basis for the complaint may be psychological, or might be defective vision of which the employee is unaware. It is a good practice, therefore, to check the eyesight of

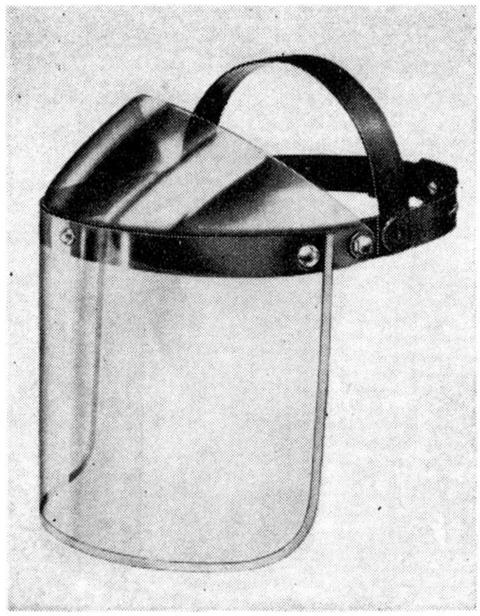

Exhibit 11–2. Full-face shields provide protection for eyes and face on such jobs as handling chemicals, sanding, light grinding, electric spot and butt welding. Face shields should not be used where resistance to severe impact is required. (Courtesy of the United States Safety Service Company, Kansas City, Missouri.)

employees required to wear safety glasses. A preliminary check can be made at the plant dispensary. Where defective vision is indicated,

Exhibit 11–3. Spectacle-type safety glasses are now available with either plastic or tempered-glass lenses. The lenses may be ground to the individual prescription of the wearer. Safety glasses are also worn with side shields where the additional protection is required. (Courtesy of the United States Safety Services Company, Kansas City, Missouri.)

the employee should be encouraged to get an eye examination from a qualified professional person. This examination would be paid for by the employee.

What should the policy be regarding the employee who will need prescription safety glasses? Many companies pursue the practice of providing prescription safety glasses without charge to the employee. However, the employee is required to provide a copy of his most recent prescription so the safety glasses can be properly ground. Also, to assure proper fit, the employee's prescription must indicate pupilary distance, bridge size, and temple length.

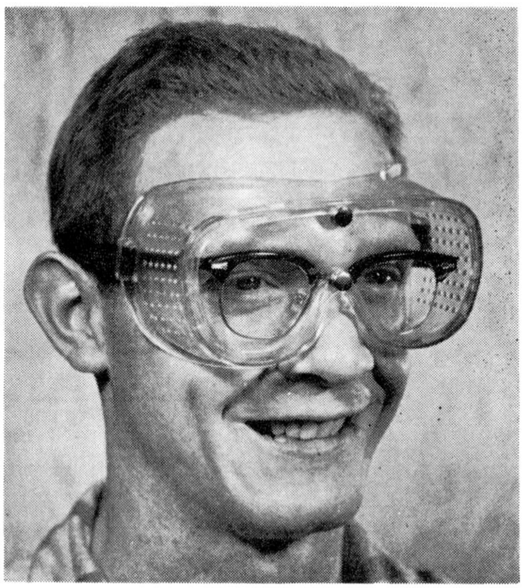

Exhibit 11–4. Plastic eye shields are designed so they may be worn over regular glasses to protect workers from dust, small particles, splashing liquids, and moderate impact from any direction. (Courtesy of the Mine Safety Appliances Company, Pittsburgh, Pennsylvania.)

It would be difficult to cover the gamut of jobs and operations which require eye protection. In general, eye protection is required in all areas where there are flying particles, dust, splashing hazardous chemicals, rays injurious to the eyes, and molten materials. The type of protection is, of course, based on the extent of the hazard involved. In areas with high concentrations of dust, flying particles, or irritating chemicals, safety glasses with side shields, cup-type goggles, full-face shields, or plastic eye protectors may be necessary. In less hazardous areas, spectacle-type safety glasses might be used. Types of eye protection required for various exposures are shown in Exhibit 11–5.

EYE PROTECTION FOR VARIOUS JOBS

TYPES OF EXPOSURE (National Bureau of Standards Handbook H24)	TYPES OF PROTECTION: CUP GOGGLES	SPECTACLES	SIDE SHIELDS	PLASTIC EYE SHIELD	PLASTIC FACE SHIELD	WIRE SCREEN SHIELD	FILTER LENSES	RUBBER OR VINYL GOGGLES	HOODS	WELDING HELMETS
Heavy impact. large particles–chipping, calking, some riveting operations, sledging in quarries.	●		●							
Moderate impact, dust and small flying particles–scaling and grinding metals, stone dressing where quartz is not involved, some woodworking operations.		●	●	●	●					
Metal sparks and spatter–electric spot and butt welding; no exposure to excessive energy or glare.			●	●	●					
Splashing metal–babbitting, pouring lead joints for pipes, casting hot metal, dipping in hot metal baths.	●			●	●	●				
Splashing liquids–acids and caustics, dipping in galvanized tanks, some japanning operations.	●				●			●	●	
Reflected light and glare–long exposure to light reflected from snow, water, roads, etc.; incidental glare from furnaces, working near acetylene welding, etc.	●	●	●				●			
Injurious radiant energy–moderate reduction in visible radiant energy–oxyacetylene welding and cutting.	●						●			
Injurious radiant energy–large reduction of visible radiant energy – arc welding.										●

Exhibit 11–5. Eye-protection chart. (Source: *National Safety News*, March, 1957.)

A successful eye-protection program

A report prepared by a safety engineer in an organization with a successful eye-protection program provides a fine example of the application of the basic principles that have been discussed.

Last December, a program to sell supervisors and employees on the wearing of safety glasses in the manufacturing area was instituted. It was culminated with the recent issuing of an amendment to the Employee Safety Instructions which requires all employees to wear safety glasses while in the work areas. The program started with the selling of all supervisors on the need for adequate eye protection. This selling was done in meetings and individual discussions conducted by the plant safety engineer. Finally, when 100 per cent of the supervisors were wearing safety glasses, they became salesmen in selling the eye protection program to employees.

Along with the selling program, the eyesight of each employee was checked. Persons with indicated defects were asked to contact a professional person.

Several meetings were held with employees for the purpose of discussing general safety matters. During these meetings, the eye protection program was given prime consideration. Finally, a secret ballot was held to determine the attitude of employees regarding the wearing of safety glasses while in the plant. The vote indicated 92 per cent of the employees favored an eye protection program.

An announcement was then made that August 1st the wearing of safety glasses at all times while in the plant would become a condition of employment. Employees understood that refusal to wear the eye protection required would mean dismissal. Significantly, only one employee refused to wear safety glasses, and he changed his mind after talking the matter over with his wife. Now, we feel the wearing of safety glasses has become a symbol of safety in our plant.

It is good business to provide employees with safety glasses, eye shields, or goggles if there is a need for such protection; employees recognize the need and the protection is provided with the understanding that it will be used.

RESPIRATORY PROTECTION

Preventing the inhalation of fumes and dusts

The need for an effective gas mask to protect military personnel against mustard gas during World War I gave impetus to the development of a wide range of respiratory devices including gas masks, mechanical-filter respirators, self-contained breathing apparatus, air-line respirators, chemical-cartridge respirators, and air-line hoods and helmets. However, the idea of using a filtering device to prevent the inhalation of dusts or fumes is not by any means new. Pliny the Elder (23–79 A.D.), a Roman naturalist, describes a gadget which was worn over the nose and mouth of pigment makers to prevent the inhalation of vermilion dust, a compound of mercury and sulphur.

Industrial hygienists and medical researchers have identified a long list of dusts, fumes, vapors, mists, and gases which, if present in sufficient volume, would be injurious to the health of workers. It has been known for many years, for example, that free silica found in sand, sandstone, granite, quartz, and other rocks is an irritant which affects the lungs, producing an occupational disease called silicosis. Lead and manganese fumes produce a systemic poisoning affecting various vital organs. Likewise, vapors of carbon tetrachloride, toluol, benzol, and many other solvents are injurious to the health of workers.

Thus, to prevent an occupational disease caused by the inhalation of such air contaminants as toxic dust, mist, gas, or vapor certain control steps must be taken. There are three principal approaches to the problem:

1. Steps can be taken to prevent the dispersion of the contaminant. This might be accomplished by enclosing the operation which produces the hazardous dusts, fumes, or gases or by segregating the operation so workers will not be in the contaminated atmosphere. Also, local exhaust systems can be used so the fumes, dust, or gas will be drawn outside the building.
2. A non-toxic or a less toxic material can be substituted for the toxic material. For example, steel shot or grit can be substituted for sand in abrasive blasting. Methyl chloroform, a less toxic material, can be substituted for carbon tetrachloride in cleaning and degreasing operations.
3. If it is not possible or practical to prevent dispersion of the toxic fumes, dusts, or vapors or to substitute a non-toxic material, then personal respiratory protective devices can be used to protect the health of those exposed to the contaminated air.

In addition to being required to protect the wearer against certain air-borne contaminants, respiratory protection is also required when there is a deficiency of oxygen in the surrounding atmosphere. Therefore, respiratory protective devices may be considered in two groups. The first group consists of the self-contained breathing apparatus, air-line respirators, hose masks, and air-supplied hoods and helmets.

Wearers of these devices are supplied with uncontaminated air from a source other than the surrounding atmosphere. The second group includes the mechanical-filter respirators, chemical-cartridge respirators, and gas masks. The wearer of these devices breathes the air from the surrounding area, but a mechanical filter or a chemical filter removes most of the contaminants before the air is inhaled.

It is not uncommon to find a respiratory protective device that is being misused. The reason for the misuse is two-fold. The function and the purpose of the device may not be fully understood, or the device may be used because it was available and the installation of proper controls such as an exhaust booth was mistakenly considered too costly or time consuming. Supervisors need to know about the various types of respiratory protective devices available, their uses, and their limitations. Adequate knowledge is required to assure proper selection, use, and care of the wide range of equipment and apparatus available. However, when a situation develops or can be anticipated where respiratory protection is required, the need for seeking expert advice is emphasized. A new toxic material, an unusual operating situation, or just a combination of usual conditions may create some rather technical problems relative to the protection required. The industrial hygienist or plant safety engineer who is contacted may be aware of a new development in the respiratory-protection field or a new control measure that has not come to the attention of the supervisor. Hence, the assistance received would be of great value.

Types of respiratory protective devices

Self-contained breathing apparatus. There are two principal types of supplied-air respirators. One type consists of compressed air or oxygen contained in a cylinder which is carried in a harness by the user of the apparatus. Air or oxygen is delivered from the cylinder to a face piece through a flexible rubber breathing tube. The wearer exhales to the atmosphere through exhalation valves in the face piece. The other type of self-contained apparatus consists of a canister of chemicals which, upon contact with moisture in the wearer's exhaled breath, start a reaction that evolves oxygen and absorbs the exhaled carbon dioxide. Because both of these devices separate the wearer from all external contact as regards the air he breathes, respiratory protection is provided in any concentration of toxic gases and in any condition of oxygen deficiency.

Employees who might use a self-contained breathing apparatus require adequate training. Misuse of the equipment could result in injury or death. One of the advantages of this equipment is the freedom of movement permitted. However, this can also be a disadvantage if users exhaust their air supply before getting out of an area deficient in oxygen. Even with a self-contained breathing

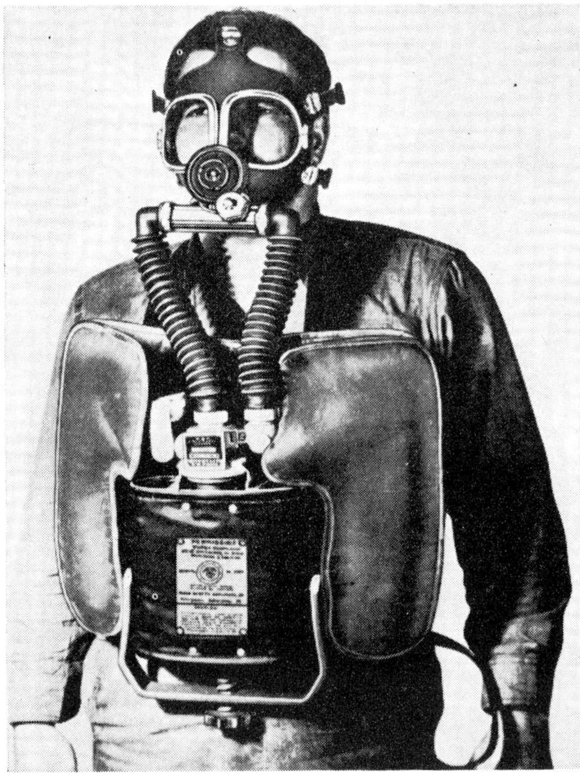

Exhibit 11–6. Self-contained breathing apparatus. Chemicals in canister react with moisture in the wearer's exhaled breath, evolving oxygen and absorbing carbon dioxide. (Courtesy of the Mine Safety Appliances Company, Pittsburgh, Pennsylvania.)

apparatus, no one should work in an atmosphere which will not support life unless at least one other person is present to give assistance in case of an accident. If to make the rescue would necessitate exposure to the hazardous atmosphere, the person standing by to render assistance should also be wearing a self-contained apparatus.

Self-contained breathing apparatus may be used for fighting fires in buildings and other enclosures, for work in unventilated tanks, for mine rescue, and for many emergency situations in industry. However, it must be stressed that self-contained breathing apparatus does not provide protection against gases which can be absorbed through the skin such as hydrogen cyanide, aniline, and carbon disulfide, to name a few.

Exhibit 11–7. Self-contained breathing apparatus. Fresh air is supplied to its wearer through a demand-type regulator from an air supply carried in a metal cylinder harnessed on the user's back. Breathing is completely independent of surrounding atmosphere. (Courtesy of the Scott Aviation Corporation, Lancaster, New York.)

Air-line respirators and hoods. An air-line respirator and an air-line hood are similar in basic design and function. Air is supplied to either a respirator or a hood from an outside source such as a compressor or an oxygen or air-pressure cylinder through a small-diameter air hose. Air-line respirators may be used for paint spraying, welding and cutting, and for exposure to fumes, dusts, gases, and vapors which are not immediately dangerous to life. Escape from the contaminated atmosphere must be possible without the respiratory protection. Air-line respirators should not be used for tank entry or other circumstances where the worker's life would be in jeopardy should the supply of air fail. Air-line hoods are the same as air-line respirators in operation except that a hood or helmet which covers the head and shoulders of the wearer replaces the half- or full-mask face piece. Hoods are used for sand and shot blasting and heavy

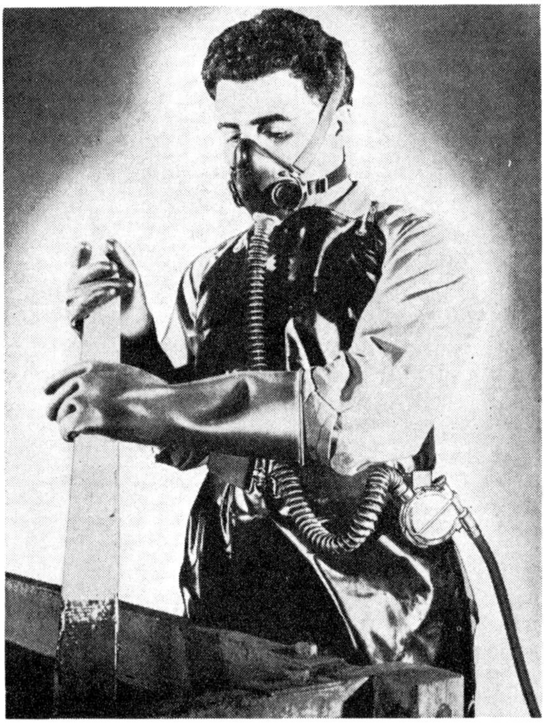

Exhibit 11–8. An air-line respirator. (Courtesy of the Mine Safety Appliances Company, Pittsburgh, Pennsylvania.)

spray painting to protect the worker's head, neck, and shoulders from rebounding abrasive or paint. Air-line respirators and hoods are best suited for continuous operations because unlike mechanical-filter and chemical-cartridge respirators, they offer little or no resistance to inhalation.

Where air-line respirators are used, a few precautions should be taken. If air is supplied from an internally lubricated compressor, care must be exercised to keep the compressor from over-heating. A hot compressor can decompose the lubricating oil, forming carbon monoxide gas. Likewise, the compressor must be located in an area free from toxic air contaminants so clean air will be available at the compressor intake. Great care should also be taken to make sure that an air-line hose is not connected by mistake to a gas line other than one supplying oxygen or air. Cases are on record where the user of an air-line respirator made the fatal mistake of connecting his air hose to a nitrogen gas line. This type of accident also emphasizes the great need for proper identification of all plant piping systems. When oxygen is supplied to an air-line respirator, the potential fire hazard must not be overlooked. A sufficient quantity of oxygen may escape from the face piece to promote or aid the burning of the face piece, the wearer's clothing, and other combustible materials. A hot spark, a hot-metal splash could supply a source of ignition. Oxygen should never be supplied to an air-line hood or helmet except under the most carefully controlled conditions.

Hose masks. Hose masks are available in two types, those with blowers (see Exhibit 11–9) for supplying air to the face piece under slight pressure and those without blowers, in which air is drawn through the hose by the breathing action of the wearer. Hose masks with blowers are approved by the United States Bureau of Mines for respiratory protection in any atmosphere regardless of the degree of contamination or oxygen deficiency, provided that air is supplied

Exhibit 11–9. Hose masks with blower.

through not more than 150 feet of hose. Without blowers a hose mask is not recommended for atmospheres immediately dangerous to life. However, hose masks without blowers are approved by the United States Bureau of Mines if used with not more than 75 feet

Exhibit 11–10. A gas mask. (Courtesy of the Mine Safety Appliances Company, Pittsburgh, Pennsylvania.)

of hose in atmospheres not immediately hazardous to life. A hose mask with a blower is ideal for entering an unventilated tank, pit, or other enclosure. When one is entering a tank or a confined enclosure, flammable gases as well as an oxygen deficiency should always be suspected. Therefore, it is highly desirable to check for flammable gases with an explosibility meter before entering a tank, sewer, or enclosed pit.

Gas masks. Gas masks are respiratory protective devices which purify air by passing it through a canister of chemicals that react with

TABLE 11–1. COLOR IDENTIFICATION OF GAS-MASK CANISTERS

Atmospheric Contaminants for Which Gas Masks Are Designed	Type	Canister Color-Code Marking
Acid gas:* i.e., phosphorus trichloride, hydrogen sulfide, hydrogen chloride, sulphur dioxide, chlorine, hydrocyanic acid.	A	White
Organic vapor: i.e., aniline, benzene, acetone, alcohol, carbon bisulfide, carbon tetrachloride, ether, gasoline, chloropicrin, formaldehyde, petroleum distillates, xylene, toluene, and so forth.	B	Black
Ammonia	C	Green
Carbon monoxide	D	Blue
Combination acid gas and organic vapor: including acidic organic vapors such as acetic acid, phosgene, and benzyl chloride.	AB	Yellow
Combination acid gas, organic vapor, and ammonia gas.	ABC	Brown
Dusts, chemical smokes, fumes, and mists.	E	One-half inch contrasting black or white stripe
Special gases: e.g., chlorine, hydrocyanic acid.	F	White with yellow stripe; white with green stripe
Combination dust, smoke, or mist.	AE, BE, etc.	One-half inch contrasting black or white stripe
Combinations of acid gases, organic vapors, ammonia, smokes, and carbon monoxide.	N†	Red

* Type A acid-gas masks are approved by the United States Bureau of Mines for only chlorine and hydrocyanic acid. However, Type A acid-gas masks obtained from a reputable manufacturer may be suggested, as indicated in the table, for certain gases.

† Type N gas, mask is called the Universal Gas Mask.

Source: *Identification of Gas Mask Canisters,* K13.1-1950, American Standards Association, New York.

or absorb the contaminants. (See Exhibit 11–10.) The gases or vapors against which a gas mask will provide protection depend entirely upon the contents of the canister. Supervisors may be aware that gas-mask canisters come in different colors. The color of the canister indicates its classification and the gases and vapors which the canister protects against. Table 11–1 contains the color code established by the American Standards Association and used to identify each gas-mask canister and the use for which it is intended. One very important point about gas masks to keep in mind is this: lives have been lost because a gas mask was used in an atmosphere deficient in oxygen. These respiratory protective devices cannot be used if there is insufficient oxygen present to support life. For this most valid reason, gas masks should not be used in tanks, pits, and sewers where there might be a lack of oxygen.

Chemical-cartridge respirators. A chemical-cartridge respirator is intended for protection in atmospheres which are contaminated but which workers may breathe without any immediate harm. However, repeated exposures to such atmospheres over extended periods may produce discomfort, irritation of the respiratory tract, or gradual injury to health. Chemical-cartridge respirators employ small cartridges containing chemicals which will remove certain gases and vapors from the atmosphere. Usually the cartridge is attached directly to a half-mask face piece. These respirators, with proper cartridges, provide protection against light concentrations of vapors from acetone, alcohol, benzine, carbon tetrachloride, gasoline, chlorine, ammonia, mercury, etc.

Chemical-cartridge respirators should be used only for the hazard for which the specific cartridge is designed. Hence, supervisors should make it a practice to check cartridges to make sure the proper type is being used. Also, it is well to stress that the chemical cartridge must be discarded when the odor of the contaminant gas or vapor is clearly detected by the wearer of the respirator.

Mechanical-filter respirators. Mechanical-filter respirators offer respiratory protection against air-borne minute particles including dusts, metal fumes, and smoke. They provide no protection against gases or vapors. Mistakenly they are often used as a chemical-cartridge respirator because of a similarity in appearance.

A mechanical filter is made of fibrous material which permits the passage of air, but removes the harmful particles by physical trapping in the filter as air is inhaled. The characteristics of these filters create some discomfort for the wearer. As the respirator is used, the accumulation of contaminants in the filter increases the resistance to air flow. This makes inhalation more difficult. Workers have been known to puncture the filter to decrease this resistance. This, of course, renders

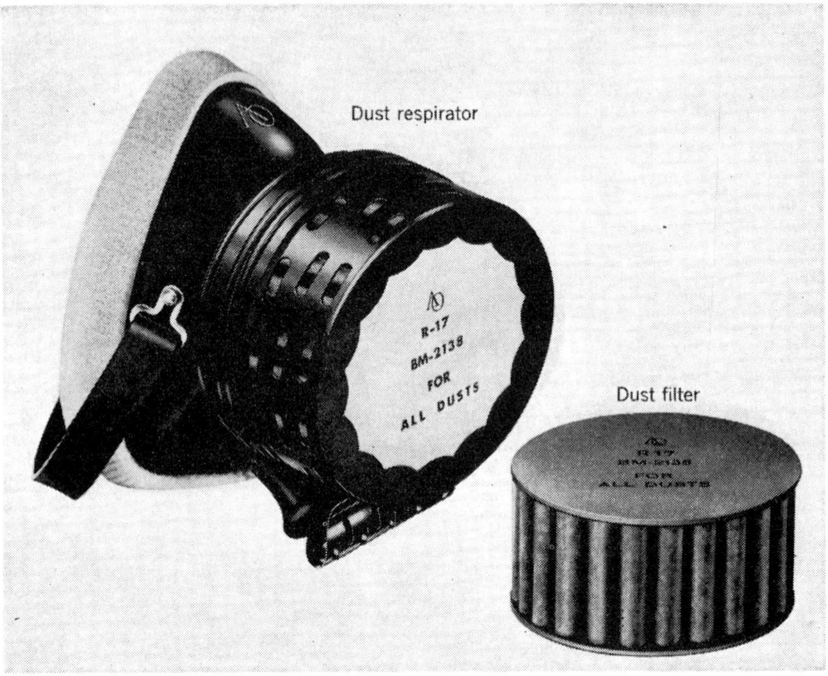

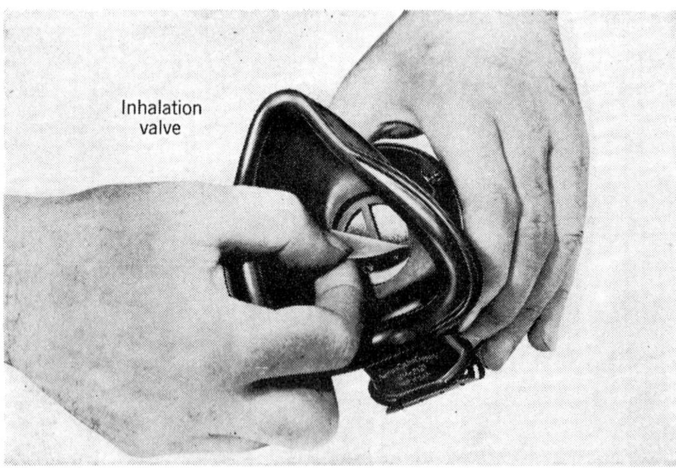

Membrane of gum rubber is designed for positive action. Air is admitted as wearer inhales and membrane returns to a tight seal as exhalation begins.

Exhibit 11–11. The principal design features of the dust and chemical respirators. (Courtesy of the American Optical Company, Southbridge, Massachusetts.)

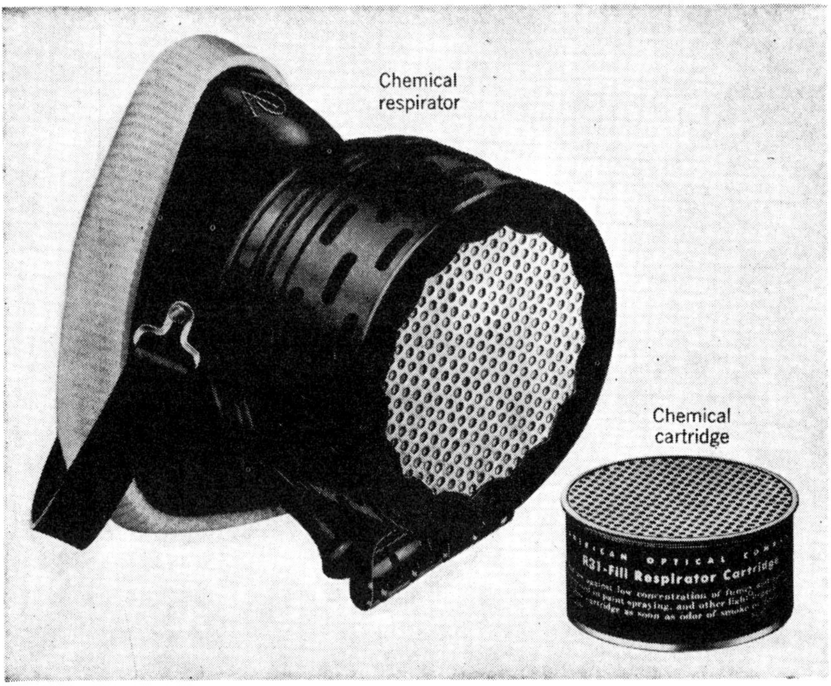

Exhalation valve assures complete expulsion of exhaled air and moisture. Valve opens when air is exhaled, closes when air is inhaled so dust or fumes cannot enter.

Exhibit 11–11. *(continued)*

the filter ineffective. To assure proper use workers should be instructed to change or clear the filter as soon as breathing becomes uncomfortable.

Mechanical-filter respirators are available in several types. Among them are dust and mist respirators and fume respirators. The basic difference between these two types is one of filtering efficiency. The dust respirators can be divided into three classes: those that provide protection against fibrosis-producing (silica dust) and nuisance dust, those that protect against toxic (lead) dust, and those that protect against all dust.

The various dust respirators may be used for grinding operations, rock drilling, handling dusty materials like plaster, grains, and cement, shaking out castings, and shoveling fine sand. Metal-fume respirators may be used in metal melting and pouring operations in foundries; in soldering, babbitting, smelting, and refining of lead, zinc, and other metals; and in welding and cutting operations.

Beryllium oxides, radioactive dusts, and air-borne particles smaller in size or more toxic than lead dust and fumes have created a need for a respirator with a filter which has a very high filtering efficiency. Manufacturers have met this challenge through the development of a filter that provides respiratory protection in atmospheres containing these more finely divided dust particles.

Selection and care of respirators

Selection of a respirator requires careful consideration of prevailing conditions. First, supervisors who are oriented in human relations will make sure a concerted effort has been made to eliminate the need for the respirators. Employees would prefer to work without them. However, for emergency situations, many temporary set-ups, and short-duration operations, the use of a personal respiratory protective device is practical. The health of the employee must be protected and adequate protection can be provided if the right respiratory device is selected and used properly. In summary, these basic facts about respiratory protective devices should be considered in making a selection:

Hose masks have a large-inside-diameter hose for connection to a supply of air from an uncontaminated source. Where the atmosphere is immediately dangerous to life and conditions permit, the hose mask used with a hand-operated blower is the most desirable form of respiratory protection. This device is suitable for non-emergency situations such as entering unventilated tanks, pits, or other enclosures.

A limiting factor is freedom of movement, which is restricted by the length of the hose.

Air-line respirators have a small-diameter compressed air-hose and a connector for fastening into the plant air supply or onto a large cylinder of oxygen or air. Where there is no immediate danger to life, but where the atmosphere is dangerous after a long exposure, the air-line respirator provides adequate protection. This device is suitable for paint spraying, welding, and cutting operations.

Self-contained breathing apparatus are available in three general types: the oxygen-cylinder rebreathing type, the self-generating type, and the demand type with air or oxygen supplied from a cylinder carried by the wearer. The oxygen-cylinder rebreathing type has not been discussed in this chapter. Such equipment consists essentially of a high-pressure oxygen cylinder with a suitable shut-off and by-pass valve, a reducing valve, and a lung-governed admission valve which supplies oxygen from the cylinder only during inhalation; a carbon dioxide scrubber and cooler; and a reservoir breathing bag connected by tubes to the mouth piece or face piece. Check valves direct the flow through the circuit so that the exhaled oxygen is purified of carbon dioxide and rebreathed from the bag with replenishment from the cylinder as required. Such equipment is more complicated to use and maintain and therefore requires more training than is the case with other types. Nevertheless, it permits the longest stay in hazardous atmospheres. Oxygen-cylinder rebreathing devices are available for either a one-hour or a two-hour duration.

The self-contained breathing apparatus is especially well suited for emergency situations such as fire, the release by accident or error of large concentrations of toxic gases, and mine and tunnel rescue work. The source of air is independent of the surrounding atmosphere and the nature of the equipment permits much freedom of movement.

Gas masks, mechanical-filter respirators, and chemical-cartridge respirators are similar in function but differ in appearance. The gas mask employs a full face piece and a large canister, whereas the cartridge respirator uses a half-mask face piece and one or two small cartridges or filters. Gas masks and respirators are air-purifying equipment suitable for use in atmospheres which contain sufficient oxygen to support life and from which the contaminant can be removed or made harmless by mechanical or chemical-reaction filters.

Bureau of Mines approval. An important feature for supervisors and safety engineers to check in connection with any respiratory protective device is whether or not it has the approval of the

United States Bureau of Mines, Department of the Interior. When a device has this approval, the user has the assurance that the device will provide adequate protection under the conditions for which the bureau has approved it. An approved device is stamped with the bureau's approval number and a reproduction of the approval certificate, which states what the device may be used for under what conditions. Lack of a Bureau of Mines approval does not mean, necessarily, that a respiratory device is not suitable for any purpose. It is possible that the bureau has not established a schedule of approval for the particular device. Also, it is not compulsory to get the bureau's approval. However, when two similar respiratory protective devices are available, one with the bureau's approval and one without, it would be a good policy to select the approved device. The approval establishes the dependability and the efficiency of the device.

Inspection and cleaning of respirators

Gas masks and self-contained apparatus are often needed for emergency purposes. Therefore, they should be placed in convenient and accessible locations in those areas where they will be needed. All respiratory devices should be inspected periodically whether used or not. Worn or damaged parts should be replaced. Gas-mask canisters usually should be replaced within one year after the seal at the bottom of the canister has been removed and after four years with the seal intact.

Proper cleaning and sanitation of respiratory devices are important to worker satisfaction and health. Face pieces in use should be scrubbed daily with lukewarm water and soap. If the respirator is not to be used again by the same person, it should also be disinfected. Disinfecting agents or the formula for a disinfecting solution can usually be obtained from respirator manufacturers. During the cleaning procedure, the equipment might also be inspected.

Finally, where personal respiratory protective devices are used, it is essential that supervisors:

1. Know the function and purpose of each respiratory device.
2. Know the type of protection provided by each device.
3. Know the advantages and limitations of each device.
4. *Carefully* instruct workers in the proper use and the reasons for the use of the respiratory devices required.

A wide variety of respiratory protective devices is available. Each device is suitable for one or more applications. It therefore becomes apparent that an orderly method of selecting the type of device to be used should be followed. Use of an improper device or misuse of a device could put the health and even the life of a worker in jeopardy.

SAFETY APPAREL

Although the primary approach in any accident-prevention effort is the development of safe working conditions and a safety awareness which leads to the elimination of all accidents, this fine goal is seldom achieved. Parts still slip from workers' hands, tools are dropped or fall from overhead locations, acid and other corrosive materials are splashed, missile-like objects fly through the air, and some materials which are abrasive or sharp-edged cut into unprotected hands. While it might not be possible or even practical to eliminate these garden-variety types of accidents, workers can be provided with a second-line defense in the form of personal protective equipment to prevent injury. Eye-protection equipment and respiratory devices have been discussed in detail. However, numerous other types of personal protective equipment are available including:

Hard hats

Hard hats are made of plastic, Fiberglas, or metal and protect the workers' heads from falling objects. The hat is held over the worker's head on a flexible suspension cradle which can be adjusted to fit any size head. The suspension helps to absorb the impact of an object striking the hard hat. Hard hats are usually manufactured to meet Federal specifications for impact, penetration, electrical resistance, flammability, and water absorption.

Hard hats are now manufactured in a variety of colors. Thus, a specific color might be used to identify teams of workers, to distinguish workers by their occupation, or to identify new workers or trainees.

Protective caps

Protective caps are usually made of net and cloth with an attached visor. These caps are designed to fully cover the hair of the head. Workers, especially women, who work at machines which have rotating spindles or parts located close to the operator's head are exposed to the danger of their hair becoming entangled in the revolving part. A safety-cap visor provides a warning when the worker's head comes too close to the danger point. The cap prevents the hair from being drawn into the machine. Hair nets, turbans, or bandannas might also be used, but these head covers generally leave part of the hair uncovered.

Gloves

Gloves for protective purposes are available in a wide variety of types. Rubber and plastic gloves are worn by workers who handle acids and other corrosive materials; asbestos gloves by those who handle hot objects; metal re-inforced gloves by workers who handle

Exhibit 11–12. A display of personal protective equipment.

abrasive and sharp-edged objects; and lead-impregnated gloves by X-ray workers. Protective gloves are also available in a wide variety of designs to meet special problems; for instance, general-purpose welder's gloves are made from specially tanned leather to combine flexibility and heat-resistance characteristics. Any discussion concerning the use of gloves for protective purposes should include a word of caution. The wearing of gloves around machinery with exposed moving parts creates a serious hazard in that the glove is likely to become caught in the rotating part and cause a serious hand injury.

Leggings, shin guards, aprons, finger cots, coveralls, and chaps are additional items of safety apparel that are used by industry. However, beyond mention of these items, there is little more that needs to be covered. Sales engineers representing various personal-protective-equipment manufacturers are available to provide consultation on the selection and application of a wide assortment of safety apparel, and each year the March issue of *National Safety News* contains a full section on personal protective equipment.[2] This section has much descriptive material and information that would be helpful to safety personnel and supervisors.

Safety shoes

Safety shoes are among the more popular and widely used items of personal protective apparel. Such foot protection consists of a regular leather shoe, either high-top or oxford, with an enclosed metal toe cap. The American Standards Association has a published Standard for Safety Footwear.[3] The standard describes a safety shoe as one of sturdy, solid construction with a steel toe box flanged at the bottom and resting on the sole of the shoe. The steel toe box must be able to support a static load of 2500 pounds and an impact load equivalent to that of a 50-pound weight dropped a distance of 1 foot. After either of these tests, there must be a clearance of at least ½ inch between the upper inside surface of the toe box and the upper surface of the shoe sole.

Many companies have a program to promote the wearing of safety shoes. Where there are such programs, it is the usual practice for the employee to pay for the shoes. This is the case even in those companies having a specific rule requiring employees to wear safety shoes as a condition of employment. This point is significant because there are some who feel a company rule requiring the wearing of safety shoes makes it necessary for the company to pay for the footwear. This conclusion stems from the fact that most companies do pay the bill for such safety apparel as rubber gloves, acid-resistant clothing, boots, leggings, and aprons, which are used for protection against specific on-the-job hazards. But there is a basic difference between these safety items and safety shoes. Rubber gloves, acid-resistant aprons, leggings, and specially treated clothing are not a normal part of a worker's wearing apparel. Shoes are, and safety shoes are merely

---

2 The Annual Safety Equipment Issue, *National Safety News*, National Safety Council, Chicago, Illinois.

3 American War Standard, *Specifications for Protective Occupational Footwear*, Z41-1944.

regular shoes with the unseen protective toe cap added. Toe injuries are common; many of them could be avoided by the wearing of safety shoes. It is in the interest of the workers for an employer to require the wearing of safety shoes. On the basis of the single fact that employees wear shoes, it is not unreasonable to require the worker to purchase his safety shoes, which today are attractive, comfortable, and lower in price than regular work shoes. As one safety engineer summed it up, "If the employees came to work barefooted, employers would pay for safety shoes. Requiring the employee to pay for the safety shoes imposes no hardship and in the long run a painful toe injury might be prevented."

There is an alternate approach to the matter of employee foot protection. Some employers have adopted a rule requiring employees to wear steel foot guards. The foot guard[4] is a metal shield which is strapped over the employee's regular shoes. The foot guards are supplied by the employer. However, where safety shoes would provide adequate protection, the employee may purchase safety shoes and wear them in place of the foot guards.

Although employers may not provide workers with safety shoes free of charge, many companies do take definite steps to make it as convenient as possible for employees to obtain this protective footwear. Safety shoes are sold at cost at an employee's store or from a mobile shoe van that is brought to various sections of the plant on a scheduled basis. Payroll-deduction plans are also available to employees wishing to purchase safety shoes.

Safety-shoe displays in the cafeteria, the employee store, and various sections in the plant, company-newspaper publicity, periodic promotions, and other techniques help to eliminate the unfounded complaints about safety shoes being too heavy, difficult to fit, and hot in summer and cold in winter. In relation to the matter of promoting the wearing of safety shoes, two clubs have been formed, a Centipede Club and a Happy Foot Club. These clubs award appropriate pins and certificates to employees who have been spared a foot injury because they were wearing safety shoes. Usually, the employee receiving such awards also receives a new pair of safety shoes to replace those damaged in the accident.

---

[4] A foot guard is a metal shield which is designed to fit over regular work shoes. The shield provides a maximum amount of protection to the entire front of the foot—not merely the toes. Such foot guards are designed to withstand a greater weight and impact than the toe box of a safety shoe. Specifications for foot guards call for the shield to withstand an impact of 300 pounds dropped a distance of 1 foot.

Work clothing

It is normally the responsibility of an employee to present himself for work appropriately clothed to perform his job. Usually, to meet safety requirements, work clothes should not be either bulky or binding. Neckties, dangling scarves, and other articles of clothing with loose ends should not be worn, especially around machinery. Hence, to serve the best interests of both employer and employee, management should establish certain safe-clothing rules when precautions are necessary. This brings up the question as to when and under what circumstances the employer should provide worker's clothing free of charge.

With regard to the issuance of clothing, many companies establish a policy which covers the subject with the aim of providing uniformity of treatment for all employees. Various types of clothing of safe design made of a specially treated material or of a specific fabric are supplied to employees free of charge. Where such clothing is provided, it is usually found that one of these three conditions prevails:

1. The company requires an employee to wear special clothing to protect himself from an unusual or unique health or safety hazard, i.e., a condition determined by the company or declared by law to be a health or safety hazard requiring special clothing as a protective measure.
2. The company requires an employee to wear special clothing to protect a process, part, piece of equipment, or product.
3. It can be established that without special protective clothing an employee's regular personal work clothes might be continuously subject to unusual damage not normally associated with regular wear and tear.

Perhaps additional reasons why employers might furnish clothing to employees should be mentioned. For example, employees may be provided with articles of clothing, free of charge, where uniformity of appearance or a standard of appearance is required by the company in order to identify a service to the public or to other employees of the company. Guards, nurses, cafeteria help would be in this category.

Generally, when a company accepts the responsibility of providing clothing, as described above, it will also accept the cost of maintenance, cleaning, and replacement of it. But where an employee is permitted to wear company clothing off the company premises because of the nature of the clothing (for example, a guard's uniform), the employee usually bears the cost of cleaning and repairing the clothing. Normal replacement of such clothing is, however, a company expense.

Undoubtedly, there are other safety problems with a much higher degree of importance, but the clothes an employee wears to work do have a bearing on the safety of the individual. Therefore, the subject is one that should not be passed over lightly by supervision. If an operation involves the use of noxious, irritating, or flammable materials, certain safety clothing may be required to assure adequate protection. Likewise, supervisors have the continuing responsibility of checking on the appropriateness of clothes worn to work, especially by women. Appearance is so important that many employees would rather run the risk of an accident than wear clothing and shoes that are safe and comfortable but perhaps not "attractive" or in keeping with a current fad. Also, it is a human tendency for some employees to wear clothing and shoes they have bought long after time and wear have made them unsafe.

It is apparent that many new fabrics now being developed and coming into use and the modern design of clothing will help to increase the safety features of clothes worn to work by employees. Also, industrialists are pressing for a wider selection of work clothes and for clothing designed for specific operations. This trend should help reduce the problems of supervisors in this area. But it is still important to recognize the matter as a problem.

SELECTED REFERENCES

Accident Prevention Manual for Industrial Operations, National Safety Council, Chicago, 1955, Section 36, "Personal Protection Equipment."

Dickenson, John A., "Tests for Safety Clothing," *National Safety News,* November, 1951.

National Safety Council Data Sheets:

D-444, "Respiratory Protective Equipment."

D-Gen. 16, "Cleaning and Sterilizing Goggles and Respiratory Equipment."

D-425, "Hard Hats."

CHAPTER

12

Accident case histories

We ought not to look back unless it is to derive useful lessons from past errors, and for the purpose of profiting by dear bought experience.

GEORGE WASHINGTON

Experience is the best teacher may be a cliché, but in the field of accident prevention much has been learned by a review of a serious or unusual accident. This might be called accident observation rather than accident prevention. Nevertheless, many safety engineers are convinced that a thorough review of accidents which have occurred in their plants or other plants has helped them locate unsafe conditions or unsafe practices that otherwise might have been missed. Likewise, circulation of a specific accident report often initiates immediate corrective action where otherwise no action would have been taken. Busy supervisors after reading an accident report might be reminded of an unsafe condition or an unsafe practice in their own areas which they had previously ignored, or they might recognize a condition previously considered safe to be on the contrary a decidedly unsafe condition. The reading of a well-prepared accident report brings various hazards and useful safety facts into sharp focus for everyone. A useful lesson can be learned.

With these points in mind, eleven accident case histories have been selected for inclusion in this chapter. Each case was selected on the basis of the accident being the type that is common to most of industry. The cases do not relate necessarily to other material in the book. However, each case does contain much useful information and practical recommendations that relate to the development of safe working conditions. The provision of these cases is expected to add to the storehouse of safety information possessed by supervisors and safety engineers. Undoubtedly, some of the cases will prove more useful than others, but the fact that there are lessons to be learned in each of them should not be overlooked. It is a known fact that the organization and the direction of safety programs require a "know-how" derived usually from formal safety training combined with practical shop experience. Therefore, if accidents which do occur are properly investigated to discover the corrective measures needed to prevent recurrence, the report of the investigation and the formulation of recommendations for control constitute valuable safety experience. This being the case, a careful review and discussion of these twelve cases should be most helpful.

GROUNDING OF PORTABLE ELECTRICAL EQUIPMENT

The accident

A millwright received a severe electric shock while using a portable electric drill. He was in the process of drilling a steel bracket which was held in a vice on a wood-top work bench. The electric drill had a lead with a pig-tail ground wire extending from the plug end. The millwright had failed to attach the pig-tail clip to a ground. Therefore, the portable tool was ungrounded. A failure in the insulation of the drill produced an accidental ground, which energized the case. In the process of applying pressure to the drill, the millwright rested his leg against a radiator under the bench. His trouser leg was damp from perspiration. The contact with ground completed the electric circuit through his body. The electric shock rendered the man unconscious, but after a few minutes of the back-pressure–arm-lift method of artificial respiration, the millwright was revived.

Discussion.

1. A provision of the National Electrical Code, 1953 revision, bans the use of flexible cords with the pig-tail type of grounding connection and establishes a grounded plug and receptacle system as the approved means for protecting users of portable tools and equipment. Although it is standard practice in most plants to ground portable electrical equipment, grounding methods vary, depending upon conditions. Compliance with the revisions of the National Electrical Code would make it necessary to equip portable tools with three wire leads and an A.S.A. type of grounding plug, and to install A.S.A. receptacles to receive these plugs. Such a change-over should be carefully planned so it will be made on a practical and an economical basis. Approved methods of grounding portables as shown in Exhibit 12–1 should be followed.

2. In many locations the two-pole receptacle is standard throughout the plant. As an expedient, some plants may elect to use an adaptor to receive a three-prong plug used with a two-pole receptacle. This adaptor includes a plate screw terminal and a ground lead and clip for attachment to the nearest ground. Where the pig-tail connection is used, experience indicates that in many cases the user neglects to connect the ground clip or the connection is accidentally broken. Thus, the desirable step would be to replace the two-pole receptacle with the new A.S.A. type of grounding receptacle.

3. With a grounded plug and receptacle system, these precautions are important:

(*a*) Design of plug and receptacle should make it impossible to insert plug in the receptacle in the wrong position. An A.S.A. type of plug and receptacle meets this requirement.

(*b*) Grounding blade on plug should be longer than other blades so the ground will be established before current can flow.

(*c*) A system for checking the ground wire on all portable tools at regular periods should be instituted. Normal operation of the tool does not indicate the existence of a ground.

(*d*) *Only authorized and qualified personnel should be permitted to make electrical repairs and replace plugs on portable tools.* Connections at the receptacle, at the plug end of the cord, and at the tool end of the cord must be all right or the frame of the portable can be energized.

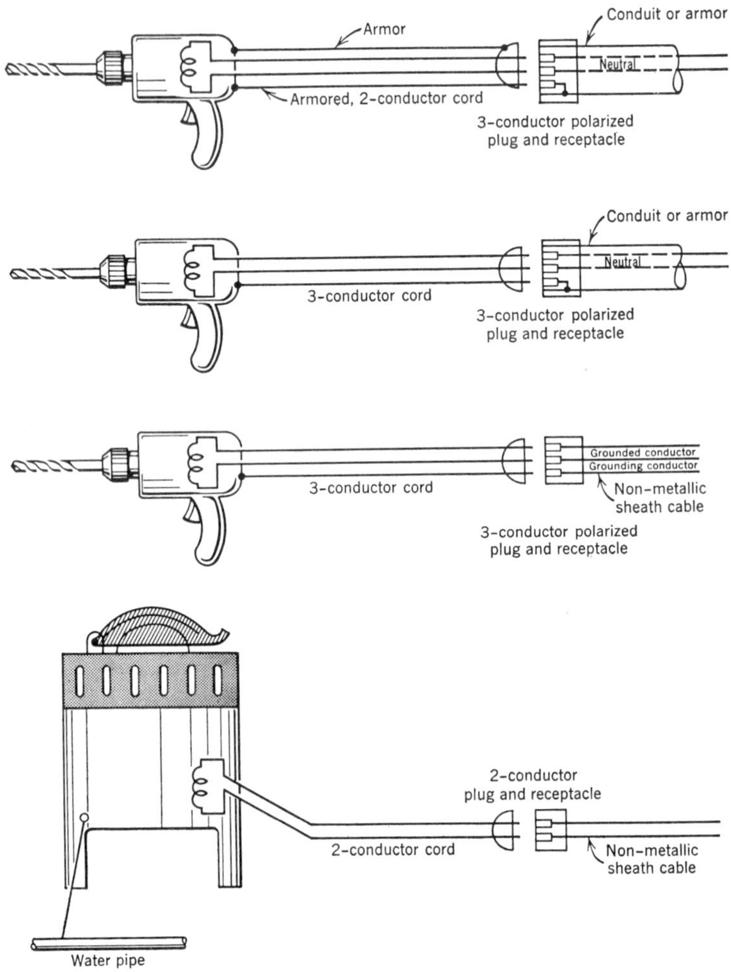

Exhibit 12–1. Approved methods of grounding portables.

(*e*) The ground circuit preferably should be a third wire and not the conduit.

4. Another consideration concerns the matter of grounding office devices. In general, the practice of placing a ground on electrical typewriters, adding machines, and similar office equipment is recommended. However, under certain conditions the hazards of electric shock may be reduced to a point where installation of a ground would be impractical. Electric typewriters that are in an office with wood floors and wood partitions and that are isolated from any grounding

point such as a water pipe or radiator may not require a ground. As a matter of fact, under such conditions a grounded typewriter in combination with a faulty, ungrounded desk lamp would actually create a hazard. Therefore, before deciding to ground office devices, it would be practical to check the matter with a qualified person in the electrical-facilities or safety-engineering section. Also, it may be discovered that certain office equipment with electronic controls will not operate with a ground. With or without a ground, good maintenance and careful inspection of all electrical equipment are essential.

5. Detailed information concerning the grounding of portable equipment may be found by referring to the National Electric Code, 1953 revision.

6. A FOUR-STEP PROGRAM TO PREVENT ELECTRIC-SHOCK ACCIDENTS

(*a*) Check all electrical test equipment to make sure that design, installation, use, and maintenance meet maximum safety standards.

(*b*) Analyze all electrical procedures and correct immediately any dangerous or unsafe work habits noted.

(*c*) Encourage supervisors to check every employee to make sure that he knows, and is following, safe operating practices when handling high-voltage electricity.

(*d*) Make sure all employees working in an area where electric-shock hazards are present are being given intensive training in the arm-lift-back-pressure and mouth-to-mouth methods of artificial resuscitation.

RADIUM AND OTHER RADIATION HAZARDS

The accident

A laboratory employee brought ½ gram of radium to a foundry to do some X-ray work; and after finishing the test, he laid the capsule on an adjacent casting, forgot about it, and went home. The next morning he realized his error and returned to the foundry. The capsule had been removed from the casting.

Every employee in the building was promptly notified of the danger involved. No one admitted having the capsule. The plant safety engineer took action. A radiation detector was brought to the building, and the capsule was located in a clothes locker. The locker belonged to a maintenance man. The maintenance man explained that he had taken the capsule because it looked like a plumb bob. He had had it in his pocket for about an hour. He was examined immediately by the plant physician. No ill effects from radium exposure were found. Two days later, however, a spot about 8 inches in diameter resembling sunburn appeared over his heart.

Discussion. Radium capsules provide just one of the many sources of radiant energy in industry that are of concern to supervisors, safety engineers, industrial hygienists, and health physicists. As atomic energy is being tamed and put to work for the benefit of mankind, radioisotopes, one of the by-products of this process, are being used by industry in research, process control, measurement, and inspection. For example, the radioisotopes cobalt-60 and iridium-192 are used frequently today for radiographic inspection of castings, welds, and other materials. Other uses for radioisotopes as they are made available include:

Measuring the rate of wear of cutting tools.
Measuring the thickness of a material.
Controlling the level of a material in an enclosed tank or an inaccessible tank.
Studying lubrication efficiency, motor wear, and corrosion.
Controlling the thickness of film coatings.
Locating movement of bulk materials in pipelines.

It is a certainty that many plants which presently do not have a radiation problem may be faced with one in the near future. As in most cases where safety is under consideration, a knowledge of the properties of the material being handled and proper use of the material are ideal tools for preventing accidents. Admittedly, many of the problems in the area of radiation-hazard control are complex. Control procedures, equipment design, health monitoring practices, radiation surveying, and other matters associated with the safe use of radioactive materials must be left to the experts. Nevertheless, supervisors and workers need to understand the basic elements of radiation-control methods, the language which is used, and the common-sense rules of safety which must be followed.

There are several different kinds of radiant energy which are of concern to supervisors and others. Two common types are infra-red rays from hot objects and ultra-violet rays from electric arc welding. However, this discussion will be confined to the kinds of radiation that are given off by the various radioisotopes now available. Seven different types of nuclear radiation have been identified, but industry, especially the atomic-energy industry, is concerned with just four of them. These are—alpha particles, beta particles, gamma rays and X-rays, and neutrons.

ALPHA PARTICLES.[1] Alpha particles are thrown off by radioactive elements such as uranium, radium, and plutonium. Tiny though they are—a hundred billion billion of them would be no larger than the head of a pin—these electrically charged particles are the largest natural radiation particles found in the atomic-energy program. They cannot damage the skin since they have very little power of "penetration." A few inches of air or even a sheet of paper will stop them. They can cause considerable damage if too much of a substance that emits them gets lodged inside the body.

BETA PARTICLES.[1] Beta particles are thrown off by many radioactive materials—radioactive carbon and phosphorus, for example. They are much smaller than alpha particles (their mass is about 1/7200 that of an alpha), and they carry an electrical charge. They are more penetrating than alphas; they can travel several yards through air and penetrate up to ⅓ inch of tissue. Over-exposure can cause severe skin burns, and, like alpha-emitting substances, materials that give off betas can cause damage if they get inside the body.

GAMMA RAYS AND X-RAYS.[1] Gamma rays and X-rays are not particles like alphas and betas but are waves of energy such as light or radio waves. Gamma rays can travel hundreds of feet through air and penetrate for many inches, going through almost anything solid (thick lead is an effective barrier against them), and over-exposure can cause severe damage deep inside the body. Gamma rays are thrown off by many radioactive substances and are generated on a large scale both in atomic explosions and in nuclear reactors. As much as 3 feet of specially prepared concrete are required to completely absorb gamma rays.

NEUTRONS.[1] Neutrons are nuclear particles, with no electrical charge at all. Their mass is about one-fourth that of the alpha particle, but, because they have no electrical charge, they can travel many feet through solid matter and hundreds of feet through the air, or can penetrate deeply into a person's body and cause damage there.

When dealing with small amounts of radioactive materials, the concern is with the accumulative effects of numerous exposures to the radiant energy. There is nothing new about this kind of problem. Carbon tetrachloride is an example of the case in point. Swallowing a quantity of carbon tet or inhaling a large volume of the fumes from the solvent may cause immediate illness, often with fatal results. Or a worker may breathe a little of the fumes each day without any apparent effects, but eventually he may become sick.

---

[1] "27 Questions and Answers about Radiation and Radiation Protection," United States Atomic Energy Commission, 1951.

Likewise, a large radiation exposure can kill; small exposures accumulate and eventually cause trouble.

EXTERNAL AND INTERNAL HAZARDS. There are two properties of radiation that are of vital interest. First, there are the external radiation hazards, and second, the internal hazards which are present if there is a possibility of getting radioactive material inside the body by swallowing or otherwise. The internal hazard is like the one associated with mercury. Being close to a quantity of mercury or even touching it is no particular hazard. But if a person breathes air containing mercury or eats food contaminated with mercury, he is subject to mercury poisoning. Likewise, if an alpha emitter gets into the body, the consequences may be serious.

External radiation hazards can be likened to the hazards of the old pot-belly stove. The closer a person got to the red-hot belly of the stove, the greater was the chance of receiving a burn; and if the stove was touched, a bad burn was assured. Also, the longer a person stood too close to the stove, the more severe the burn. If the stove is considered a beta-particle or gamma-ray emitter, the safety precautions become obvious. By staying away from the stove, limiting the time of exposure, or placing a shield between the stove and the person, the hazard of a burn is controlled. Likewise, radiation hazards are controlled by three factors: distance, time, and shielding. But unlike the fire in the pot-belly stove, alpha, beta, and gamma radiation cannot be detected except by special instruments.

MONITORING DEVICES. Radiation monitoring for determining the amount of exposure to which a worker is subject is an important aspect of the radiation-protection program. There are several types of monitoring devices available. Perhaps the best known is the film badge, which contains a packet of X-ray film, which will darken in proportion to the amount of radiation that strikes it. This badge will give a cumulative record of radiation exposure over any given period. The film badge has a filter portion which consists of a film between two metal shields. The metal absorbs beta rays and permits only gamma rays to strike the film. An unfiltered portion of the badge absorbs both beta and gamma rays.

A second type of monitoring device is the pocket dosimeter. This device looks like a large pocket pen. It is worn by persons in areas where radioactive materials or X-rays are present. Such devices utilize the principle that two bodies with a like electrical charge repel each other. Presence of radioactivity causes ionization of the air between the two charged bodies in the dosimeter chamber. This discharges them causing them to move closer together. The displacement is calibrated to a direct reading of roentgen dosage. However, high humidity or dropping of this monitoring device will cause an erroneous reading.

The Geiger-Müller counter is still another type of radiation-detecting and -measuring device. The Geiger counter gives a direct reading of the roentgen-dosage rate. Thus a survey at any given time will detect an existing radiation hazard. This permits precautionary steps to be taken before damage is done.

EMPLOYEE EDUCATION. A necessary step in any radiation safety program is the education of employees. First, employees must understand that radiation hazards can be controlled. For example, the safety record in the atomic-energy industry is outstanding. This enviable safety performance has been made possible by adequate employee training and strict adherence to all established operating procedures. Employees must know what is being done to protect them and what they must do to protect themselves. Beyond the matter of employee education, each plant will have problems peculiar to it alone in the area of radiation safety. Some plants like those in the atomic-energy field will have widespread problems from the reactor to the handling, storage, and disposal of large quantities of radioactive materials. In other industries the problem may be no more than the handling of a single cobalt-60 capsule for radiographic inspections. The significant point is that the problem, big or little, must not be ignored. Assuming the existence of various radiation hazards produced by radioactive materials and X-ray, these specific safety steps are suggested:

1. Make sure proper articles of protective clothing, remote-handling equipment, shielding materials, and film badges are provided and properly used for work that involves the use of radioactive materials or for work that may expose personnel to radioactive hazards.

2. Establish for approval by a health physicist or other qualified person such rules and procedures as are necessary to prevent the exposure of personnel to greater-than-permissible amounts of radioactive material.

3. Notify the medical unit promptly in every case of an accident involving individuals engaged in work with radioactive materials.

4. Enforce the posting of approved "Radiation Hazard" signs where radiation hazards exist, and prevent the indiscriminate posting of the signs where no hazard exists. (See Exhibit 12–2.)

5. Make sure employees adhere to a schedule of periodical medical check-ups.

6. Make a periodic check of radiation survey and monitoring programs to be assured they are being conducted as planned.

The above list is not inclusive, and it is not implied that whenever radioactive material is used, all the steps outlined above are necessary. The extent of the hazard, prevailing working conditions, the time element, and other factors should always be taken into consideration in determining required safety measures.

Exhibit 12–2. An official design and symbol for warning tags, labels, and wall signs which indicate a radiation hazard. (Standard colors are purple on yellow.)

Again referring to the specific accident involving the use of a radium capsule, these safety steps are suggested. To prevent accidents in the use of radium capsules:

1. Personnel should be thoroughly instructed in the dangers involved and the necessity for handling the radium carefully.
2. The use and storage of radium should be under effective supervision. The location of all radium containers should be known at all times, and storage should be under lock and key.
3. The equipment provided for handling the radium containers, particularly when mechanical in nature, should be designed so that containers will not be subject to mechanical shock.
4. Suitable monitoring equipment should be available for detecting any unusual condition such as that resulting from breakage or loss of a container. Meters which respond only to beta and gamma radiation are unsatisfactory and may give a false feeling of security when used to detect radium exposures. Alpha meters of the ionization or scintillation type are satisfactory, although their calibration is difficult.
5. Containers of all types should be examined regularly to make certain that they are intact and are not leaking.
6. Personnel should be properly instructed in the procedure to be

followed in case of breakage of a container so that the contamination will not be spread.

THE HEALTH PHYSICIST. In the preceding discussion on radiation hazards, reference was made to the health physicist. This job title may still be an unfamiliar term. Hence, an explanation is in order.[2] The title originated during the early years of the super-secret Manhattan Engineering District. This historic atomic-research project, which led to the first atomic bomb, was conducted under the seating section of the old Chicago University football stadium, Stagg Field. In an effort to maintain complete secrecy regarding the nature of the research, any reference to radiation was forbidden. Hence, the title health physicist was chosen rather than radiation safety engineer or any other more descriptive name.

At one time the nuclear physicist provided needed radiation protection and established radiation safety standards. But since World War II, college graduates with degrees in biology, engineering, chemistry, arts and sciences, and other fields have been recruited into the work. For a time it was necessary for those entering the radiation-safety field to receive their training and experience on the job. Now, however, the Atomic Energy Commission has set up fellowship programs at several universities. These programs are designed to provide a source of technically trained people with a background desirable in the health-physics field.

The formulation of standards for radiation exposures is one of the principal functions of the health physicist. These standards include the permissible levels and amounts of radiation exposure of workers on a daily or weekly basis, limits on the amount of radioactive materials that may be retained on a worker's clothing or on equipment after decontamination, and limits on the amount of radioactivity that may be released to the atmosphere or into a stream of water.

It is part of the daily routine of the health physicist to formulate radiation-safety instructions that specify areas where radiation warning signs, protective clothing, film badges, or respiratory protection is required. He also makes periodic checks of personnel exposures through the film badges or other radiation-detecting and -measuring devices. Where film badges indicate exposures above the prescribed limits, the health physicist makes a thorough investigation and recommends corrective measures.

When a new radiation facility is planned, the health physicist

[2] L. J. Cherubin, "Health Physics: Protecting Man from Radiation," *General Electric Review*, November, 1956.

studies the layout to assure adequate radiation safeguards. He makes sure that there are no radiation leaks, that the shielding is adequate, and that adequate consideration is given to the safe disposal of radioactive wastes. Thus the health physicist must concern himself with many technical problems, ranging from a study of the effects of radioactive wastes on plant and animal life to the problems of calibrating radiation-measuring devices.

INSPECTION OF HOISTING EQUIPMENT AND DEVICES

The accident

A large steel casting that weighed over 3000 pounds was being raised from the foundry floor by a 10-ton overhead crane. As the lift was made the crane hook broke, and the casting dropped to the floor. Although there were no injuries or property damage, production was delayed for several hours while the crane hook was being replaced.

Discussion. Where the safety of people is involved, a regular inspection of all hoisting devices and equipment must be made.

CRANE HOOKS. A crane hook is subject to many stresses and strains that will cause cracks and flaws to develop, but these defects can be found before a fracture occurs. Recommended inspection procedures include a visual check of the hook and a magnetic-particle test or a red-dye-penetration test.

These inspections are worthwhile. For example, in an inspection of twenty-five crane hooks in one large heavy-apparatus plant, these defects were found:

Seven hooks showed surface defects.
Four hooks were scrapped after X-rays showed deep internal cracks.
Eight crane-hook nuts showed deep cracks and were scrapped.

CHAINS. The heart of any chain-safety program is inspection. The inspection procedure should include a magnetic-particle test on main and connecting links and a link-by-link inspection. Defects most commonly found in such inspections are twisted, distorted, nicked, gouged, or excessively worn links. On the basis of the extent of these defects, the chain should be either repaired or discarded.

WIRE-ROPE SLINGS. A periodic visual inspection of all wire-rope slings should be made. Broken strands and sharp kinks are an indication that the sling needs to be replaced. Exhibit 12–3 shows the more common causes of wire-rope damage (see page 222).

Inspection Elements:

1. *A qualified inspector* properly trained and required to make a formalized inspection on a regularly scheduled basis.
2. *Records of inspections* which indicate date unit was placed into service, date of each inspection, all defects found in the inspection, nature of repairs made, and dates worn or damaged parts were replaced.
3. *Reminder system* that is tied in with the record system to signal when the next inspection is to be made.
4. *Semi-annual inspections* of all hoists, cranes, slings, and chains by a trained inspector.
5. *Daily inspection* by hoist and crane operators, and crane followers or hookers. This is a visual inspection. Defects are reported to the appropriate supervisor.
6. *Engineering recommendations* regarding size and type of hoisting equipment suited for various plant operations. Unusually rigid standards must be established for the in-plant fabrication of lifting hooks and other hoisting and sling attachments. Because of the many problems involved regarding selection of the proper metal, the heat-treating process, the problems of proper design, etc., it is wise to purchase such equipment from reliable manufacturers.

GAS WELDING IN CONFINED SPACE

The accident

A welder, while using a cutting torch in a confined space, was fatally burned. It was assumed from the rapidity with which the welder's clothes burned that there was a high concentration of oxygen present. An investigation revealed that the source of the oxygen was a break in the oxygen hose close to the cutting torch of the gas welding unit.

This tragic accident emphasizes the need for following well-formulated safety procedures whenever it is necessary to work in a confined space. Also, careful attention should be given to the care and maintenance of all welding equipment, especially the oxygen and acetylene hoses.

Discussion. These steps are suggested:

1. Review the American Standards code Z49.1-1950, "Safety in Gas Welding and Cutting Operations." Sections 7.4 and 8.6, "Work in Confined Spaces," and Section 3.11, "Hose," should receive particular attention.

HOW CABLES ARE DAMAGED

		Description of Damage	Major Causes of Damage	How to Avoid Damage
SCUFFED	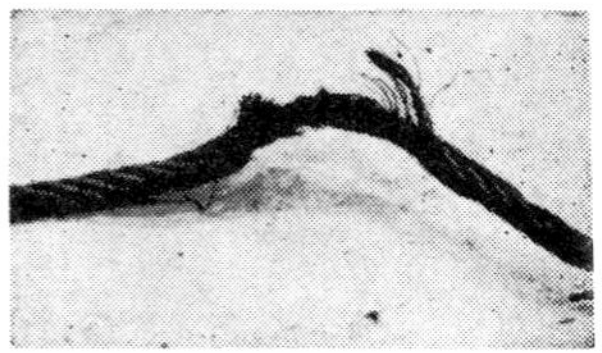	Cable scraped and torn	Turning in a basket hitch Turning into a loose cable Turning with cables on the outside of a job	Use choker hitch for single-hook turning Always turn into a tight cable Attach cables so there is no relative motion between job and cable
SQUASHED	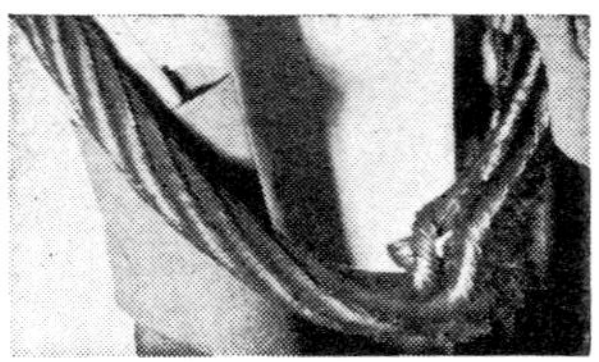	Core of cable forced up through outer strands	Load is placed on floor with cable between floor and load Cable is wrapped around a sharp corner	Use blocking to support all loads Use cable guards
CUT OFF	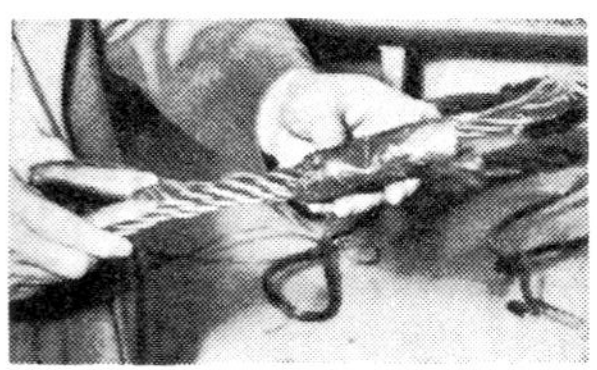	Cable cut partially or completely	Turning load over on cable Lifting with cable directly against a sharp edge	Use blocking Use cable guards

KNOTTED		Two cables are joined and cannot be separated	Using a chocker hitch to pull a cable out of a job or to lengthen a cable	Use correct joining methods
BIRDCAGE		Permanent kink in cable—generally in the center of cable	Cable with twist in it has been pulled tight	Check cables for twist before lifting, particularly cables inside the job
KINKED		Outer strands of cable longer than inner strands, causing permanent bend	Lifting with cable against a sharp edge and with an included angle less than 45 degrees	Use cable guard Keep angle greater than 45 degrees

Exhibit 12–3. Sources of cable damage. (*Source:* Frank Sherman, "How to Lift with Overhead Cranes," *Modern Materials Handling,* December, 1955.)

2. Discuss with employees the need for proper maintenance and inspection of all welding equipment. Point out the hazards of pulling the welding hose over sharp objects or leaving it in a path where it might be run over by an industrial truck or other vehicles. These specific recommendations regarding the maintenance of welding hose are made by the Linde Air Products Company in the booklet "Precautions and Safety Practices in Welding and Cutting with Oxy-Acetylene Equipment":

(*a*) Examine hose carefully at least once every week for leaks, worn places, and loose connections. This can be done by immersing the hose under normal working pressure in water. Leaks in the hose at the nipple connection should be repaired at once by cutting off the hose a few inches from the end and remaking the connection. Leaks at other locations should be repaired by cutting off the bad section and inserting a hose coupling as a splice. Leaks not only waste acetylene and oxygen, but may become a source of hazard. Acetylene escaping from a hose is apt to become ignited and start a fire or set fire to the operator's clothing. It is a good practice after about two months of daily use, to cut off the hose 2 inches from each end and remake connections even though there is no apparent sign of wear.

(*b*) Do not attempt to repair hose with tape.

(*c*) Should a flashback occur and burn the hose, discard that length of hose. A flashback renders a piece of hose unsafe because it burns the inner wall. Sooner or later the damaged hose will disintegrate and cause trouble by clogging or otherwise interfering with proper operation of the blowpipe.

Procedure for underground, tank, or confined-space work. Before a man enters any confined space such as a manhole, each of the following requirements should be met:

1. The area to be entered should be checked visually to insure that the water level is below 6 inches and a dry wooden platform is available for use of workmen.

2. The air in the area should be checked for:

(*a*) Explosive gases and fumes, with an explosimeter.

(*b*) Oxygen content, with an oxygen analyzer.

(*c*) Carbon monoxide, if any burning or products of burning have been involved, with a colorimetric carbon monoxide tester.

3. If any of the above tests show significant deviation from normal, the area must not be entered until ventilation has been made by blowers or sufficient inerting gas (such as nitrogen or carbon dioxide) added to reduce the explosion hazard to not more than 0.2 per cent of the lower explosive limit. If inerting gas is used, or an oxygen

deficiency exists, entry should be made only while using a Bureau of Mines approved breathing apparatus.

4. No man or group of men should enter a confined space unless a watcher familiar with the job and instructed in rescue work (including the use of the breathing apparatus and artificial respiration) is in the immediate vicinity, in fresh air, and is in contact with the men at regular intervals. Breathing apparatus must be available for the rescuer.

5. No smoking or open lights, torches, arcs, or flames are permitted in confined spaces without previous written permission of the fire chief or safety engineer, who will first inspect the area to insure that fire or explosion possibilities have been minimized.

6. No spraying or painting using volatile solvents or oils should be undertaken in confined spaces without written permission of the safety engineer, who will specify and provide the necessary respiratory and other protection depending on the job.

7. All electrical equipment, such as temporary lights, ventilators, and power tools should be in first-class condition and conform to established standards of grounding and guarding.

8. Any manhole, tank opening, or other opening which must be left unattended should be protected by day by barricades, and by night by barricades plus lanterns or flashers. An opening must never be left without such protection. (The barricades must be in place *before* the opening is made.)

DRY-ICE HAZARDS

The accidents

Two accidents provide convincing evidence that dry ice must always be used with a clear understanding of the hazards involved.

1. In order to repair a main bearing on a 74-inch Bullard, a repairman went into a pit to pack the bearing with dry ice. After the bearing had been removed, the dry ice was left in the pit. The following day, another repairman went into the pit to replace the bearing. The dry ice left in the pit the day before had evaporated. The resulting carbon dioxide had replaced the good air. After a brief exposure, the repairman became affected by the lack of oxygen. A co-worker, noting his unsteady action, helped him out of the pit. This prompt action prevented what might otherwise have been a death due to asphyxiation.

2. A supervisor went to a chest-type freezer to get a steel shaft that

had been packed in dry ice, preparatory to a shrink fit. The freezer-chest was empty except for one shaft which was in a far corner of the chest. The supervisor in reaching for the shaft placed his head and shoulders in the chest. He later reported, "It was just like somebody cutting my breath off with a knife. I seemed to black out and when I came to, I was standing about 10 feet away." Carbon dioxide in very high concentration is known to produce almost-immediate unconsciousness and sometimes death. The supervisor was lucky in that his weight pulled him out of instead of into the chest.

Discussion.

1. Freezer chests used for dry ice should be so arranged that it is not necessary to reach bodily into the chest. Tongs can be used.
2. Gloves should be worn so it is unnecessary to make body contact with dry ice.
3. Pieces of dry ice should not be put into air-tight containers such as bottles or canisters because when the ice changes to the gaseous form, sufficient pressure can be built up in the container to cause an eruption.
4. Dry ice should not be used in a pit or a small enclosure unless some form of forced ventilation is provided.

THE HAZARDS OF WORKING ON LIVE CIRCUITS

The accident

An experienced electrician received a serious electric shock while making a "hot tap"—that is, connecting a lead to a feeder line with power on. In making the tap, the electrician stood on a ladder resting against a steel roof girder. He was 20 feet above the floor.

Instructions are that when a man is tapping a live line, a rubber blanket must be used to cover the girders, trusses, and all electrical-current-conducting material within reach. In this case, conducting material within reach, including a steel girder, was not covered.

In accordance with instructions, the electrician made his first tap on the wire farthest from him to avoid working over a tap. He was in the process of tapping a cable clamp when he apparently made contact with ground. That is, he touched the steel girder.

At the hospital, the electrician reported that his hand had slipped and hit the girder. In this way, a circuit was completed through his arm and across his chest. He received severe electrical burns.

Discussion. When work is done on energized high-voltage lines, the odds are that four out of five accidents will be serious, often fatal. Undoubtedly, the best solution to the problem is the elimination of the need for making hot taps. However, this might pose a problem, especially in an older plant. Therefore, where hot taps must be made, safe practices must be taught and scrupulously followed.

In view of the circumstances of the above accident, it would be appropriate to ask these questions:

1. What is the extent and quality of the safety instructions received by the plant electricians? Are they shown step by step how to make a hot tap safely?
2. Is it really necessary to make hot taps? Can the number of such hot taps be reduced by proper planning?
3. When working on live circuits should electricians be required to wear rubber gloves?

In reference to the first question, it is significant that a sixty-year-old maintenance supervisor insisted it would be difficult to get an experienced electrician to listen to safety instructions. Safety personnel should accept this challenge and give the necessary impetus to the safety training of skilled people. Using job-hazard analyses, electrical supervisors can prepare step-by-step routines for doing each electrical assignment safely. It cannot be assumed that skilled people learn all the safety requirements of their jobs when they learn their trade. This would be wishful thinking.

Investigation of numerous electrical accidents reveals these principal causes:

1. Working energized circuits.
2. Accidentally contacting open busses or exposed energized parts.
3. Inadequate operation of disconnecting switches, short-circuit conditions, or overload.

Accidents from these causes can be reduced to substantially zero by installation of modern equipment and by systems so designed that flexibility can be obtained without requiring working electrical circuits with power on or exposure to live parts. There is available economical and safe equipment to overcome these causes of electrical accidents. Modern equipment, however, is not enough. Elimination of electrical accidents depends upon an adequate educational program too.

In specific reference to the second question (Are hot taps necessary?), these recommendations emerge:

1. If a hot tap must be made, all grounds surrounding the tap and within reach should be insulated with rubber blankets, etc. Work should be done only by a person familiar with the hazards.

2. All workers required to make hot taps should be properly instructed regardless of previous experience, and their procedures should be checked periodically.

3. In all plants where hot taps are now being made, steps should be taken to encourage the modernization of existing distribution systems and the installation of an adequate number of disconnecting switches in the feeder systems to permit opening a circuit in front of a tap without disrupting a large section of the operating plant.

Now what about the third question: Are rubber gloves necessary when working on a live circuit? In many plants where hot taps are made on an infrequent basis, it is an established policy not to permit electricians to wear rubber gloves. This does not mean there is anything wrong with a policy requiring the use of rubber gloves. Public utilities insist on the use of rubber gloves where work on live circuits is involved. However, carefully supervised procedures and routines for controlling the use of the gloves and a daily inspection of the gloves have been established in cases where the utilities work on live circuits occurs several times each day. But in many plants, a hot tap is made much less frequently. Because of these infrequent occurrences, established controls regarding the use and inspection of rubber gloves are likely to break down. Under such conditions an electrician is likely to use a rubber glove with a defect. With the electrician not knowing about the defect, the glove would provide a dangerous false sense of security. As this chapter was being written, a story appeared in a local newspaper which provided an example of the case in point:

> **HOLE IN GLOVE SPELLS DEATH**
>
> Griffith, Ind., Dec. 10: A tiny hole in a rubber glove spelled death for a utilities repairman. The repairman drove into a filling station Saturday and noticed an ice storm had knocked down an electric wire across the street. He put on a pair of rubber gloves he kept in his car and crossed the street to move the wire. He was electrocuted. Later examination of the gloves revealed a small hole in the right forefinger.

Where hot taps are made at infrequent intervals, where electricians work in isolated areas of the plant, and where electricians are unsupervised, it is usually considered impractical to require the use of rubber gloves. With the gloves, the electrician is likely to take unnecessary chances. A small pin hole in the glove might lead to tragic consequences. The positive approach is to eliminate the need for hot taps.

GRINDING WHEELS—OVER-SPEED AND IMPROPER MOUNTING

The accident

A portable-grinder operator was struck in the mouth and a passer-by was struck in the forehead with flying pieces of a grinding wheel that had disintegrated. Investigation revealed that the wheel was running at 25 per cent above rated speed. The bore of the grinding wheel was $1\frac{1}{4}$ inches. The motor shaft was $\frac{1}{2}$ inch. Washers had been used to compensate for the difference between the two diameters. Also, rough washers had been used to hold the wheel instead of properly designed flanges. Paper spacers were not used between the wheel and the washers. There was no guard on the wheel.

This accident was the result of a violation of about every safe practice for grinding wheels. Following the accident, other portable grinders were found in a similar condition—over-speed, improperly mounted, washers used instead of flanges, and no guard.

Discussion. Listed below are a few of the recommendations made by the National Safety Council and by the American Standards Association for safe operation of grinding wheels.

1. As soon as a grinding wheel is received from the manufacturer, it should be unpacked and carefully inspected for the possibility of damage suffered in shipment, and it should also be given the "ring" test. Before being mounted, the wheel should be given the ring test again.
2. An abrasive wheel should never be mounted without compression washers to compensate for the slight unevenness of wheel or flanges. Blotting paper, rubber, or leather may be used for this purpose.
3. If the spindle is smaller than the bushing of the wheel, the wheel should be rebushed by the manufacturer or by experienced people in the plant.
4. Abrasive wheels should always be mounted between flanges. Flanges for the same wheel, whether straight or tapered, should be of the same diameter and thickness.

5. Work rests should be substantially constructed and securely clamped in position not more than $\frac{1}{8}$ inch from the abrasive wheel.

6. A competent person should be assigned to the mounting, care, and regular inspection of grinding wheels and machines.

7. To insure maximum safety to operators, they should know the specific type of work which each grinding wheel is intended to do. A close supervision should be maintained over the equipment.

8. Where possible, sturdy guards should be placed over the grinding wheels that will retain flying parts in case the wheel breaks.

9. A careful check should be made of all wheels to be sure they are not being operated at speeds above the rated speed for a particular wheel.

For detailed information concerning grinding-wheel safety, reference should be made to the American Standards Association code *The Care, Use, and Protection of Grinding Wheels* and to the National Safety Council's Safe Practices Pamphlet No. 13, *Grinding Wheels.*

EXPOSED CRANE AND HOIST FEEDER LINES

The accident

An electrician was instructed to repair an overhead light fixture which was located 3 feet above the 440-volt feeder lines of the plant crane. He used a ladder to reach the light. To make the repair, he unfastened a portion of the metal light shade. He was about to take the shade down the ladder when it hit against the feeder lines. The electrician's left shoulder was pressed against an overhead pipe. This completed an electrical circuit. As a result of the electric shock and the fall, the man died.

Other crane-feeder accidents have been reported. A millwright carrying a steel pipe through the plant upended the pipe, bringing it against an energized feeder. A crane operator left the crane cab via a column rather than the regular crane ladder and without thinking, grasped a feeder line for support. The elevator carriage of an industrial truck raised to its maximum height hit against the energized feeders of an overhead hoist. The end results of each of these cases was an electric shock.

Discussion. The hazards of exposed crane and hoist feeder lines vary in degree depending upon location. Unsafe conditions associated with crane and hoist installations may be grouped as follows:

1. Unprotected hoist and crane feeders which are 14 feet or less above floor level. (Employees handling long metal pipes or rods might accidentally bring these conductors of electricity into contact with the feeders. Likewise, the elevating carriage of a fork truck and similar equipment might make contact with the energized lines.)

2. Feeders that are located high above the factory floor but adjacent to crane ladders, platforms, beams, catwalks, light fixtures, and other overhead installations. (Employees replacing light bulbs, using the crane ladder, or repairing overhead equipment might come into dangerous proximity to these feeders.)

To prevent accidental contact with crane and hoist feeder lines, which may be energized by 110 to 575 volts, steps should be taken to provide adequate but practical protection of all personnel. The following program is suggested:

1. Make a plant survey to locate and classify existing hazardous conditions involving crane and hoist feeders.

2. Take steps to enclose or guard all crane and hoist feeder lines that can be reached by the carriage of a fork truck, by a long pipe, from a platform, or from the floor.

3. Where crane feeder lines can be reached from a fixed ladder, a catwalk or a platform, take steps to eliminate the hazard by relocation or by the installation of adequate barriers.

4. Place "High Voltage—Danger" warning signs on all feeders at 10-foot intervals.

5. Take steps to assure adequate protection of feeders on all new crane and hoist installations—specify enclosed feeders in the purchase order.

THE HAZARDS OF HAND AND PORTABLE TOOLS

The accidents

1. An employee operating a portable pneumatic grinder discovered he could speed up the job of grinding large castings by changing the governor on his grinder. After making the change, he continued to grind for a few minutes and then the wheel burst. A large piece of the wheel struck him in the chest, crushing the breast bone and severing his lung. Another piece struck a steel wall 200 feet away and left a dent $5/16$ inch deep. Investigation revealed that the wheel had been running at a 10,000-rpm over-speed.

2. While cutting identification marks in steel stock with a cold chisel, a workman was struck in the eye by a flying chip from the mushroomed head of the chisel. An eye was lost. Another worker lost an eye when a chip flew from the head of a chisel. He had fashioned the chisel from a discarded air-hammer bit. The head of the homemade hand chisel was too brittle for safe use. A hammer blow caused it to splinter.

3. An operator was tightening the gear puller on a vertical milling machine with a crescent wrench. The gear puller loosened suddenly and the wrench slipped off, striking the operator on the head. Although the wrench fitted properly, the worker was not prepared for the unexpected.

4. An employee was using an air hammer to break up concrete flooring. He was standing near a window of the building, and the handle of the air hammer extended over the window sill. When the bit of the hammer cut through the flooring, the handle of the hammer jammed against the window sill and crushed the worker's fingers.

5. A welder, having finished one job, picked up a stepladder to move to another job. Someone had left a wrench on top of the ladder; it fell, striking the welder on the head.

Discussion. A survey of industrial processes will indicate extensive use of hand tools and portable power tools in the repair and maintenance of equipment, in the performance of many hand operations, and in the packing and crating of the finished product. Included in the category of hand tools are screw drivers, chisels, drills, saws, hammers, clamps, wrenches, files, and knives; and the powered portable tools such as grinders, polishers, chippers, circular saws, and hoists. Misuse of these tools, use of the wrong tool, use of defective tools, and leaving tools in unsafe places are some of the usual causes of hand-tool accidents.

PURCHASING HAND TOOLS. Safety men and industrial supervisors should take an interest in the selection of all hand tools. The person doing the purchasing should always take into consideration the safety features of each product offered for sale. Quite often an attempt to buy the low-cost article necessitates a reduction in quality which introduces an accident cause. Naturally, better quality usually means a sturdy, better-built product with less chance for the unexpected to occur and, therefore, less chance for an accident.

In large organizations, hand tools are carefully inspected by engineering departments and laboratories before they are approved for purchase or placed on an approved purchasing list. Safety personnel would be remiss not to work closely with such agencies in order to be assured that the safety factor has been given careful consideration. In some of the smaller plants, the person responsible for the safety program could well afford to make independent investigations of the various types of hand tools used in his plant to ferret out inferior articles, which invariably result in inferior work and increase the accident hazard.

An appropriate list of safety factors which might be considered in the selection of hand tools and portable power tools follows:

1. Electrically powered tools should be equipped with automatic cut-off (dead-man control).
2. Control switches should be of sturdy construction and adequately protected to prevent accidental starting of the hand tool.
3. All cords on electrically powered tools should be equipped with ground wires or the standard A.S.A. grounding plug. (Generally speaking, electrically powered portable tools should have Underwriters' Laboratory approval.)
4. Handles of hammers, shovels, axes, and picks should be of straight-grained wood, free from slivers, and preferably of ash, hickory, or maple.
5. Proper tempering and the use of the correct grade of steel in the heads of hammers, chisels, stamps, punches, and other tools should be carefully considered.
6. Design and construction should be considered in terms of safe use.
7. Methods of packing and shipping employed by the vendor should be considered in order to preclude damage of the hand tools in transit.

HAND-TOOL INSPECTION. An adequate routine for the inspection of all hand tools when they arrive at the tool crib is essential. Preferably, the tool-crib attendant should be responsible for these inspections. However, in spite of the competence and sincerity of the tool-crib attendant, certain follow-up is essential. At regular intervals, supervisors and safety men should check the hand-tool control procedure as well as the hand tools in use.

An example of an inspection routine followed by a large manufacturer to determine the safety of hand tools arriving at the tool crib will indicate the importance attached to this subject by safety-minded management. In the case to be discussed, a safety inspection of portable power grinders will be reviewed. Similar inspection procedures can be established for all types of hand tools. These are the steps taken by the large manufacturer in the interest of hand-tool safety.

Before an order is placed for a grinder, the tool department checks the manufacturer's specifications pertaining to operating voltages, rpm, wheel diameters, and general construction of flanges, spindles, and chassis. By checking these specifications, the purchase of a grinder which would operate at an over-speed or one of unsafe construction is avoided.

When the portable grinder is received, it is given a visual inspection. Name-plate data pertaining to operating characteristics are carefully observed, and if a ground wire on a three-prong grounding plug is needed, one is attached; the grinder is then ready for a speed test. Rpm is measured by using a tachometer for grinders operating at less than 10,000 rpm. For higher speeds, a stroboscope is used.

A report covering the actual operating characteristics of each machine tested is compiled and compared with the manufacturer's name-plate data. If any conditions are found that would affect the safe operation of the grinder, necessary corrections are made before the machine is released for operation.

On grinders which may be set up and operated with various pulley combinations, the speed of the spindle and the motor belted together for each combination of pulleys is checked as well as the motor speed with no load at an over-voltage.

The procedure for checking pneumatic grinders is practically the same as the set-up for checking the electrically powered units. However, all pneumatic grinders that will operate at a speed greater than 5500 rpm on a 90-psi air supply are painted a bright red (see page 343).

Grinding wheels have been known to burst because of a manufacturing defect, damage in shipment, improper storage, or mishandling during installation. Therefore, such wheels are carefully inspected when placed in the tool crib, and at the time they are handed to an employee for use, a visual inspection and a "ring" test are made.

IN-USE HAND-TOOL APPRAISAL. At regular intervals, supervisors, safety engineers, and others should plan to make a systematized appraisal of hand tools in use throughout the plant. A check list similar to the one on p. 235 may be used to advantage as a reminder of unsafe acts and conditions to look for.

SPECIAL HAND TOOLS. The list on p. 235 does not, of course, cover all hand tools that may be found in use today. Numerous tools have been developed to perform special functions. But, regardless of the

HAND-TOOL-APPRAISAL CHECK LIST

Unsafe Conditions	Unsafe Acts
Screw Drivers	
Badly worn, splintered, or broken handle Bent blade or shank Dull or poorly shaped blade	Using screw driver as a chisel, pry, or punch. Holding screw driver in one hand and work in the other Using wrong-size screw driver
Knives	
Dull blade Worn handle	Cutting toward body Placing in unprotected position Not using protective sheath
Chisels and Punches	
Head mushroomed Head and point over-tempered (Look for chipping at the cutting point.) Body of tool too short to allow safe grip	Not wearing safety glasses Not holding tool in safe manner
Mallets and Hammers	
Loose, split, or rough handle (Tape should not be used on handle because it covers defects.) Head poorly or loosely fitted to handle	Using wrong type of hammer (carpenter's hammer for machine work) Exposing free hand to hammer blows
Files	
Handle missing File teeth covered with foreign material or dull	Using file as pry or punch Hitting file with hammer
Wrenches	
Jaws worn or sprung Mechanical defects	Using wrong type or size of wrench Using pipe on handle to get more leverage Using wrench as a hammer
Saws	
Improper set Loose or splintered handle	Using crosscut saw as a ripsaw Starting saw with a down instead of an up stroke
Lifting Jacks	
Worn threads, etc. Poor and inadequate base Jack filled with dirt and grit Jack standing under load with handle in socket	Using jack rated below load Failing to place jack on firm foundation Standing over handle of jack
Electrically Powered Hand Tools	
Ground wires missing or not connected Guards defective or missing, cords left across passageways, causing tripping hazards Defective leads Brushes sparking	Misuse of powered tool Failure to get a firm footing before starting work

purpose of the tool, the probability of an accident exists if ordinary care in the use of the tool is not exercised.

In industries subject to explosion hazards or fire hazards the use of non-sparking hand tools is essential. A non-sparking tool is made of a non-ferrous alloy, such as beryllium copper.

Another special hand tool is the soft-metal or plastic pliers, which are particularly useful for the removal of parts from between punch-press dies. A ferrous metal should not be used for two reasons. First, if hard-metal pliers are caught between the dies, the dies will be badly damaged. Second, the pliers will shatter and flying particles will endanger the operator and other employees in the area.

An air hose may be considered a special hand tool. It presents several hazards. Under no circumstance should it be used as a substitute for a brush to clean machines, clothing, or the person. Any form of horseplay should be prohibited with severe penalties for violation of the rule. In those cases where an air hose is essential for blowing out fixtures and jigs, eye protection should be provided. Likewise, the air-line pressure should be reduced to the minimum required for doing the job. Special reducing valves may be placed in the line or in the hose nozzle. It is desirable to place screens around work to confine particles blown from the fixtures.

EMPLOYEE AND SUPERVISOR EDUCATION. Employees will quite often fail to recognize the importance of hand-tool safety because such devices are simple in construction and are not ordinarily thought of as dangerous agents likely to produce injury. Therefore, adequate training to develop the proper attitude toward the use and maintenance of hand tools is essential. A discussion of hand-tool accidents and hand-tool hazards at supervisor and employee safety meetings will help to maintain interest in the subject.

Job training should stress the right method for using hand tools and the need for keeping all tools in proper repair. Basically, the attitude of each supervisor toward hand-tool safety will determine the attitude of employees.

FALLS—A MAJOR CAUSE OF INJURIES

The accidents

1. A plumber required a ladder to reach an overhead pipe. He took a 20-foot straight ladder from the storage rack and carried it to the location of the job. He positioned the ladder and climbed to the

fifth rung from the top. Just as he started to work, the rung he was standing on broke. The feet of the ladder kicked out and the plumber fell. He received a head injury and a broken right arm.

2. A maintenance employee climbed a 6-foot ladder to adjust a water-line valve that was 14 feet above the floor. To reach the valve, he stood on the top of the ladder. His wrench slipped off the valve, and he lost his balance. He fell to the floor, sustaining several bruises and a strained back.

3. A mail boy got behind schedule, so to make up lost time he ran between buildings. A construction crew had just opened a pit and had left to get a barricade. The mail boy did not see the opening; he fell in. There was no injury sustained. However, the accident once again demonstrated the hazards of running and also the need for placing a barricade around a pit opening before the opening is made.

Discussion. The effectiveness of those responsible for safety is in part dependent upon their ability to divide their time proportionately between the major and minor safety problems confronting them each day. Although all supervisors and safety personnel are primarily concerned with the prevention of accidents, especially those resulting in injury, it does not follow that the safety problems are the same within each industry. In order to make a decision regarding the type of safety program required for any operating unit, a complete analysis of existing facts is needed. Accident case histories, safety appraisals, and a study of existing safety programs are a basis for the analysis, which must be followed by an orderly solution of the indicated problem.

An analysis of national accident statistics will indicate that falls from elevations and on the level are a leading accident cause. After reading that over 26,000 people lose their lives in falls each year, one might first think of inaugurating a vigorous campaign to prevent falls. However, it is obvious that national statistics do not provide a reliable guide for planning the accident-prevention program for a specific plant. Further study of the national record might reveal that of the 26,000 persons dead from falls, 15,000 were over sixty-four years of age, and 1000 were under fourteen years of age. There were, however, 4600 industrial fatalities resulting from falls, and this is 25 per cent of the total work fatalities for one year. It can be assumed that the prevention of falls in most plants is a big problem. However, the actual cause of falls in each organization must be found before a suitable program can be planned. In some manufacturing organizations, the fall problem may be of minor consequence. In other industries, it will rank first among the major accident causes. Regardless of the variation in the magnitude of the fall problem from plant to plant, numerous general facts concerning falls deserve careful consideration.

HOUSEKEEPING AND PLANT LAYOUT. The prevention of falls begins at the drawing board and in the planning department. The construction of a building, the design of stairs and inclines, the arrangement of machinery and the choice of lighting equipment are factors which may contribute to the frequency of falls.

Aisles should be wide enough to permit the free movement of material and people. They should be free of material and other obstacles. To help keep aisles clear, it is desirable to mark them with a 4-inch-wide yellow line. If possible, blind corners, especially in a manufacturing plant using industrial trucks, should be eliminated or adequately protected by mirrors or warning signs. Employees must be instructed never to place material on the floor next to a corner or intersection or next to a door opening into an aisle. An employee rounding a corner is likely to trip over the material before he sees it.

Material should not be placed in warehouses or on manufacturing floors in such a manner that employees must crawl over it. Usually, haphazard piling or storage of material increases the time required to get at the material needed. Much time is spent moving material around and injuries result because of the falling and tripping hazards created.

RUNNING AND UNDUE HASTE. Although manufacturing plants are largely populated by adults who should know the hazards of running through buildings and up and down stairs, falls resulting from running are numerous. Such unsafe conduct in a manufacturing plant is especially dangerous; and, in addition, it denotes a lack of managerial control of the work force and an ineffective safety program.

As a first step, supervisors should attempt to discover the reasons why workers run. They might be running for these reasons:

Bus and train schedules not coordinated with exit periods.
Bottlenecks at gate or in parking lot.
Inadequate restaurant facilities.
Long pay lines.
Inadequate transportation facilities.
Unbalanced work loads.

WEARING APPAREL CONTRIBUTES TO FALLS. Worn soles and heels, high heels, tangling laces, and poor-fitting shoes cause falls because of bad balance, tripping, and slipping. However, it is difficult to control the wearing of the hazardous apparel mentioned. Women are usually reluctant to discontinue the wearing of high heels in spite of the foot discomfort and tendon strain produced, and it is understandable that some employees prefer to wear their oldest shoes to work.

However, carefully planned publicity concerning proper footwear, the sale of safety shoes at cost, and the establishment and enforcement of practical safety rules will help to solve a footwear-safety problem. For example, one large manufacturer has seen fit to place the following recommendation in his safety book: "Shoes with high heels, house slippers, canvas shoes, sandals, and open-toe shoes are not to be worn while working in the plant. Comfortable and attractive shoes with a protective toe and ideal for work are available at the Employees' Store."

CONDITION AND CARE OF FLOORS. Lack of proper maintenance is another prevalent cause of falls on floors. In a plant this is a major problem because of the heavy traffic over the floors each day. Under severe conditions produced by heavy trucking, wood floors deteriorate rapidly. Boards pry loose, nails protrude, and the flooring splinters. Hence, careful inspection, followed by prompt repair, is necessary to keep floors in safe condition.

In addition to necessary repairs being made, floors must be cleaned at regular intervals and the spilling of oil and grease and dropping of small parts on the floor must be avoided. To eliminate these unsafe conditions, the best approach is to get at the source. Drip pans, splash guards, and adequate maintenance of rolling equipment will eliminate most oil and grease.

An interesting story which illustrates the importance of careful selection of floor-cleaning agents and waxes is found in the files of a large insurance company.

> In one of the largest buildings in New York City, the entrance hall has a beautiful marble floor, the last word in art decoration. From time to time, people fell in this hall and some were severely injured. Careful study revealed a film on the marble after the janitors had cleaned the surface. A change to another washing detergent containing a slight abrasive left a film of marble dust instead of grease on the floor, and the falls in this hall were practically eliminated.

In some instances, it is impossible to keep slippery material off the floor, but in such cases a paint containing an abrasive material, corrugated mats, an abrasive floor covering, or special shoes may be used to advantage. However, safety personnel should be cautioned that the use of a resistive material on the floor may create rather than eliminate fall hazards. Studies indicate that people walking along a smooth surface will become unbalanced when their feet strike an abrasive surface which produces excessive foot resistance.

STAIRS. The construction, illumination, and maintenance of stairs deserve careful attention. Falls on stairs and steps often result in serious injury. The causes of such falls are numerous. Failure to use handrails, running on stairs, defective stairs, objects left on steps, poor lighting, and irregular risers and treads are among the leading causes. The space allotted the subject in this chapter permits only a bare outline of this important problem. Therefore, the reader is urged to refer to the National Safety Council's Safety Practices Pamphlets No. 2 and No. 99 and to other references on stairs and steps.

A few general rules for the construction of stairs follow:

1. Stair risers should all be of the same height and treads of the same width.
2. Pitch of stairs should be between 30 and 39 degrees.
3. Risers should not be more than 8 inches or less than 5 inches high.
4. Treads should be not less than $9\frac{1}{2}$ inches deep.
5. Stairways should have landings at least every 8 or 9 feet of vertical height.
6. Handrails should be placed on all stairs in accordance with the American Standard, Safety Code for Floor and Wall Openings, Railings and Toe Boards, A 12-1932.

The location of a mirror, display, poster, or bulletin board might be the underlying cause of a fall. For example, falls have occurred shortly after an eye-catching poster was placed at the foot of a short flight of stairs. An employee walking toward the stairs has been attracted by the poster, or rather, distracted. He has missed the first step of the stairs and has fallen. Windows placed at the head or foot of stairs can have an equally distracting effect, and in addition employees using the stairs in early morning or evening may be blinded by the sun shining through the window; this temporary distraction causes them to make a mis-step. Likewise, the variation in light in adjoining rooms can create a fall hazard because of the inability of the human eye to adjust immediately to the variation.

PORTABLE LADDERS. Working on a ladder above floor or ground level is seldom without hazard, even when normal precautions are taken. But the risk can be minimized where ladders are the right type for the job, where suitable ladder shoes and stabilizers are used, and where the ladders are well maintained and properly used.

To assure approved ladder design and construction, a reliable guide is the American Standard, Safety Code for Portable Wood Ladders, A 14.1-1952. Metal ladders at present are not covered by a code. However, there are several reliable manufacturers of metal ladders who are following the exacting requirements of the specifications for magnesium and aluminum ladders established by the Metal Ladder Manufacturers Association. Where metal ladders are used, however, it is well to keep in mind that these ladders are conductors of electricity and should not be used around electrical equipment.

Whenever a portable ladder is used, there is always the danger of the feet slipping. This hazard can be avoided by the use of ladder shoes suited for the prevailing conditions. There are two types of shoes available, those that grip the surface by friction and those with sharp points which dig into the ground or floor. One point to keep in mind is the matter of adequate ladder-shoe inspection and maintenance. Worn friction-type ladder shoes are ineffective.

Regular appraisal and maintenance of ladders is essential. Things to look for in the appraisal include damaged and badly worn rungs or rails, missing rungs, worn and damaged ladder shoes, and broken or damaged ladder attachments. Defective ladders should be tagged and taken out of service. If beyond repair, it is best to immediately destroy the ladder. Care in the storage of ladders should also receive adequate attention and should be noted in the ladder-appraisal report.

Supervisors must insist upon the observance of safe practices at all times when portable ladders are used. The following safe practices must prevail:

1. Defective ladders should not be used.
2. Whenever it is necessary to place a ladder in front of a door opening toward the ladder, the door must be blocked or locked or otherwise guarded by a second person.
3. Ladders placed in a busy aisle or corridor must be barricaded or roped off. This precaution is necessary to keep pedestrians or a vehicle from running into the ladder.
4. Employees must not reach out from a ladder more than arm's length.
5. Employees must face the ladder and use both hands when climbing up and down.
6. Employees subject to dizzy spells or with a heart condition should not be permitted to use ladders.

ELECTRICAL-TESTING HAZARDS

The accidents

1. In a small plant of the ABC Electrical Manufacturing Company, a high-voltage test of an electrical control device was performed in a small room in an isolated section of the plant. During the actual tests no one was allowed in the room except the tester and his helper. A control switch for the electrical-test circuit was located on a wall of the room about 10 feet from the actual test area. Each time a device was brought in for test, the helper and the tester would make the necessary connections, using bulldog clips. The tester would make a final check of all connections and then instruct the helper to step back. The tester would then close the control switch on the wall to make the test. This test had been operated for many years without an accident. One day on a late shift the usual procedure had been followed. The tester asked the helper to step back and then turned to walk toward the control switch. Almost in the same moment, the helper noticed that one of the bulldog clips had not been connected properly. He went back to correct the connection; the odds were against him. He still had the clip in his hand when the tester energized the test circuit by closing the wall switch. The helper's return to the device had been unnoticed by the tester. The 5000-volt electric shock was fatal.

2. To eliminate as far as possible the chance of human failure, a manufacturer of electrical control devices had isolated all electrical hazards in interlocked enclosures. This meant that the actual tests were performed in a permanent test enclosure. To enter the enclosure the tester had to open a door. Opening the door broke the electrical test circuit both mechanically and electrically. Thus, when the tester entered the enclosure, power would always be off even though he might have forgotten to open the control switch. To make each test, the tester would shut the enclosure door and reconnect the plug and receptacle of the interlocking circuit. To short cut this last step, a tester put a jumper around the interlocking circuit. Thus, opening the door did not break the circuit. The operator had to remember to open the control switch each time he entered the enclosure. The tester fell behind the production line, and in his rush to catch up, he forgot to open the control switch. With power on, he entered the test enclosure. The terminals of the control device were energized when he touched them. The high-voltage electric shock was fatal.

Discussion. When a plant needs a high-voltage test station, the station must be designed to do a good production job. And for safe, efficient use, the set-up must eliminate as far as possible the chance of human failure or mechanical or electrical failure that leads to accidents such as the two described.

This means isolating electrical hazards within interlocked enclosures and providing devices that automatically remove power and eliminate hazard in an equipment failure or malfunction. Basic rules for incorporating safety into the design of an electrical-test set-up follow:

1. In any electrical-test enclosure, input power has to be wired through a primary disconnect that can be seen from the test area.

2. All non-current-carrying metal parts of a high-voltage-test set-up, like transformer tanks, must be grounded. This provides a low resistance path to ground if a faulty ground develops in the system.

One end of the high-potential transformer's high-voltage winding must be grounded. So must the equipment under test. This affords a return path between the high-voltage winding and the unit under test should the unit fail.

3. All gates, doors, or access points to the test enclosure must be interlocked by a method that breaks the circuit mechanically as well as electrically. For example, a plug and receptacle may be used. Test personnel should be trained to check interlocks at the beginning of each work period.

The interlock must break both sides of the line except where one side of it is grounded. In this case, it is sufficient to have the interlock break only the ungrounded or "hot" side of the line.

Interlocked circuits must always be used so accidental grounding of one line will not cause the safety devices to become inoperative.

4. Red flashing warning lights should be used to indicate an electrical-test area. Two lights should point out every avenue of approach. The lights should be wired so they are in parallel and operate only when there is a hazard in the area and the primary disconnect is closed. Test personnel must assure themselves that everyone is clear before applying voltage.

5. "Danger—High Voltage" signs must be used at every access point to the test area.

6. Conductors other than ground connections cannot pass through, over, or under the enclosure in a way that permits bringing power in or out of an interlocked area without full benefit of the safety devices.

For example, one enclosure should never be run with power from another. Under such conditions only the protective devices at the power-source enclosure would be operative. Anyone entering the second enclosure would be unprotected by the interlocks.

7. Where possible, all equipment, power sources, etc., should be enclosed within the protective area. Low- and high-voltage circuits must be separated by grounded barriers, isolating transformers, or by some other method to stop high-voltage feed-back.

Exhibit 12–4. An electrical-test enclosure which provides positive worker safety. The test circuit cannot be energized until the sliding gate is closed. The design of enclosure and also of the test panel is such that there are no exposed electrical conductors within reach of workers. (Courtesy of the General Electric Company.)

Instrument circuits extending from the enclosure must be within a panel or metal shield connected to the enclosure and grounded. Instruments connected to these circuits have to be within an auxiliary interlock or behind a barrier which keeps them out of reach of all personnel.

8. For a temporary set-up, or in open areas, the testing area has to be indicated with white tape, temporary fence enclosures, etc.

9. Foot switches should be used for temporary enclosures—one for the operator, one for each assistant. Foot switches must be near the work under test and connected in series. Either the operator or an assistant can remove the high potential in an emergency.

10. If voltage permits, the high-potential cable from the transformer high-voltage winding to the unit under test must be armored. This guards against possible contact with control cables. If armor cable cannot be used, the high-potential line must be kept separate from all control cables, and it must be included within the enclosure.

The basic safety objective in electrical testing is to prevent personnel from contacting live electrical parts. This objective is best accomplished by isolating the hazard so power is automatically removed from the equipment and remains off when a hazardous part of the circuit is exposed or can be reached.

Use adequate safety devices and procedures to isolate hazards in all areas. This means following the same safe practices in laboratory and development work as in production set-ups.

Respect for electricity must be developed and maintained through training before a man can accept responsibility for his own safety in a testing area. A man must appreciate what an interlock is and does if he is to resist the temptation to short cut it.

Training can be tailor-made to meet specific needs. Rules and regulations, diagrams, and actual demonstrations can be used in the training. New employees should first work as helpers or observers with a more experienced tester. Good supervision and a continuing check-up of all test set-ups are required even in those cases where adequate safety devices have been provided.

SELECTED REFERENCES

ABC of Radiation, Brookhaven National Laboratory, Associated Universities, Inc., Upton, New York, 1949.

"Are You Equipped to Fight Falls," *National Safety News,* August, 1957.

Electrical Accidents and Their Causes, published annually for the Factory Department, Ministry of Labour and National Service, Her Majesty's Stationery Office, London.

Inskip, L. S., and H. H. Watson, "Grounding of Portable Electric Equipment," *Electrical Engineering,* April, 1955.

Sherman, Frank, "How to Lift with Overhead Cranes," *Modern Materials Handling,* December, 1955.

"They Backed the Attack on Falls," *National Safety News,* August, 1957.

PART IV

APPRAISING, ANALYZING, AND MEASURING SAFETY PERFORMANCE

CHAPTER

13

Plant and equipment safety appraisals

The safety engineer should be held accountable for pin-pointing unsafe work areas, unsafe equipment, and unsafe practices and bringing them to the attention of the proper line supervisor with practical recommendations for improvement. In the performance of these duties and where necessary to discharge his functional responsibility, the safety engineer should have the right to look at any area and to discuss safety with any person. He should not have the authority to order or direct, but should carry out his responsibilities by appraising, teaching, counseling, and advising, relying on his authority of facts well marshaled rather than the power to command.

AMOS E. NEYHART
The Pennsylvania State University

Every machine and operation in a plant can be properly safeguarded, housekeeping excellent, and personal protective equipment adequate, but there is no assurance that this fine state of affairs will continue. An emergency, substitution of material or a tool, and time and wear may alter conditions drastically. Some follow-up is required so conformance with accepted safety standards will be maintained. Therefore, regular safety appraisals conducted by safety personnel and supervisors should be a part of the plant accident-prevention program. The nature of such appraisals will, of course, vary depending upon the type of industry, the size of the plant, the variety of equipment and machines, and the materials used.

A principal function of a plant safety engineer is to pin-point unsafe conditions and make recommendations for their correction, but supervisors have a responsibility for looking for unsafe conditions and unsafe practices too. Thus, an understanding of the objectives of a safety appraisal and the procedures for making the appraisal is essential.

Objectives of safety appraisals[1]

Naturally, the primary objective of any safety appraisal is to discover hazardous conditions and to initiate correction of them. Accomplishment of this goal would bring the plant or any operation in the plant up to approved safety standards. Numerous "hazard check lists" are available to facilitate the plant safety appraisal. But to be practical and useful, such check lists should be tailor-made for each plant. The check list must relate to existing plant operations and conditions, not to a lot of generalities. In preparing a hazard check list it would be helpful for supervisors to keep in mind the various factors which are normally covered in a plant safety appraisal. In brief, the basic goals of a plant safety appraisal would be:

1. To see that equipment, machines, tools, and parts are in good condition, are properly safeguarded, and have not become worn or damaged so as to create a hazard.
2. To make sure materials used in the manufacturing process do not create an uncontrolled health, fire, or explosion hazard.
3. To see that personal protective devices, fire equipment, first-aid

[1] The term "safety appraisal" is used instead of "safety inspection" because of the broader meaning of the word "appraisal." To inspect means to look upon. To appraise means to look upon and in addition to bring together facts, to exercise judgment, and to evaluate as to quality and status.

equipment, machine guards, and safety appliances are adequate and are being used properly.

4. To make sure aisles, floors, stairs, elevators, ramps, and plant layout are being maintained in a safe condition.

5. To check illumination, ventilation, and noise levels.

6. To check all work practices to make sure that they conform to approved safety standards.

TYPES OF SAFETY APPRAISALS

Supervisors are constantly alert for any unsafe conditions, but these day-to-day observations must be supplemented with formalized and regularly conducted safety appraisals. The following types of appraisals are an essential part of the plant safety program:

1. Plant-wide safety tours conducted by the plant manager, safety personnel, and others.
2. Safety appraisals of sections of the plant by teams of line supervisors and safety personnel.
3. Periodic, regularly scheduled safety appraisals of specific types of equipment and machines by trained personnel.
4. Special appraisals such as a procedure for releasing all new and relocated equipment.
5. Safety appraisals conducted by employees or by employees and their immediate supervisors.
6. Appraisals conducted by state labor and health department engineers, insurance engineers, fire-prevention specialists, and industrial hygienists.

Plant safety tours

An important by-product of a safety appraisal conducted by the president of a company, the plant manager, and other plant executives is the opportunity the plant tour provides for management to demonstrate its personal interest in the safety and welfare of employees. Hence, supervisors should take full advantage of these periodic plant tours by being quick to join the appraisal team when it reaches their section and by taking prompt corrective action on any unsafe conditions that might be discovered. Employees knowing that top management and immediate supervision have a real interest in safety will respond favorably. The net results should be fewer accidents.

Whenever the chief executives of the plant or company make a plant safety appraisal, they provide an excellent opportunity for increasing safety interest among all personnel. In general, these plant tours produce the most good when they are announced in advance. There is nothing gained by the unannounced executive plant tour that catches a supervisor with his guards up and his section in disorder. Ample notice of a planned safety appraisal will prevent embarrassing occurrences. Of course, the house will be in order when the big boss arrives, but this is all for the good. On the other hand, no amount of sweeping and polishing will eliminate unsafe practices or an unhealthy safety attitude. These are the factors which should be of concern to the plant manager or company president.

A briefing session before these plant tours will pay good dividends. The safety engineer can review various safety problems with members of the appraisal team. He can tell them about supervisors who have done outstanding safety jobs and about employees who have submitted unusually good safety suggestions. During the tour these people can be pointed out so the executives in the appraisal team may compliment them. The impact of a few words of praise, provided the praise is earned, will be immediate and wide-spread. Likewise, the appraisal team's interest in a particular safety problem is sure to motivate prompt action.

Sectional appraisals

At times familiarity with a section of a plant creates a state of satisfaction with things as they are. Thus, it is not uncommon for certain hazards to become an accepted part of the job. To protect himself against the dangers of such complacency, a supervisor may wish to get help from other supervisors and the plant safety engineer in making a periodic safety appraisal of his area. Many companies use safety-appraisal teams for sectional safety appraisals. These teams might be composed of:

1. A foreman or general foreman from another section,
2. the foreman of the section, and
3. the plant safety engineer.

Such teams, in making the safety appraisal, are concerned with the housekeeping in the section, the methods of handling material, the condition of safety devices, and the observance of safety rules. In general, such superficial factors as dust on lockers, employees' clothes in the work area, oil on the floor, a pallet in the aisle, and other minor items which are sure to change from day to day are not included in the report of the safety-appraisal team. In many plants the appraisal team may actually rate the supervisor in charge of the section. Various point rating systems may be devised for facilitating these ratings.

Periodic safety appraisals of specific equipment

Supervisors, because of their understanding and knowledge of their own work areas and their familiarity with operations, are well qualified for general types of safety appraisals. But they might not be qualified or have the time to make a specialized safety appraisal of particular equipment. For example, the safety appraisal of such equipment as pressure vessels, power presses, cranes and hoists, slings and chains, elevators, portable power tools, ladders, and fire extinguishers requires special knowledge and training. Also, a great deal of time is required to complete such appraisals. Therefore, specially trained personnel are usually assigned these specialized duties.

Although the supervisor may not make these specialized safety appraisals, he does have responsibility for seeing that such appraisals are made by competent people and on time. Likewise, he must make a follow-up so needed repairs and corrections will be made and defective equipment taken out of service.

An important aspect of these safety appraisals is their close tie-in with a preventive maintenance program and the maintenance of production. For example, power-press appraisals made by a qualified maintenance mechanic in a metal-container plant turned up such defects as a cracked pitman, pulverized bearings of a flywheel, and a drive belt about to break. It is unlikely that any of these conditions would have led to injury of an employee. But in each case, a long production delay, damage to an expensive die, and possible additional damage to the equipment were avoided because of the appraisals. Likewise, the periodic safety check on cranes, hoists, and pressure vessels may prevent down-time during peak production periods. The essentials of periodic safety appraisals of specific equipment are:

1. A qualified, properly trained person.
2. A check list for making the appraisal.
3. A safety-appraisal schedule.
4. A record of the appraisal which indicates defects found, repairs made, and date of appraisal.

Periodic special safety appraisals of the following equipment are recommended:

1. Power presses.
2. Cranes and crane hooks.
3. Slings and chains.
4. Fire equipment.
5. Respiratory equipment.
6. Pressure vessels.
7. Elevators.
8. Industrial trucks.
9. Portable power tools.
10. Hoists.
11. Ladders.
12. Pull-out press guards.
13. Gas-fired ovens.
14. Hand tools, etc.

Safety appraisals of new and relocated equipment

A new hydraulic press of modern design equipped with two-hand controls was installed in a branch plant of a large manufacturer. Soon after the installation an operator had a thumb and one finger amputated. An investigation revealed that two men had been placed on the press. One man operated the two-hand controls. The other man stood in back of the press to help position the part being formed. The man on the back of the press was injured because nothing had been done to keep his hands out of the danger zone. A cardinal rule of power-press operation had been violated. Any qualified safety engineer or press-room supervisor would have recognized the hazard immediately. But in this case the supervisor was not familiar with press operations and press safety. This case provides an example of the day-to-day activity in the plant which cannot be controlled by the routine periodic safety appraisals. New equipment, machines, and processes and all relocated or modified machines and equipment should be carefully checked for compliance with existing safety standards before being put into operation. A qualified safety engineer, because of his broad knowledge of accident-prevention methods and state and local safety requirements, can render valuable assistance to the supervisor by making a safety appraisal of all new and relocated equipment. However, such appraisals do not relieve the supervisor

MACHINE INSTALLATION TAG

DO NOT OPERATE
UNTIL THIS TAG IS REMOVED

This tag should be placed on all new or moved machines by the millwrights. This tag can only be removed by the safety engineer or his authorized representative *There is no other authority to remove this tag.*

MILLWRIGHT'S INSTALLATION APPROVED

Type of machine ______________________

Location ______________ Bldg. ______________

This machine has been properly installed and the guards provided have been put in place

Date ______________ Signed ______________
(Millwright)

ELECTRICIAN'S WIRING APPROVED

This machine is properly wired for safe operation

Temporary ☐ Permanent ☐

Date ______________ Signed ______________
(Electrician)

OPERATION APPROVED

This machine is approved for operation.

Date ______________ Signed ______________
(Maintenance Supervisor)

This machine has been accepted from the safety viewpoint and is released for operation.

Date ______________ Signed ______________
(Safety Engineer)

Date ______________ Signed ______________
(Supervisor)

Exhibit 13–1. A machine-installation tag which would be used in a large plant having separate groups of millwrights, electricians, etc.

of any responsibility for safe working conditions. In effect, the safety engineer releases the equipment to the supervisor. The supervisor, in turn, releases the equipment to the operator. Special "Do Not

No. 142

NEW OR RELOCATED APPARATUS

DO NOT OPERATE

UNTIL THIS TAG IS REMOVED

BY THE SAFETY ENGINEER

OPERATION APPROVED

Machine .... Bldg ....

Date ....

Signed ....

TO BE FILED BY SUPERVISOR OF DEPT SAFETY ENGINEER

OPERATION APPROVED

Machine .... Bldg ....

.... No. 142

Insp. Date .... Signed ....

TO BE FILED BY SAFETY ENGINEER SAFETY ENGINEER

Machine .... Bldg ....

Ready for Inspection

No. 142

Date .... Signed ....

TO BE SENT TO SAFETY ENGINEER

Exhibit 13–2. A machine-installation tag which could be adapted for use in a small plant.

Operate" tags, which may be used to insure the safety appraisal of all new or relocated equipment, are shown in Exhibits 13–1 and 13–2. Also, a practical procedure for use of the tag is outlined as follows:

Procedure for Use of "Do Not Operate" Tag

1. It is required that all installations of machines, equipment, or apparatus, whether new or relocated, shall be appraised and approved by the safety engineer before regular operation is begun.

2. A "Do Not Operate" tag shall be placed on the equipment by the person (millwright, machinist, electrician, etc.) who makes the installation and the supervisor of maintenance notified when the installation is complete.

3. The supervisor of maintenance shall check the installation, sign the bottom stub (see Exhibit 13–2), and send it to the safety engineer. This stub is notification that the equipment is ready for a final safety appraisal.

4. The safety engineer shall make a personal check of the equipment, and if it is satisfactory, he shall sign the stub and place it in his file.

5. The top of the tag also shall be signed and dated by the safety engineer and shall be given to the supervisor. This indicates to the supervisor the safety approval of the safety engineer. However, final approval for safety of the equipment still rests with the supervisor.

Employee safety appraisals

Safety appraisals made by workers are desirable because they help promote employee participation in the safety program. Because knowledge of the work area is essential, such appraisals should be confined to the employee's own section or at least to sections doing the same type of work. Likewise, employee safety-appraisal assignments should be made by the immediate supervisor, not the safety engineer or someone else. To facilitate the employee safety appraisal, the supervisor may wish to supply the employee with a check list that also becomes the appraisal report, such as the one shown in Exhibit 5–3, p. 90. Such check lists must be prepared specifically for the section involved. A standard form is seldom satisfactory. For example, items like stops on bench drawers, boards with nails, and unsafe hand tools are hazards characteristic of a particular type of operation. Such hazards obviously would not be found in all plants.

Another recommended method to use in conducting the employee safety appraisal is to take a specific unsafe condition such as defective hand tools and make this the appraisal target. Other specific items for target safety appraisals might be housekeeping, personal protective equipment, fire hazards, or defective equipment. An instruction period prior to the appraisal might be used to brief the employees on the unsafe conditions to look for. For example, during a defective-hand-tool appraisal, employees would be instructed to look for mushroomed tool heads, splintered or broken tool handles, use of the wrong tool, and like hazardous conditions. Safety-instruction cards prepared by the National Safety Council on a wide variety of subjects provide useful guides for the employee safety appraisal. (See Exhibit 13–3.)

HAND TOOLS
Inspection Check List

CHISELS
- Heads safe-ended or dressed? ☐
- Cutting edges sharp and square? ☐

FILES
- Tangs protected with handles? ☐
- Teeth sharp and clean? ☐

HAMMERS
- Handles tight, unbroken, and clean? ☐
- Face of head smooth, not mushroomed? ☐

KNIVES
- Sheaths, or racks provided? ☐
- Handles guarded? ☐

SCREWDRIVERS
- Handles smooth and clean? ☐
- Bits sharp and square? ☐

WRENCHES
- Jaws sharp, not spread? ☐
- Right type for job? ☐

SAFETY INSTRUCTION CARD **No. 772**
National Safety Council PRINTED IN U.S.A.

Exhibit 13–3. A check list to be used by employees looking for unsafe conditions.

Safety appraisals by outside agencies

Insurance-company safety engineers, industrial hygienists of state health departments, state safety engineers, and fire marshals by the nature of their work gain a large amount of knowledge regarding injury and health hazards common to industry. Hence, the recommendations and safety suggestions made by these qualified people should not be taken lightly. A friendly and sincere cooperation with state and insurance-company engineers and specialists is recommended. Usually these specially trained people have a valuable service to offer. Industrial hygienists from state health departments and insurance companies might discover various health hazards in a thorough review of manufacturing operations. But in addition, because of their knowledge and experience, their investigations may bring to light many good ideas for improving a job method. A recommendation to eliminate a toxic-fume hazard by the application of more efficient exhaust methods, for example, might also lead to a considerable saving of the cleaning solvent and also to more efficient operation of the degreaser. Likewise, the recommendation to use a less toxic material to minimize a health hazard might mean also that a less expensive material could be used. In a sense, the price of safety is "eternal vigilance." This being the case, it would appear logical to make full use of the various safety services which are available. For this reason, where past performance warrants such consideration, these outside people should be used to full advantage. They should be given all the facts, an opportunity to study the plant operations, and an audience with key people so their recommendations might be discussed.

LADDER NO. ....

UNSAFE

Repair ....

Return to .... Bldg. .... Door ....

Date .... Signed ....

- - - - - - - - - - - - - - - - - - - -

Mr. .... Bldg. ....
(Tool Crib Attendant)

Ladder No. .... has been found unsafe, and will be sent to Carpenter Shop for repair and return

Date .... Signed ....

- - - - - - - - - - - - - - - - - - - -

CARPENTER SHOP
BUILDING NO. 76

Call for Ladder No. .... at Bldg. .... Door ....

Repair ....

Return to .... Bldg. .... Door ....

Date .... Signed ....

Exhibit 13–4. A tag for marking defective ladders. (Courtesy of the General Electric Company.)

Defective-equipment tags

Closely associated with plant safety appraisals are the methods common to industry for tagging-out defective equipment and for tagging or locking equipment controls to protect personnel. It is essential that supervisors understand the basic principles of these tagging procedures. A definite policy is needed for placing defective equipment out of service. A system including the use of "Do Not

Operate" tags is suggested. These tags, in order to make the system effective, must be supplied to supervisors, safety men, and certain maintenance employees only. When defective equipment is dis-

DO NOT OPERATE

DO NOT USE OR OPERATE THIS EQUIPMENT UNTIL THE DEFECT NOTED HAS BEEN CORRECTED AND THIS TAG HAS BEEN REMOVED BY THE SECTION SUPERVISOR.

Tag placed: Date ______________ Time ______________

Tag placed by ______________________________

Reason for placing tag ______________________________

____

____

ANY EMPLOYEE OPERATING EQUIPMENT TO WHICH THIS TAG IS ATTACHED, UNLESS AUTHORIZED, WILL BE SUBJECT TO DISCHARGE.

Exhibit 13–5. A defective-equipment tag.

covered, the tag is attached with the strict understanding that the equipment is not to be used until the tag has been removed by an authorized person. Examples of defective-equipment tags are shown in Exhibits 13–4 and 13–5. Any person attaching a defective-equipment tag to a machine or equipment should do so with the express approval of the supervisor responsible for the equipment.

Personnel-protection tags

An electrician opened the primary disconnect on an overhead crane and then proceeded to the crane bridge to make a minor electrical repair. A few minutes later, the crane operator reported for work. Noting that power had been shut off on his crane, he closed the control switch. The electrician working on the bridge was electrocuted. This tragic accident emphasizes the need for a sound and strictly enforced procedure for protecting personnel required to repair, inspect, and clean power equipment and tools controlled by valves, switches, and levers. To provide the necessary protection of personnel, these steps are taken:

1. No employee is permitted to work on a power machine or power equipment until power is removed and the control is tagged at the primary disconnect (for example, at the line switch, not at a push button). (For positive protection, the switch or valve may be padlocked so power cannot be restored until the padlock is removed.)
2. Tags and padlocks are removed only by the person whose name appears on the tag.
3. If two or more persons are working independently on a machine or circuit, each should affix a tag or lock to the control.
4. Tags for protection of personnel should not be used for other purposes such as tagging defective equipment.
5. Prompt disciplinary action is required for any violation of the above procedure.

No matter what method of tagging- or locking-out equipment is used, effective control can be maintained only by constant supervision and adequate training of employees. Safety posters and discussion of the tagging methods in employee safety meetings will acquaint new workers with the rules for tagging equipment and will be a helpful reminder to the longer-service employees too. (See Exhibit 13–6.)

Conclusions

Well-planned safety-appraisal procedures systematically and regularly applied are an effective means of discovering hazardous condi-

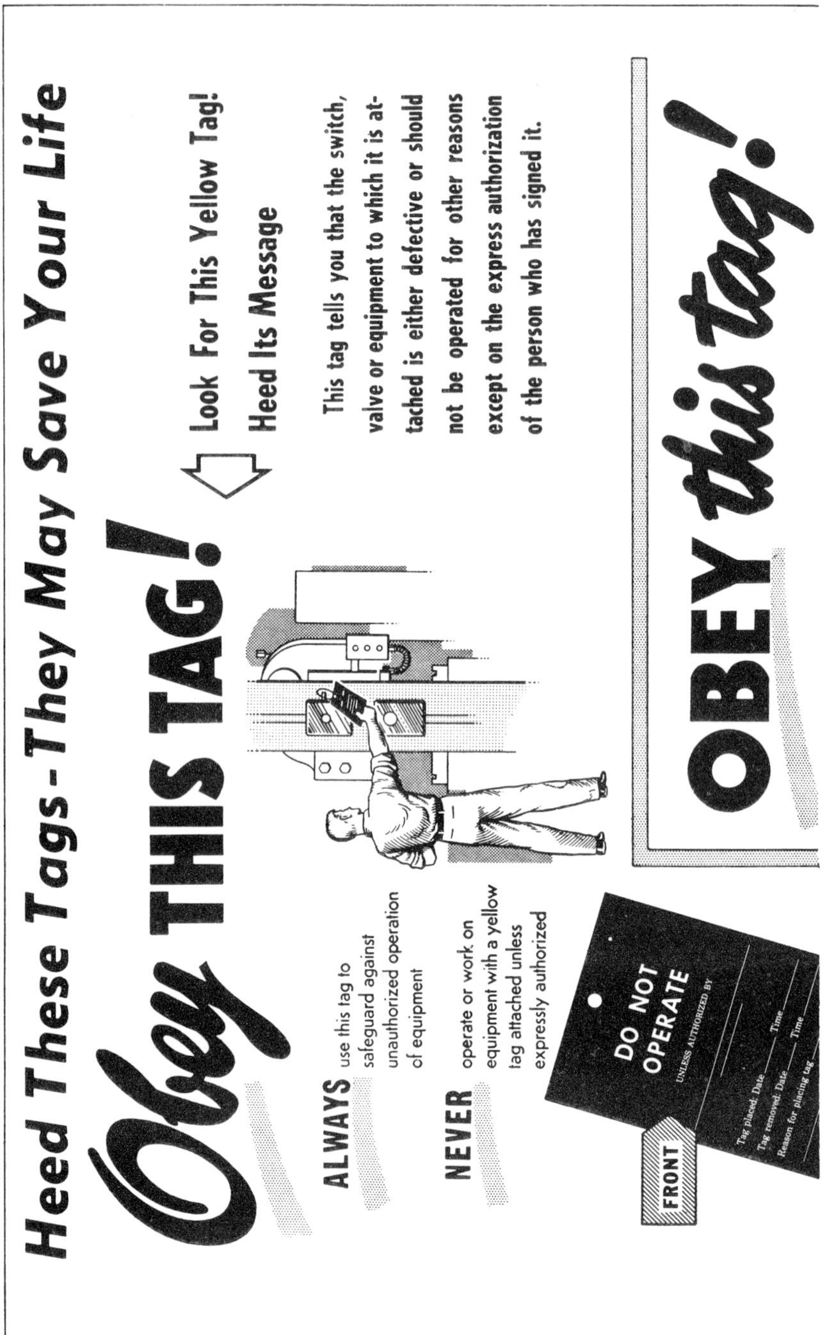
Heed These Tags - They May Save Your Life
Obey THIS TAG!
Look For This Yellow Tag!
Heed Its Message
This tag tells you that the switch, valve or equipment to which it is attached is either defective or should not be operated for other reasons except on the express authorization of the person who has signed it.
ALWAYS use this tag to safeguard against unauthorized operation of equipment
NEVER operate or work on equipment with a yellow tag attached unless expressly authorized
DO NOT OPERATE
UNLESS AUTHORIZED BY
Tag placed: Date Time
Tag removed: Date Time
Reason for placing tag
FRONT
OBEY this tag!

Exhibit 13–6. A safety-tag poster.

tions that if not corrected are likely to lead to an accident which produces personal injury, a production delay, or property damage. In conducting the appraisal, the need for gathering pertinent facts about existing conditions and exercising sound judgments regarding the required corrective action is the point of focus. In keeping with the basic concept that the supervisor has the major responsibility for safety, any unsafe conditions which are found are reported to him with logical recommendations for correction. The action to be taken, however, usually is decided upon and taken by the supervisor.

It is well to recognize that there are different types of safety appraisals which can be made—each with a specific purpose. In summary, these types of safety appraisals have been discussed:

1. Plant-wide safety appraisals conducted by:
   (*a*) Chief executives of the company.
   (*b*) Safety engineer.
2. Safety appraisals of a section of the plant conducted by appraisal teams (employees, supervisors, etc.).
3. Periodic safety appraisals of specific equipment conducted by trained specialists.
4. Safety appraisal of new and relocated equipment made by the safety engineer.
5. Safety appraisals by outside agencies.

Unless prompt corrective action is taken following a safety appraisal, the effort and time required to make the appraisal have been wasted. Well-planned and -maintained safety appraisals will help keep unsafe conditions and practices at a minimum. Such appraisals are worthwhile. They are a continuing activity in any successful safety program.

CHAPTER

14

Accident investigation and cause analysis

The value of any accident investigation must be judged by the practicability of applying the remedy. The investigation of an accident is a fact-finding job. Fact-finding, however, is not the simple accumulation of a mass of data. It is an exploration of what actually happened, a sifting of data, a consideration of the reasons for the accident.

RALPH J. CROSBY
Marsh and McLennan, Inc.

In modern safety programs accident investigation is regarded as a definite responsibility of the first-line supervisor. By reason of his familiarity with the worker and the work area, his knowledge of machines and materials, his direct relationship with the work group, and his personal interest in safety, the first-line supervisor is in a good position to conduct an accident investigation. However, to pin-point the various causes of an accident and to decide what corrective steps are required, assistance is available to him, if needed, from the plant safety engineer, technicians, insurance-company engineers, and others,

Although the supervisor makes the investigation of a particular accident, it is the plant safety engineer who has responsibility for formulating a practical procedure for finding the true causes of an accident, then helping the supervisor develop a skill in making the investigation.

The basic reason for an accident investigation is to find the causes of the accident so prompt corrective action can be taken. Although unsafe acts and unsafe conditions will be apparent, finding the contributing causes, especially the mental and physical condition of the employee which influenced the unsafe act, may be a little more difficult. But inasmuch as the goal of the accident investigation is to acquire as much information as practical, the investigation should not stop until the human factors involved have been identified. Finding out what the worker was doing at the time of the accident is, of course, essential. But knowing what the worker's activities, his training, his state of mind, his physical condition were before the accident might have an important bearing on the corrective action which will be taken to keep the same type of accident from re-occurring.

Regardless of the course the investigation takes, a general rule of promptness and an open-minded approach should prevail. What were the contributing and the immediate causes of the accident? What steps need to be taken to prevent the same type of accident from re-occurring? These are the principal questions to be answered. Perhaps the six questions that teach all that is known can be applied to accident investigation.

WHO was injured?
WHERE did the accident happen?
WHEN did the accident occur?
WHAT were the contributing and immediate causes of the accident?
WHY was the unsafe act or unsafe condition permitted?
HOW can a similar accident be prevented?

Before discussing a set procedure for investigating and finding the causes of accidents, it would be well to point out three concepts in safety work which often are misleading or tend to obscure the need for positive action: (1) the practice of classifying accidents by the type of injury sustained; (2) giving "carelessness" as the cause of the accident; and (3) avoiding the fixing of blame in the accident investigation.

Types of injuries

The first of these concepts—the classification of accidents by the type of injury—might be a long-established practice in many companies. Supervisors and other members of management might be receiving reports on a weekly or monthly basis which indicate the number of lacerations, burns, fractures, amputations, foreign bodies, abrasions, and contusions treated at the plant dispensary. This information could be interesting, but it provides few guides to the prevention of similar accidents. Such information would be more useful to the plant nurse and physician than to the supervisor who must take corrective action. To keep the safety program on a sound, result-producing basis, supervisors must concentrate on the causes of the accident rather than on the type of injury which resulted.

Carelessness

The second concept, or perhaps it would be more descriptive to say misconception, concerns the overuse of the word "carelessness" in safety work. Carelessness, according to Webster, means free from care, untroubled, indifferent, heedless, and thoughtless. It is obvious that the definition has a wide breadth of meaning. It could be used to describe a wide variety of circumstances which are in no way related. But ask a group of industrial supervisors to state the major cause of accidents, and it is likely that the answer will be "carelessness." Hence, it is not surprising that about seven out of ten accident reports give for the cause of the accident "carelessness" and for corrective action "will talk to the injured employee and tell him not to be careless again." However, ask for specific examples of accidents caused by carelessness, and these typical answers are obtained:

Reached around guard while machine was in motion.
Running down flight of stairs.
Used ladder with worn safety feet.
Improper use of knife, was cutting toward hand.
Was not giving adequate attention to job—daydreaming.
Didn't realize what he was doing was unsafe.
Disregarded safety rule.
Inexperienced and improperly trained for the job.

Obviously, "carelessness" has been used to describe a wide variety of accident causes. It means almost everything or almost nothing, depending upon the point of view. Carelessness then as a given cause of an accident neither defines nor describes prevailing conditions or practices. When told that the cause of an accident was carelessness, there is nothing to go on in determining needed corrective action. Then too, it is likely that the indiscriminate use of the word tends to place the blame for the accident on the employee and ends any attempt to really get down to the actual cause. On the other hand, stating the specific cause of the accident such as "reaching around guard while machine was in motion" describes an unsafe condition and an unsafe act. Corrective action can be taken. It is likely that with such specific information the guard will be redesigned so the employee can't reach into a pinch point. Thus, to do a good job of accident investigation and identification of accident causes, it will help to avoid the use of the word "carelessness."

Fixing responsibility

The third misconception concerns the recommendation sometimes made that the idea of fixing blame should definitely be avoided in the accident investigation. Admittedly, the primary reason for an accident investigation is to find the *contributing* and *immediate* causes of the accident, to demonstrate the sincere concern management has for the safety and welfare of each employee, and to identify the corrective steps required to develop safe working conditions and to prevent the same type of accident from re-occurring. And supervisors by their conduct and attitude during the accident investigation must convince employees that the investigation is intended primarily to find the accident cause. However, the investigation will also indicate whether or not responsibility for safety has been fully assumed by supervisors and employees. In reference to this point, there are some who would prefer to view the matter of blame with their heads in the sand. The suggestion is made that in the investigation no attempt should be made to place blame or fix responsibility for an accident because where responsibility is fixed, an attitude of "covering up" develops. This is poppycock. If decisions made following the investigation are fair and impartial, employees will cooperate in the investigation and be willing and straightforward in giving information to their bosses. Where a line supervisor is responsible for safety, he is also accountable for good results. Modern management requires operating policies based on measured performance, enforced standards, and appropriate action for incapacity or poor performance. Ignoring this concept in the accident investigation is unsound. For example, if a supervisor has failed to correct an unsafe condition which he knew about, or if an employee has deliberately violated a safety rule, a need for action is indicated. Ignoring such conduct would be hard to justify. Poor safety performance must be treated in the same manner as poor production performance would be treated. (It is not implied here that all accidents would require some form of disciplinary action.) In fixing responsibility, the accident or the extent of the injury are not the factors to consider. It is the conduct of the supervisor or employee which contributed to the accident that really counts.

If the responsibility for safety is placed squarely on the shoulders of the first-line supervisor, he must determine where the fault lies when an accident occurs and, if necessary, correct his own shortcomings. Likewise, if employees are instructed to perform their jobs in a safe manner and are paid accordingly, the supervisor has every right to expect compliance with his instructions and established safety rules.

Of course, where it is necessary to fix responsibility, an open mind and good judgment must prevail. For example, if a press operator is injured because he tied down one button of a two-hand control, where does the fault lie? If the control had been tied down for several hours and the supervisor had observed the condition but had taken no corrective action, then the supervisor's failure to enforce a safety rule is the basic cause of the accident. His failure to take corrective action as soon as he observed that the control had been tied down signified to the employee that he sanctioned making the control inoperative. But if the supervisor had no knowledge of the control being tied down, if the supervisor had taken corrective action for such violations in the past, and if he had been sincere and consistent in his efforts to enforce safety rules, responsibility for the accident rests squarely on the employee. Definite action is required. Where blame for the accident rests on the employee, an unsafe act is usually involved. Definition of an unsafe act may be a matter for debate. In general, however, an unsafe act is a violating or avoiding of a commonly accepted safe procedure which might directly permit the occurrence of an accident. Selection of the unsafe act would involve consideration of the following:

1. The selected unsafe act may be something a person did which he should have done differently, or it may be his failure to do something which he should have done.
2. The person who committed the unsafe act may be the person

who was injured, or he may be some other person who was not injured.

3. The person who acted unsafely may have done so deliberately with full knowledge that he was doing something unsafe, or he may not have known that he was acting unsafely.

In deciding on the unsafe act, it is helpful to ask, "Would a cautious and well-trained person have done the same thing under the same circumstances?" In general, a personal action should be designated as an unsafe act only when there was a reasonable and less hazardous procedure which could have been followed. For example, if a person's work requires him to use a machine for which no guard has been provided, his use of the machine should not be considered an unsafe act for which he has personal responsibility. However, if a guard were provided but the operator removed it before using the machine or made it inoperative, then his act should be considered unsafe and a failure to assume personal responsibility for his own safety.

Without extending the discussion, it might be helpful to point out to those who still feel that the fixing of responsibility should be avoided that there is full agreement that the principal objective of accident investigation must be to find the cause factors involved. But it would be highly impractical to ignore the fact that an employee had made a safety device inoperative just because recognition of the fact would fix blame.

Accident types

Four types of accidents require investigation. They are:

1. Disabling-injury accidents.
2. Minor-injury accidents (those requiring first-aid treatment or doctor's care).
3. Accidents involving equipment or material damage.
4. Near-injury accidents.

These types of accidents are self-explanatory except for the disabling-injury accidents. The American Standards Association code Z 16.1-1954, *Recording and Measuring Work Injury Experience,* classifies disabling injuries as follows:

1. Fatality—a work injury which results in death.

2. Permanent total disability—a work injury which permanently and totally incapacitates an employee from following any gainful employment.

3. Permanent partial disability—a work injury which results in a loss or loss of use of any member of the body except teeth, fingernails, and finger tips without bone involvement. An example would be the amputation of a finger. Such an injury is considered disabling although there might be no time lost from work.

4. Temporary total disability—a work injury which renders an employee unable to perform his job or any regularly established job which is open and available to him on any one or more days following the date of the injury.

The American Standards Association publication Z 16.2, *Classifying Accident Causes,* defines accident types according to the source of the injury. Hence, to avoid any confusion regarding use of the term "accident type" and also to provide supervisors with additional useful information, the A.S.A. accident types are listed below:

1. Caught in or between—includes those cases in which the injured person is pinched, squeezed, or crushed between a moving object and a stationary object or between two moving objects.

2. Struck by—where a blow or an impact caused by an object in motion causes the injury.

3. Struck against—where the injury is caused by a person in motion striking against a stationary object.

4. Fall of person (same level)—includes, in general, those injuries which result from a slip, trip, or stumble.

5. Fall of person (different level)—where a person falls from one level to a lower level.

6. Abraded, punctured, scratched—where injury results from a penetrating object or the injury of tissue by constant rubbing against a rough, pointed, or abrasive object.

7. Overexertion—includes sprains, strains, ruptures, etc., resulting from sudden or more than normal physical effort.

8. Contact (electrical current)—injury resulting from contact with any energized electrical conductor.

9. Contact (temperature extremes)—injury resulting from contact with objects which are either too hot or too cold.

10. Contact (radiation sources, caustic, toxic, and noxious substances)—includes cases of asphyxiation, drowning, food poisoning, skin rashes, etc.

Accident-type classifications are used primarily for the coding of accident-cause data. However, supervisors might find it helpful to memorize the ten accident types and then use them as a check list of conditions to look for in their safety appraisal of working conditions. Could a worker be *caught in or between* machines and equipment; is there any likelihood of being *struck by* a moving object; what are the probabilities of a *fall of a person;* what *contacts* might be harmful? These would be key questions for supervisors to ask themselves.

Identifying accident causes

Ability to discover the principal causes of an accident is a skill that can be developed by acquiring a basic knowledge of the causes of accidents and by experience in accident investigation. Most accidents result from a combination of contributing causes and one or more unsafe acts and unsafe conditions. Seldom is the immediate cause of the accident a single unsafe condition or a single unsafe act. Knowing the various unsafe conditions and unsafe acts that cause a majority of accidents will provide a supervisor with a good foundation from which to start his investigation. With a list of unsafe conditions and unsafe acts in mind, the supervisor can check each accident to determine which of the commonly known unsafe conditions or unsafe acts may have caused that particular accident.

The American Standards code *Classifying Accident Causes* also contains lists of typical unsafe acts and unsafe conditions. By permission of the A.S.A. these lists are reproduced below:

IMMEDIATE CAUSES OF ACCIDENTS

Unsafe Acts

1. Operating without authority, failure to secure or warn.
2. Operating or working at unsafe speed. (Too slow, too fast, throwing materials, etc.)
3. Making safety devices inoperative. (Removing, misadjusting, disconnecting, etc.)
4. Using unsafe equipment, hands instead of equipment, or equipment unsafely.
5. Unsafe loading, placing, mixing, combining, etc.
6. Taking unsafe position or posture. (Under suspended loads, lifting with bent back, etc.)
7. Working on moving or dangerous equipment. (Cleaning, adjusting, oiling, etc.)
8. Distracting, teasing, abusing, startling, etc. (Quarreling, horseplay, etc.)
9. Failure to use safe attire or personal protective devices. (Goggles, etc.)

Unsafe Conditions

1. Improperly guarded agencies. (Unguarded, inadequately guarded, etc.)
2. Defective agencies. (Rough, slippery, sharp, inferior composition, etc.)

3. Hazardous arrangement, procedures, etc., in, on, or around the selected agency. (Unsafely stored, congestion, overloading, etc.)

4. Improper illumination. (Insufficient light, glare, etc.)

5. Improper ventilation. (Insufficient air change, impure air source, etc.)

6. Unsafe dress or apparel. (Unavailability or absence of gloves, aprons, shoes, respirators, loose clothing, etc. (This includes defective personal protective equipment and clothing.)

The A.S.A. lists are actually categories in which unsafe acts and unsafe conditions may be grouped. In stating the cause of an accident, a supervisor would want to be more specific than to state, for example, that the cause of the accident was "working on moving or dangerous equipment." Rather, the supervisor's report would indicate the specific cause such as cleaning bolster plate while drill revolved, walking on roller conveyor, or jumping off moving truck.

Likewise, specific examples of "using unsafe equipment" would be using defective power drill, using screw driver for hammer, and using mushroomed chisel.

Specific examples of "hazardous arrangement" would be boxes improperly stacked, aisles congested, and machines too close.

Finally, specific examples of "unsafe dress or apparel" would be lathe operator wearing finger ring, loose clothing on drill-press operation, and not wearing eye protection.

Tabulating accident causes

Investigation of an accident to determine the contributing and the immediate causes will show what must be done to keep the same type of accident from happening again. But from time to time all the accidents which have occurred should be tabulated according to the indicated cause. This tabulation will show which accident causes predominate. Then, supervisors will know the accident-cause factors requiring increased attention. Generally such tabulations are prepared by the safety engineer and sent to all supervisors with a good interpretation of the statistics and recommendations for action. In preparing the tabulation, the various accident causes may be grouped in the unsafe-condition and unsafe-act categories found in the American Standard, or accident-cause categories might be devised which are more applicable to a particular plant or operation. The tabulation in Table 14–1 was prepared by the safety engineer of a large manufacturing operation. He devised his own accident-cause categories rather than using those listed in the A.S.A. Standard.

TABLE 14–1. SEMI-ANNUAL SUMMARY: THE PRINCIPAL CAUSES OF INJURIES

To: All Supervisors and Managers — Date: July 16, 1958

Accident Cause	Disabling Injuries		Total Injuries	
	Number	Per Cent	Number	Per Cent
Instruction—(To include all cases where supervision did not insure that the employee was thoroughly trained and suited to the job, also where specific safety instructions were not given prior to the start of any new or irregular job.)	14	29	467	31
Housekeeping and Arrangement—(To include all cases where poor arrangement or housekeeping was the underlying cause.)	0	0	193	13
Safety Device—(To include all cases where an applicable safety device should have been provided but was not or where the safety device was inadequate or improperly maintained.)	0	0	105	7
Maintenance of Equipment—(To include all cases caused by equipment in need of repair or where maintenance work was improperly or inadequately done.)	4	7	0	0
Improper Tools or Equipment—(To include all cases where the use of improper tools or equipment resulted in the injury.)	0	0	45	3
Insufficient Safety Morale—(To include all cases where the employee injured himself or another through a lack of extreme care and desire to prevent accidents.)	18	36	600	40
Physical Deficiency—(To include all cases mainly attributable to an unknown physical deficiency in the person involved in or causing the accident.)	4	7	0	0
Methods or Process—(To include cases caused by the nature of the process or the methods of doing the job in question, not directly chargeable to personal causes or supervision.)	3	7	31	2
Materials—(To include cases caused by the nature of the materials being handled except those directly chargeable to personal causes or supervision.)	0	0	30	2

TABLE 14–1. (*Continued*)

Accident Cause	Disabling Injuries		Total Injuries	
	Number	Per Cent	Number	Per Cent
Improper Construction or Design—(To include cases caused by improper construction or design of equipment or machinery.)	3	7	30	2
Risk of Employment—(To include only such cases as are clearly caused by some condition of employment which could not have been reasonably foreseen or guarded against.)	3	7	0	0
TOTAL	50	100	1501	100

Information in Table 14–1 was obtained from the safety engineer's copies of the "Supervisor's Report of an Accident." The statistics in the tabulation are for an entire plant. However, similar tabulations could be made for various operations in the plant so the information would be even more specific. By reference to such tabulations, the supervisor gets some valuable leads for planning his own safety activities. Using the above tabulation as an example, supervisors would learn that about one-third of all reported accidents were the result of faulty instruction, 40 per cent of insufficient safety morale, and more than 10 per cent of poor housekeeping and arrangement.

Exhibit 14–1 is another example of an accident-cause breakdown prepared by a safety engineer to meet the specific needs of his company. In addition to a summary of unsafe acts and unsafe conditions, three other categories are included in the accident-cause-analysis report form: supervisory safety failure, occupational diseases, and unclassified injuries. The category, supervisory safety failure, was added to the report because a concerted effort was being made to establish supervisory accountability as well as responsibility for accident prevention. Accident statistics prepared for a specific plant with accident-cause classifications selected according to the past accident experience of the plant, help to pin-point existing accident problems. On the other hand, mass statistics prepared on a country-wide or an industry-wide basis might be misleading or of little value to the individual supervisor. Supervisors must learn to deal effectively with the specific causes of accidents in their own plants. For this reason, the accident-cause classifications in Exhibit 14–1 were selected by the safety engineer after a careful study of the past accident experience of his plant.

ACCIDENT CAUSE ANALYSIS
FOR SUPERVISORS

Month ______________ Prepared by ______________

	NUMBER OF CASES	PERCENTAGE OF TOTAL
1. SUPERVISORY SAFETY FAILURES		
a. Safety instructions not adequate.	4	15
b. Safety rules not enforced.	42	
c. Necessary personal safety devices not provided for job.	1	
d. Corrective action indicated but nothing done.	0	
Sub-total	47	
2. UNSAFE ACTS OF EMPLOYEES		
a. Protective equipment or guard provided but not used.	4	52
b. Unsafe method of handling, (Failure to allow for sharp, slippery objects, pinch points, loose grip, wrong lifting.)	86	
c. Improper tools or equipment used although proper tools were available.	0	
d. Unsafe movement, (Running, jumping, stepping on, climbing over, throwing, etc.)	16	
e. Inattention, (Walked into, struck self, etc.)	56	
f. Failed to follow instructions.	3	
Sub-total	165	
3. UNSAFE CONDITIONS		
a. Ineffective safety device.	2	11
b. No safety device although one needed.		
c. Equipment, tools, or machines defective.	6	
d. Unsafe storage or piling.	14	
e. Unsafe housekeeping, (Material on floor, ruts, projections, etc.)	11	
f. Lack of personal protective equipment.		
g. Guard removed and not replaced, (Not by employee injured.)	1	
Sub-total	34	

4. UNCLASSIFIED ACCIDENTS (NO DEFINITE CAUSE APPARENT)			
a. Back strains (Not including improper lifting cases.)		4	20
b. Trick knees.			
c. Bursitis.		2	
d. Neurosis.			
e. All other.		56	
	Sub-total	62	
5. OCCUPATIONAL DISEASES			
a. Dermatitis.		6	2
b. Gas poisoning.			
c. Silicosis.			
	Sub-total	6	

Total injury frequency rate	42	Total	314	100%
Last year's total injury rate	36	Rate, year to date		45
Base = 10,000 manhours.				

This report summarizes the causes of all accidents which were reported last month.

Increased attention should be given to those accident causes which are accounting for the greater number of injuries.

Please contact the safety office if assistance is required in planning your safety activities.

Plant Manager ______________ Date of Report ______________

Exhibit 14–1. A report of accident causes prepared for supervisors by the safety engineer. This form is intended to serve as a guide to the preparation of a more suitable form for other plants and operations. The statistics and facts presented in the above form are taken from the "Supervisor's Report of an Accident" and reports of all injuries and occupational diseases treated at the plant dispensary.

A bar chart (Exhibit 14–2) provides a graphic presentation of the cause classification of 4226 injuries. It is of particular significance that the chart shows that 16.8 per cent of the injuries were not classified as to cause. Especially in the investigation of minor injuries, it is

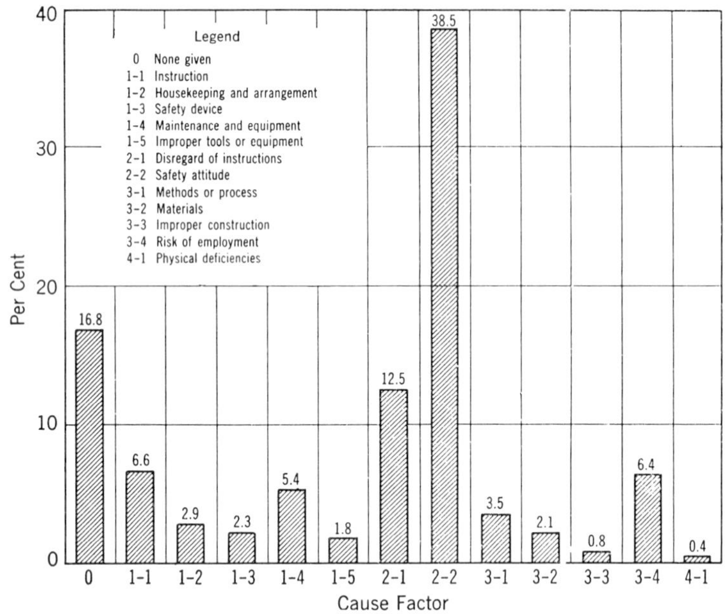

Exhibit 14–2. Cause classification of injuries (data on 4226 injuries). (*Source:* Fred McKinnon and L. W. Smith, General Electric Company, Hanford Atomic Products Operation, Richland, Washington.)

understandable that the cause of some injuries will not be apparent. Consider, for example, the employee who reports, "I noticed blood on my finger and realized I had cut my hand," or "I bent over to pick up a pencil and felt a kink in my back." Although a diligent effort should be made to find the cause of each injury, it would be impractical to insist upon a cause classification for every injury. In some cases there would be nothing basically unsound or wrong about the admission that a cause could not be found.

Investigating disabling-injury accidents

Whenever an accident occurs which results in an injury, damage of equipment and material, or both, prompt accident investigation by the immediate supervisor is important. Depending upon the circumstances involved, higher levels of supervision would be notified and participate in the investigation too. For example, in all cases involving an amputation or fractured bone, most machine accidents, and, of course, any fatal accident, the first-level supervisor should immediately notify the general foreman, superintendent, and plant manager along with the plant safety engineer. This group would then proceed with a tactful and thorough investigation of all the circumstances associated with the accident. The function of the staff safety engineer—who participates in the investigation at the request of the line supervisor—is to render expert advice and assistance on the technical aspects of the case. The safety engineer's knowledge of toxic materials, hazardous chemicals, electrical hazards, safety codes, machine guards, protective equipment, and mental and physical factors will help to guide the investigation to a satisfactory conclusion.

A supervisor will find it helpful to keep a written report of each accident he investigates. Thus, following the accident investigation and preferably not later than the end of the shift on which the accident occurred, a "supervisor's report of the accident investigation" should be prepared. One copy of the report is normally retained by the first-line supervisor. Additional copies are made for the safety engineer, general foreman, superintendent, and plant manager. This procedure will allow all interested persons to review the findings of the investigation and to determine whether or not the investigation has been complete and impartial and the causes of the accident have been adequately identified. In particular, attention should be directed to the corrective action recommended. Responsibility for correcting the situation must be assigned, material requisitions approved, retraining instituted, other sections of the plant notified, and employees informed regarding steps management intends to take in an effort to prevent future accidents. Of course, whether or not each of these steps is necessary will depend upon the circumstances of the accident.

The accident-report form

The type of industry, the peculiar nature of various plant operations, or unusual environmental factors may prompt management to ask for certain specific information on the accident-investigation-report form. For these reasons, the report forms used by industry vary widely. It is essential, however, that the form, regardless of detail or arrangement, provide adequate coverage of the accident causes and the corrective action to be taken. Information which is pertinent to cause and correction includes:

1. Name, occupation, and sex of injured worker.
2. Place and time of accident.
3. Description of how accident happened.
4. Immediate causes of accident—unsafe acts and unsafe conditions.
5. Contributing causes—supervisor safety performance, mental and physical condition of worker.
6. Corrective action to be taken—when.

Three carefully planned accident-investigation-report forms are shown on pages 281, 282, and 283. These forms were selected because the information required to complete them relates directly to accident causes and correction. Such forms can be completed by a supervisor at the conclusion of his accident investigation without reference to personnel or payroll records. Thus, delay in completing the form is avoided. This last point has particular significance because many accident-report forms require supervisors to supply extraneous information such as:

1. Average weekly wages of injured employee.
2. Nationality.
3. Home address.
4. Kind of wage plan.
5. Number of dependents.
6. Married or single.
7. Language spoken.
8. Severity of injury, etc.

It is apparent that the supervisor would be required to contact the personnel department for the employee's home address, the payroll for his average wages, and plant doctor for the severity of the injury. This would take a lot of his time, and such information is unrelated to the specific purpose of the report—a statement of the cause of the accident and the corrective action to be taken.

Workmen's compensation and certain insurance reports might require much of the so-called unrelated information, but supervisors seldom prepare these reports. They are prepared by personnel or payroll departments, and details regarding average wages, number of dependents, and so forth are obtained from central office records and not from the supervisor's accident report. Although details and arrangement may vary, it is sufficient to say that the supervisor's report of accident investigation should include information relating to cause and correction; unrelated information should be omitted, generally.

SUPERVISOR'S REPORT
OF
ACCIDENT INVESTIGATION

The purpose of the accident investigation is to find the causes of the accident and to state what steps need to be taken to prevent the same type of accident from reoccurring

Injured employee name James Hazard Pay No. 39-3314 Sex Male
Date and hour of accident Jan. 15, 10:30a. m. Place of accident Woodworking Shop
Occupation of employee Model maker How long with Company About 8 years
Will injury be disabling Yes

Describe the Injury
Right index finger was cut off at second joint. Also a deep cut on right hand.

Describe the Accident (State what the injured was doing and the circumstances leading to the accident)
Hazard was ripping a pine board 6" wide and 3' long. There was no guard on circular saw. At end of cut employee's hand slipped and hit against saw blade. Hewas not using pusher stick.

Mental and physical condition (Explain if mental or physical condition of employee contributed to accident.)
Hazard had on previous occasions expressed the belief that model makers could work without guards.

Unsafe Condition (Describe as oily floor, poor light, lack of guards, broken part, etc.)
No guard over saw blade and pusher stick had not been used.

Unsafe Act (Describe as removed guard, running, inattention not following rules, etc.)
Not using pusher stick and inattention

Please answer all questions:
1. Have the safety rules applying to this case been properly enforced No - "pusher stick"
2 Was the injured employee instructed on HOW to do job safely No
3. When did the employee last attend a safety meeting January 4
4. Has a job hazard analysis been prepared for the job Yes
5. Were you aware of the unsafe condition involved Yes

COMMENTS· Agree skilled workers require adequate safety instruction.
What will be done to Prevent a Recurrence Guard replaced, Safety rules will be enforced and an effort made to develop a much healthier safety attitude
When By March 1
DATE: 1/15/58 MADE OUT BY: A. L. Brown APPROVED: W. R. White
Prepare in triplicate· original to Manager second to Safety Engineer, third for file

SUPERVISOR'S

ACCIDENT INVESTIGATION REPORT № 1148

Lukens Steel Company . . . . Coatesville, Pa.

THIS ACCIDENT INVOLVES (CHECK ONE OR BOTH)

☒ PERSONAL INJURY   PROPERTY DAMAGE ☒

DEPARTMENT General   DATE 4-1-57   TIME: 9:00 A. M. ____ M.

IF PERSONAL INJURY, WHO WAS:		IF PROPERTY DAMAGE, WHAT WAS:	
Person Injured	John Doe	Equipment Involved	Window and Frame
Nature of Injury	struck shoulder	Nature of Damage	completely destroyed
His Position	Helper	Estimated Cost to Repair or Replace	$22.00
His Check Number	0000	Actual Cost to Repair or Replace	(to be filled in by Safety)

DESCRIBE HOW THE ACCIDENT OCCURRED Victim placed plate hooks on a load and as the crane operator lifted the load one of the hooks flew off the load striking him and smashing into the window of the office nearby.

WHAT WAS DONE UNSAFELY? (USE REVERSE SIDE AS GUIDE TO UNSAFE ACTS) The worker assumed an unsafe position and placed one hook on the load with a twist in its chain. The crane operator should not have lifted the load with the worker in an unsafe position

WHAT WAS DEFECTIVE, OR IN UNSAFE CONDITION? (USE REVERSE SIDE AS GUIDE TO UNSAFE CONDITIONS) When suspended together one of the hooks hung six inches lower than the other indicating that improper equipment was being used.

THIS IS THE ACTION I WILL TAKE TO PREVENT THIS TYPE ACCIDENT FROM HAPPENING AGAIN The crane operator was given a proper warning by his supervisor and properly reissued his crane operation rules. The victim will be properly warned of his violation of hook-up rules and properly reissued a rule booklet. Written instructions will be given all workers concerned that equipment they are handling is to be inspected for defects before use. A daily inspection program of this equipment has been set up.

SUPERVISOR DIRECTLY IN CHARGE Tom Boe   DEPARTMENT SUPERINTENDENT D. J. Jones

ALL ACCIDENTS -- including fires -- which result in Personal Injury or Property Damage MUST BE REPORTED & INVESTIGATED AT ONCE

DISTRIBUTION OF FORMS — SUPERVISOR keeps GRAY COPY; YELLOW COPY to DEPARTMENT SUPERINTENDENT; BLUE COPY to SAFETY DEPARTMENT

CENTRAL FOUNDRY DIVISION
GENERAL MOTORS CORPORATION

FOREMAN'S ACCIDENT REPORT

Department __________ Name of Foreman__________

Name of Injured Employe__________ Clock No.__________

Regular Occupation__________

What was employe doing when injured__________

What specific instruction was given the employe as to the safe method of doing this work?__________

____

By whom__________Date of last safety contact__________

When did accident happen? Date__________Time A.M. P.M.

Did injured employe stop work?__________Time A.M. P.M.

Describe how accident occurred:__________

____

____

What caused this injury (your version)__________

____

What caused this injury (injured's version)__________

____

If injured on machine, give name__________ Location__________

Was machine properly guarded__________ Can it be guarded__________

Give names and statements of all eye witnesses on back of report__________

Did employe return to his regular job following injury __________

If not, state reasons__________

What was his job following injury?__________

What would you recommend to prevent future injuries of this kind?__________

What has been done to prevent future injuries of this kind?__________

Name of person making this report__________ Date__________

Superintendent's Signature__________ Date__________

NOTE:—

1. This report must be turned in before the end of shift on which the accident occurred.
2. One copy to be retained by Superintendent. One copy to be sent to Safety Department.
3. Submit any additional comments on back of report.

Applying the principles of accident investigation

Principles of accident investigation that have been discussed can now be applied to an actual accident which led to a disabling injury. These facts were discovered by a supervisor, plant manager, and safety engineer in their investigation of a circular-saw accident:

James Hazard, an experienced model maker, had worked in the same shop for ten years. At 10:30 A.M., January 15, he was ripping a pine board 6 inches wide and 3 feet long. At the end of the cut, his hand slipped and contacted the revolving saw blade. The small finger of his right hand was amputated and the ring finger deeply lacerated.

Immediately following the above accident, the supervisor notified his plant manager and the safety engineer. The three met at the scene of the accident and proceeded with the investigation. The unsafe conditions and the unsafe act were obvious, but the investigation group was also concerned with the contributing causes of the accident. Two witnesses were asked to give their version of the case, and a check of the work area was made. The injured employee had been rushed to the hospital and he was in a state of shock so he was not questioned.

The investigation revealed these additional facts: Three years before, following a similar accident a guard was placed on the circular saw. This fact came to light when the guard was found under a work bench, broken and covered with dust. About four months prior to the accident, the guard had been taken off for repairs and not replaced. The supervisor in discussing the accident commented, "This is the first saw injury in three years." This comment led to a check-up which revealed that in the last four months, two model makers had been treated for small cuts sustained from contact with the saw blade. The supervisor's reference was to the last *serious* accident; he wasn't aware of the two minor injuries. The investigation also revealed that Hazard had not been using the pusher stick provided for the job.

After cc ıpleting the investigation, the supervisor prepared the report which appears on page 281. A copy was sent to the general foreman for approval. Then copies were sent to the plant manager and the safety engineer.

The safety engineer's review of this report and those received from supervisors in other sections of the plant indicated that the same type of accident was occurring more frequently than had been previously apparent. This finding pin-points one of the valuable services the safety engineer is able to render. A high number of accidents might be occurring on specific machines or operations scattered throughout the plant. Certain unsafe acts which cause injuries may be committed repeatedly, at different locations in the plant and at different times, but their importance as accident causes may be overlooked because each supervisor is aware only of the accidents occurring on his machines or in his section. By summarizing accident causes on the basis of a review of injury reports received, the safety engineer is able to pin-point accident problems for supervisors and to recommend specific corrective measures.

In summary, the steps taken following the circular-saw accident were as follows:

1. The supervisor was notified that a serious accident had occurred in his section.
2. He called the general foreman, plant manager, and safety engineer to notify them of the accident.
3. The investigation team went to the scene of the accident.
4. The supervisor prepared his accident report. (Same day.)
5. He sent a copy to the general foreman for approval. (Same day.)
6. After approval, he sent copies to the plant safety engineer and the plant manager. (Within forty-eight hours.)
7. The safety engineer reviewed the report and decided that pertinent facts should be communicated to all other supervisors.

The safety engineer, after deciding that other supervisors would profit by a review of the circular-saw case, prepared a report for company-wide circulation. However, in his report he avoided any mention of the names of the injured employee and the supervisor. Most supervisors prefer this company-wide reporting on an impersonal basis. An example of a typical report prepared by a safety engineer appears on page 286. (Reports of accidents in other companies might also be circulated on a plant-wide basis.)

By a review of the foregoing report, supervisors will be prompted to re-appraise their own safety activities and, if necessary, take corrective action. The reporting procedure is approved by supervisors because, by the omission of names, no one is embarrassed or held up as the bad example. However, these omissions in no way distract from the value of the report.

Investigation of minor-injury accidents

Most accidents which result in an injury, even a so-called minor injury such as a cut, bruise, or burn, might be an indication of some-

TO: SUPERVISORS AND MANAGERS **November 7, 1958**

FATAL ELECTRICAL ACCIDENT

A 51-year-old pipefitter was electrocuted on Nov. 6. He was repairing the water supply line to a resistance welder when the accident occurred.

The cause of the accident was his failure to remove power from the welder before commencing to repair it. The cover plate was not interlocked and, before removing it, the pipefitter did not take the power off the welder.

There are several steps that might be taken to prevent similar accidents:

1. Establish a definite procedure for maintenance and use of electrical equipment to assure optimum safety.
2. Provide interlocks on panels or openings on welding machines, test tables, control panels, and other types of electrical manufacturing equipment to remove primary power when the cover is removed.
3. Provide locks on control panels and other electrical equipment where interlocks are impractical.
4. Establish a tag-out procedure for the protection of employees working on hazardous equipment.
5. Schedule artificial-respiration training for employees in areas where work is done on electrical equipment.

You might wish to check your section and determine if adequate precautions are being taken to prevent a similar accident.

Harold Vann
Safety Engineer

thing wrong, and an opportunity for corrective action. Therefore, in an effort to obtain more productive results in the accident-prevention program, greater attention by supervision must be accorded the so-called minor injury. As a foreman so aptly put it, "There is no such thing as a minor accident, although some of them do result in only a minor injury."

The circular-saw accident involving Jim Hazard is an example of what the foreman had in mind. The accidents causing the minor cuts suffered by two other men before Hazard's injury were major accidents, but minor injuries resulted. Correction following the first minor injury would have prevented the finger amputation. A similar situation is revealed in this report:

A pneumatic press operator caught her right middle finger between the stroke limit bar and the ram-housing on the up-stroke of a midget multiple press used for a riveting operation. The tip of her finger was amputated. The existing hazard had not been recognized previous to the injury.

One interesting aspect of the investigation was the story told by an adjacent operator doing the same job. A few weeks previous she had caught her finger in the same manner; in her case the gap between the limit bar and ram-housing on her press was greater, so her injury was a minor bruise. If the minor injury had been investigated, a serious hazard would have been discovered and eliminated.

At first the investigation of a slight injury like a blister, small cut, or sliver may appear to be a waste of time for the busy supervisor. Some line operators have doubted the merits of the practice. A careful survey has revealed these benefits:

1. By investigating minor injuries, the supervisor demonstrates his personal concern and interest in the welfare of his associates. (Many supervisors reported that the favorable reaction and the rapport established when they discussed minor injuries with employees convinced them that a total-injury investigation procedure was worthwhile because the practice provided for good employee relations.)
2. By checking a minor injury, conditions or practices might be discovered that would eventually lead to a more serious injury.
3. Checking all injuries keeps the investigation of the serious injury from becoming a "five star" search for a fall guy that would be resented by employees—it avoids the comment, "You have to get half killed around here before they get interested in safety."
4. Minor injuries are a large part of the total injury problem.

In many companies the total cost of minor injuries computed in terms of time lost from work, first-aid, and treatment expense is two or three times the total compensation and medical expense which results from disabling injuries. While statistics regarding minor injuries would vary considerably from plant to plant, the evidence indicates economic justification for taking a serious look at the minor injury. Treatment of each minor injury will usually require two or three visits to the plant first-aid room. Cost of each visit will fall somewhere between $2.00 and $12.00. Time away from the job will vary between 15 and 90 minutes. Aside from the humanitarian considerations, by controlling minor injuries, dollars can be saved.

The following article, which appeared in a "Foreman's Forecast," points up the minor-injury problem. It was written by a safety engineer in a plant with 9000 employees.

IS IT SAFE?

Yesterday I cut my thumb on an insidiously dangerous and a cleverly unguarded "safety" razor. I have been shaving since the first crop of peach fuzz appeared on my upper lip, so undoubtedly I was lulled into a false sense of security that a safety razor was safe. However, after looking at the warm blood oozing from the end of my thumb and the gob of skin clinging to the blade of the razor, there is doubt in my mind regarding the safety of a safety razor. Yesterday, it took me five minutes longer to shave; I splotched a white shirt with red blood, I couldn't get a decent knot in my tie, and all day my thumb stuck out—well, like a sore thumb. All of this made me stop to think of the tremendous amount of time that must be lost because of minor injuries each year.

A quick check of our records revealed that during the first six months of the year there were an amazing total of 16,657 work injuries treated and that there were 81,300 dispensary visits made by our employees. Assuming that each dispensary call required at least ten minutes of the employee's time, 13,550 production hours were lost in six months. Undoubtedly, we can multiply this tremendous total by three when we take into consideration the time lost by the employee preparing to go to the dispensary, the time lost getting back to work, the impaired efficiency of the employee, and the time lost by the supervisor checking the injury. Therefore, instead of an actual loss of 13,550 hours, we probably lost at least 40,000 production hours during the first six months of the year because of the so-called minor injury.

Paradoxically, minor injuries are important because they generally are not considered important. A minute lost here, a minute lost there may be insignificant if considered alone, but when we add all the minutes together, they become hours and hours become days, weeks, months and years. Forty-thousand manhours are equivalent to one man working for fifteen years. How much more of our fine product could have been produced if, through conscientious effort, the minor-accident toll could have been reduced by 50%.

The minor injury cannot be dismissed as an uncontrollable factor in the production scheme. In fact, investigation of the minor injury is of considerable importance. It is generally a matter of chance that the minor injury is not of a more serious consequence. For example, one person may fall from a chair and get up without a scratch while another less fortunate individual will sustain a broken neck. A small cut may require a single treatment, or it may be neglected and result in an infection causing death. Considerably more production time is lost each year because of the so-called minor injuries than because of disabling injuries, yet supervisors sometimes fail to give the minor injury the attention it necessarily deserves.

Reporting minor injuries

The same cause analysis that is applied to the disabling injury might also be applied to the minor injury. However, the reporting procedure may be simplified. What happened and what will be done to prevent a similar accident are the principal questions to be answered. A report form like the one shown in Exhibit 14–3 might be used.

The form originates in the plant dispensary or first-aid room when an employee reports for treatment of an injury. The above form is the triplicate copy of the dispensary case record. The reverse side of the form is shown in Exhibit 14–4.

All information on the front of the form is filled in by the plant nurse. The original is retained in the dispensary file, the duplicate goes to the plant safety engineer, and the triplicate to the injured employee's supervisor, the same day the injury is reported. In some plants the employee takes the third copy to his supervisor. Following an investigation, the supervisor completes the form and sends it to his boss for approval. If a satisfactory investigation has been made, the report is forwarded to the safety office where it is matched with the duplicate copy. This provides a check on how well the procedure is working. Also, the safety engineer in his review of the reports might discover an opportunity to be of service to the supervisor by suggesting additional control measures or by noting an elusive type of hazard that was overlooked in the investigation.

Near-injury accidents and material-damage accidents

A crane hook broke and the falling load narrowly missed hitting two employees. A salt-pot erupted spraying molten material in all directions, but there was no one in the area at the time of the accident. A locker fell over in the shower room; fortunately it missed hitting anyone. These are near-injury accidents. In each case, because of luck, no one was injured, but there was material damage that can be computed. Such accidents might go unnoticed, but when they do come to the attention of supervisors, a check should be made to determine the cause and initiate corrective action. For example, following the crane-hook accident, a check revealed that no procedure had been established for a periodic inspection of crane hooks, slings, and chains. The supervisor called the matter to the attention of the safety engineer. A formalized program for inspecting all crane hooks every six months using a red-dye-penetration test and a magnetic-particles test was started. Investigation of near-injury accidents may provide some valuable leads for accident prevention.

Conclusions

Discussion in this chapter and all other chapters of this book assumes the existence of a sufficient degree of executive support of

DETAILED DESCRIPTION OF ACCIDENT TO BE COMPLETED BY SUPERVISOR

Describe the accident

What will be done to prevent a similar injury?

INVESTIGATED BY	SECTION	DATE	APPROVED
SUPERVISOR			GENERAL FOREMAN

SUPERVISOR'S COPY

Exhibit 14–3. This is the triplicate copy of a three-part form. It is sent to the supervisor from the dispensary. The duplicate is sent to the safety engineer.

NAME LAST FIRST INITIAL | SEX M F | MEDICAL NUMBER | PAY NUMBER

WORK AREA | JOB TITLE | SUPERVISOR PHONE

DATE REPORTED | TIME A.M. P.M. | DATE OF ONSET IF DIFFERENT FROM REPORT DATE | ☐ IND ☐ PERS. ☐ OBSV

HISTORY IN PATIENT'S OWN WORDS

DIAGNOSIS

TREATMENT

DISPOSITION
☐ REGULAR WORK
☐ RESTRICTED WORK
☐ SENT HOME
☐ SENT TO HOSPITAL
☐ DISCHARGED

X-RAY TAKEN? ☐ YES ☐ NO
DISFIGURING? ☐ YES ☐ NO
PERM. DISAB.? ☐ YES ☐ NO

PROBABLE DURATION
SIGNED R.N. M.D.
I P

TO RETURN
FORM FILED
CODE
DAY MO. YR.

DISPENSARY CASE RECORD

Exhibit 14–4. This is the reverse side of the form shown in Exhibit 14–3. Information requested is filled in at the dispensary. (Courtesy of the General Electric Company.)

the safety program. Little good could be achieved if the practical and sound safety decisions and activities of first-line supervisors were not approved and supported by upper levels of management. There is full agreement that the first-level supervisor can become qualified and is in the best position to find the immediate and the contributing causes of accidents. Likewise, the supervisor is the person upon whom plant executives must rely to take corrective action. However, the safety program is likely to be a planned failure if the supervisor's requisition for a necessary machine guard or safety device is ignored or canceled without an adequate explanation. On the other hand, supervisors should avoid becoming discouraged just because occasionally a request for a safety device is not granted. After all, management is people. Hence, there might be many reasons why the apparently reasonable request has been rejected. Perhaps the boss does not have all the facts. Perhaps the boss resents the suggestion to safeguard a machine because he feels he should have had the idea first. But nothing is gained by giving up. On the second or third try the request might be granted.

Accident investigation, cause analysis, and correction are three basic steps in accident prevention, but the point of emphasis must be, necessarily, on correction. It is not enough to decide *what* must be done and *how* it must be done—actually making the correction is what really counts.

CHAPTER

15

Measuring safety performance

There is a great difference between judgment and measurement. To judge is to arrive at a conclusion or decision by weighing or comparing. To measure is to ascertain quality, dimensions, or quantity by comparison with a standard. In judging things they are compared one with another. In measuring them all are compared with the same thing, namely, the standard. Comparison is common to both, but the use of an agreed-upon standard as the basis of comparison distinguishes measurement from judgment. Paintings are judged, pistons are measured. Judgment is the more widely applicable process. Measurement is possible only where a standard can be used. Measurement where applicable is the more definite and satisfactory because all agree to compare with the same thing, the standard.

PROFESSOR JOSEPH W. ROE
New York University

A manager of a large progressive steel mill with an outstanding safety program said, "Each supervisor must be convinced that the safety of his people is his responsibility, and that as an operating man he has the ability to stop accidents." But by what standards does a supervisor measure his safety performance? How does he know whether or not he has done a good or a poor safety job? What facts and statistics are available to convince him that he has the ability to stop accidents? Admittedly, where no standards exist, safety performance is measured according to the judgment of each supervisor. Such judgment, in turn, can be warped by prejudice, false premises, erroneous opinion, or a lack of adequate information. As an example, an owner of a medium-sized foundry was sure that his shop had a good safety record. His injury rate was 50 per cent better than the national average for foundries. What the owner did not know was that the average injury rate for foundries is 2½ times worse than the rate for steel mills, and 30 per cent higher than the average for all industry. When he compared his rate with the injury rates of foundries doing a good safety job rather than with the average rate, he was no longer satisfied.

A supervisor's production, cost, or quality performance is measured by comparison with various fixed standards. Likewise, certain standards and statistical data are needed to measure safety performance. Measurements are needed to show what has been accomplished compared to what should have been accomplished. Measurements are needed to help supervisors decide where they must concentrate their efforts.

Disabling-injury frequency rates

Disabling-injury[1] frequency rates can be used as a measurement of accident-prevention performance—provided that it is understood what "frequency rate" means and how it is computed.[2] This measurement is a fairly good indicator of safety performance of a plant or company, but it has little value as a measure of safety performance of a supervisor. Nevertheless, the method for measuring disabling-injury experience needs to be understood fully because of the wide use of such statistics throughout the United States and the frequent reference to disabling-injury rates in many safety publications.

---

[1] "Disabling injury" is defined on page 270.

[2] The methods of computing frequency and severity rates are outlined in the American Standards Association publication, *Recording and Measuring Work Injury Experience,* Z 16.1-1954.

Disabling-injury frequency rate is defined as the number of disabling injuries per million manhours worked. For example, a plant of 750 people will work about 1,500,000 manhours each year. If during the year 6 disabling injuries are reported, the *disabling-injury frequency rate* for the plant would be:

$$\frac{6 \text{ injuries} \times 1{,}000{,}000}{1{,}500{,}000 \text{ manhours}} = 4 = \text{frequency rate}$$

Hours worked are the total number of hours worked by all employees in the plant including production and office, salaried and hourly people. If an actual count of manhours worked is not available, manhours may be estimated by taking the total number of employees times the normal hours in the work week times the number of weeks in the period.

When the number of employees in a group is low, for example, a supervisor with 25 people, the manhours base for computing the frequency rate will obviously be small. Thus, one accident would produce a high frequency rate.

$$\frac{\text{One disabling injury} \times 1{,}000{,}000}{25 \text{ employees} \times 40 \text{ hours} \times 50 \text{ weeks}} = \frac{1{,}000{,}000}{50{,}000} = 20$$

Twenty disabling injuries per million manhours worked is the disabling-injury frequency rate for the above supervisor. But this rate is not a good indication of the supervisor's safety performance. One accident produced the high rate. It would be wrong to conclude that a supervisor with no disabling injuries and a zero frequency rate had done a better job. Statisticians feel that a frequency rate computed on a base of less than 500,000 to 1,000,000 manhours is unreliable. Thus, disabling-injury rates are indicators of progress made in accident prevention only when the manhour base is sufficiently large. If the manhour base is so small that one disabling injury produces a high frequency rate, the statistic has little value.

Disabling-injury severity rates

Severity rate is the number of actual days lost and charged for disabling injuries per million manhours of exposure. The computation is based on actual calendar days lost because of temporary total disabilities and scheduled days charged for fatalities, permanent total disabilities, and permanent partial disabilities. The charge ranges from 6000 days for a death or a permanent total disability to 35 days for amputation of the tip (distal phalanx) of a toe. (See Table 15–1.)

TABLE 15–1. SCHEDULED CHARGES*

A. For Loss of Member—Traumatic or Surgical

Fingers, Thumb, and Hand

Amputation Involving All or Part of Bone†

	Thumb	Fingers			
		Index	Middle	Ring	Little
Distal phalange	300	100	75	60	50
Middle phalange	. . .	200	150	120	100
Proximal phalange	600	400	300	240	200
Metacarpal	900	600	500	450	400
Hand at wrist					3000

Toe, Foot, and Ankle

Amputation involving All or Part of Bone†

	Great Toe	Each of Other Toes	
Distal phalange	150	35	
Middle phalange	. . .	75	
Proximal phalange	300	150	
Metatarsal	600	350	
Foot at ankle			2400

Arm

Any point above‡ elbow, including shoulder joint	4500
Any point above wrist and at or below elbow	3600

Leg

Any point above‡ knee	4500
Any point above ankle and at or below knee	300

B. Impairment of Function

One eye (loss of sight), whether or not there is sight in the other eye	1800
Both eyes (loss of sight), in one accident	6000
One ear (complete industrial loss of hearing), whether or not there is hearing in the other ear	600
Both ears (complete loss of hearing), in one accident	3000
Unrepaired hernia (for repaired hernia, use actual days lost)	50

* *Source:* Standard Z 16.1, *Method of Recording and Measuring Work Injury Experience,* American Standards Association, New York.

† If the bone is not involved, use actual days lost, and classify as temporary total disability.

‡ The term "above" when applied to the arm means toward the shoulder, and when applied to the leg means toward the hip.

Hence, the severity rate of the plant with 6 disabling injuries and 1,500,000 manhours of exposure would be determined by first determining time charges[3] for each injury and total days charged for the 6 disabling cases. A list of the 6 disabling injuries and the time charges follows:

TYPE OF INJURY	TIME CHARGES
1. Temporary total disability[4]	50 days lost
2. Temporary total disability	34 days lost
3. Temporary total disability	6 days lost
4. 50 per cent functional loss, left ring finger	240 days charged
5. Amputation, right ring finger between distal and middle joints	120 days charged
6. Lost sight, one eye	1800 days charged
Total:	2250 days

Thus, the severity rate for the plant with 6 disabling injuries is:

$$\frac{2250 \times 1{,}000{,}000}{1{,}500{,}000} = 1500 = \text{severity rate}$$

Average severity rates by industry range from about 100 days per million manhours of exposure for the communications industry to over 6000 days for coal mining. Opinion regarding the value of severity rates as a measure of accident-prevention performance varies widely. Some agree that the rate is an important indicator of the quality of the safety program. Others are convinced that the rate is meaningless because chance is such a large factor in determining the severity of an injury. Admittedly, the severity of an injury might at times be limited by the type of accident which produces it. Certain types of accidents seldom produce more than a minor injury, while other types of accidents often produce serious injuries. But beyond this point, there is little that man can do to control the severity of the injury once the accident is in process. Two men fall from a scaffold; one walks away unhurt, the other is killed instantly. In the case of the first man, the accident does not get into the records. In the case of the second man, the fatality necessitates a charge of 6000 days.

Finally, the severity rate measures only the total days charged per

[3] Time charge for a temporary total disability is the actual calendar days lost counting Saturadys and Sundays, but not the day of the injury or the day the injured employee returns to work. When a scheduled charge is made, such as 240 days for a right ring finger, a permanent partial disability, the actual days lost are not counted.

[4] "Temporary total disability" is defined on page 271.

million manhours of exposure with no reference to the number of injuries involved. For example, ten injuries, each with one day of disability, yield the same severity rate as one injury with ten days of disability, provided the manhours of exposure are the same. Obviously the latter injury was much more severe than the other ten. Thus, it is incorrect to assume that the severity rate is a measure of the severity of injuries—it is more nearly a weighted frequency rate.

The American Standards Association

To assure that disabling-injury frequency and severity rates mean the same thing regardless of the industry, the company, the plant, or part of the country, the method for computing these rates has been standardized by the American Standards Association and published as Standard Z 16.1-1954, *The American Standard Method of Recording and Measuring Work Injury Experience.* The standard presents a method of calculating injury rates which is used by most of industry, the National Safety Council, and the Bureau of Labor Statistics. Knowing something about the background of the American Standards Association and how various standards are formulated may provide a better appreciation and understanding of the Standard for Measuring Work Injury Experience and other standards published by the A.S.A.

The American Standards Association is the American clearing house for standards activity. Founded in 1918, it is a federation of more than 100 trade associates, technical societies, professional groups, and consumer organizations. Some 2300 companies are affiliated with the A.S.A. as company members. Each standard, such as the one for measuring injury experience, represents general agreement among interested groups as to the best current practice with regard to a specific problem. A standard is developed by a committee made up of representatives from associations, professional organizations, and government agencies. For example, representation on the committee which developed the standard for measuring injury experience included the American Society of Safety Engineers, the National Safety Council, the National Electrical Manufacturers Association, the American Federation of Labor, the U.S. Department of Labor, the Bureau of Labor Statistics, the Association of Casualty and Surety Companies, and many others. The original standard came into being in 1937 and was revised in 1945 and again in 1954. This in brief is a history of the A.S.A.

Again in reference to the standard for measuring work-injury experience, in addition to understanding the method for calculating injury frequency and severity rates, supervisors also should know how various provisions of the standard have been interpreted and applied. It is important to know which injuries should be included in the calculations. As a case in point, it is still thought by some that the matter of counting an injury as disabling is determined by the state workmen's compensation boards. This was true from 1937 to 1945. If a board ruled that an injury was compensable, it was charged to the plant's injury experience. Although this provided a simple method of reporting, it failed to provide a uniform experience between states with widely different workmen's compensation laws. In an effort to formulate a national standard for comparison of injury rates, the 1945 revision became independent of state and federal requirements for reporting injuries for purposes of workmen's compensation and rulings as to disability by workmen's compensation agencies. This necessitated inclusion in the standard of a series of definitions of what constituted a disabling work injury. By following the revised standard it is a relatively easy task to determine which work injuries should be counted and which work injuries should not be counted in calculating injury frequency and severity rates.

In general, a work injury includes any injury or occupational disease that results from an employee's work activity or the environment of his employment. *The fact that the employee or employer did not have control over the cause of the work injury does not exclude the injury from the records.* In general, if an employee is injured while at work and loses a full day (beyond the day of the injury) because of the resulting disability, or if there is a permanent partial loss, there is no question that the case should be counted. However, there are some border-line cases that might cause a supervisor to wonder why he has been charged with a disabling injury.

Back injuries, especially those of a nebulous origin like, "I bent over to pick up a pencil and . . . . " must raise doubts regarding the efficacy of the standard. This shortcoming was recognized in the 1954 revision. The present standard specifies that back injuries shall be considered work injuries only if there is a clear record of an accident or incident such as a slip, trip, or fall, sudden effort or over-exertion, or a blow on the back and in the opinion of the employer's authorized physician the injury could have resulted from the claimed accident or incident.

Classification of an inguinal hernia also proved troublesome in the past, so the subject was given special attention in the 1945 revision of the standard. To be considered a work injury, an inguinal hernia must be precipitated by an impact, sudden effort, or severe strain and meet all of the following conditions:

1. There is a clear record of an accident or an incident such as a slip, trip, fall, sudden effort, or over-exertion.
2. There is actual pain in the hernial region at the time of the accident.
3. The immediate pain is so acute that the injured employee is forced to stop work long enough to draw the attention of his supervisor or fellow employee, or the aid of a physician is secured within twelve hours.

Another problem in the use of the standard arises when an employee sustains a disabling injury during a period of the working day when he is not engaged in the performance of his regular duties. Under such circumstances, there might be questions as to whether or not the injury should be counted. A review of the two lists which follow may help answer any such questions. The first list contains examples of cases that would be considered work injuries and reportable under the standard. Examples in the second list are not classified as work injuries and, therefore, are not reported.

WORK INJURIES WHICH ARE INCLUDED IN DISABLING-INJURY STATISTICS

1. An injury which occurs during normal travel of the employee in the interest of the employer would be included in the disabling-injury statistics if it occurs between the time such travel starts (either from the employee's home or from a fixed place of work, like the central office if there is one) and the time such travel is ended. (Applies to traveling salesmen, bill collectors, appliance repairmen, etc.)
2. If a regular place of work is inaccessible to ordinary transportation and the company furnishes special transportation from a designated meeting place, an injury would be included if it occurs between the time an employee is picked up at such a meeting place and the time he is returned to the same place.
3. An injury to an employee who does not have a fixed place to work such as a member of a public-utility line crew would be included if it occurs between the time the employee reaches a designated meeting place for the crew and the time he is dismissed from duty at a point where the crew disbands.
4. An injury which occurs while an employee is entertaining a customer or client or while the employee is being entertained for the purpose of transacting or discussing business is included.

5. An injury is included if it occurs while an employee is going from the entrance to plant property to his work place or from his work place to the exit from plant property before and after working hours or if it occurs while the employee is going from one part of the plant to another.

6. An injury which occurs during a coffee break or other rest period is included.

7. An injury is included which occurs while an employee is going to or coming from a shower or wash room or which occurs while the employee is using the shower or wash-room facilities before, during, or after working hours on company premises if use of the facilities was occasioned by the employee's work.

8. An injury is included if it occurs while an employee is on a personal errand for his supervisor either on or off plant property.

9. An injury which results from an external activity such as fighting a fire outside the plant is included.

WORK INJURIES WHICH ARE *NOT* INCLUDED IN DISABLING-INJURY STATISTICS

1. Back injuries and inguinal hernias which do not meet the specific conditions of the standard are not included in disabling-injury statistics.

2. An injury is not included if it occurs during normal routine travel from an employee's home to the employee's regular place of business and vice versa. (Normal routine travel includes travel which is occasioned by overtime, special, or emergency work.)

3. An injury which occurs on a common carrier (bus, streetcar, subway, etc.) on which the employee is traveling as a passenger is not included.

4. An injury which occurs during the employee's regularly and specifically defined lunch period is not included. (An injury which occurs on company property while going to or returning from a lunch area is counted.)

5. An injury which occurs on a parking lot maintained by the company for convenience of employees is not included unless it occurs while an employee is performing duties of his employment such as grading the parking lot, erecting directional signs, etc.

6. An injury which results *solely* from a pre-existing physical deficiency is not included if an employee without such physical deficiency would not have experienced the incident which resulted in the injury.

Because frequency rates are expressed in terms of a common unit of exposure, companies of varying size and with varying working hours may be compared without imposing a problem. However, for practical reasons, the injury rate of a single establishment or plant should be compared with organizations doing similar work and, preferably, with the frequency rate of the plant in previous years so injury trends will be revealed.

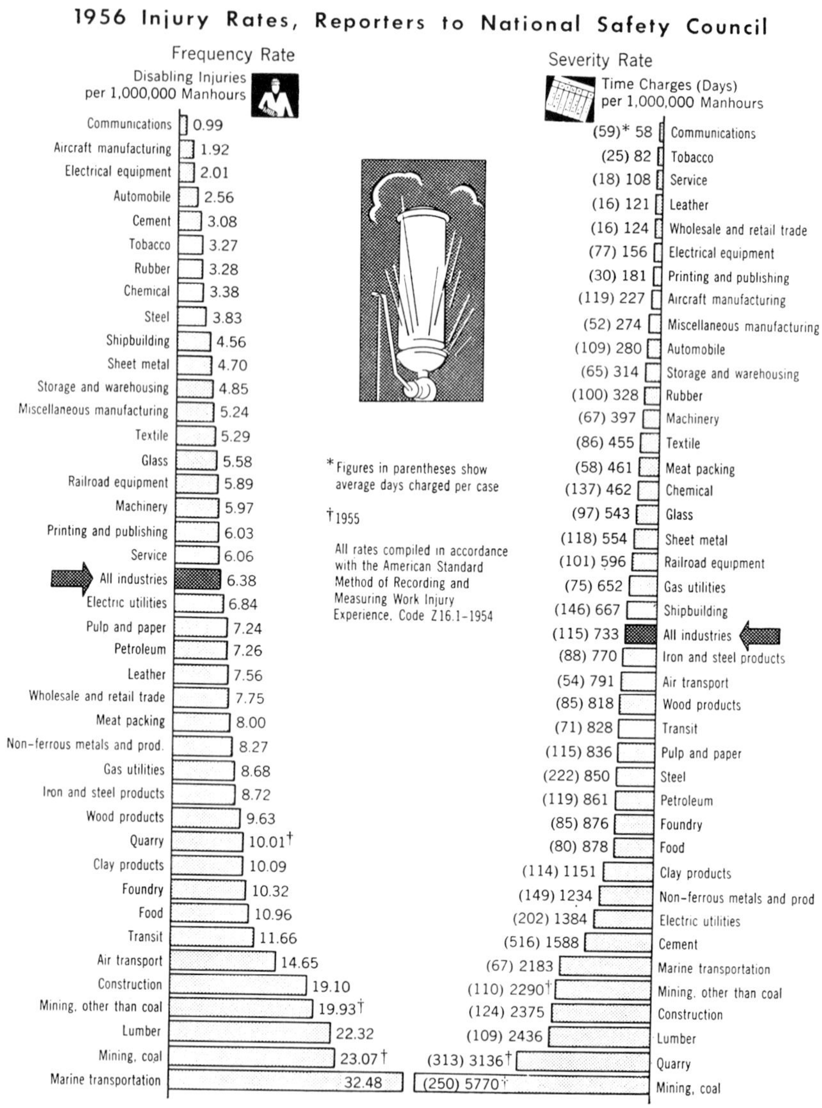

Exhibit 15–1. Frequency and severity rates by industries. (Source: *Accident Facts,* 1957 edition, National Safety Council, Chicago, Illinois.)

Exhibit 15–1 provides bench marks for evaluating the disabling-injury experience of a plant by comparison with the rates of its particular industry. The left-hand column shows the disabling-injury frequency rate by industries of member-companies reporting to the

National Safety Council. The right-hand column shows severity rates by industries and average days charged per case.

Total injury experience

To say a plant or company has a good safety record does not mean necessarily that every section of the organization has done a good accident-prevention job. As a matter of fact, even a zero rate might have little meaning because minor injuries, which comprise a large part of the total-injury problem, are not reflected in disabling-injury frequency rates. To really pin-point the accident problem, a look at total-injury experience is needed. The use of total-injury frequency rates, which include even the minor injuries such as a small scratch, provides a sensitive barometer of accident-prevention performance by sections of the plant or by supervisors. Such a measurement is needed if supervisors are to be held accountable for safety.

Total-injury rates are widely used but, as typically reported, are the least valid of all accident statistics. But this need not be the case. Total-injury statistics can become most useful if the pitfalls of the usual total-injury reporting methods are avoided while some fundamental principles of supervisory-performance measurement are incorporated.

Obviously, the first step in avoiding the pitfalls is to recognize the factors that tend to detract from the usefulness of total-injury statistics. For example, the practice is widespread to report total-injury experience on the basis of the type of injuries which resulted from accidents instead of by the cause of the accidents. A second pitfall to avoid is the reporting of total injuries by the number of injuries charged to each supervisor rather than by a frequency rate of such injuries as calculated from some predetermined base, such as 10,000, 100,000, or 1,000,000 manhours or the number of injuries per 100 employees.

Here is an example of the case in point. One supervisor has 50 people, they have 25 injuries; another supervisor has 100 people, they also have 25 injuries. When the cases are stated in number of injuries, supervisor *A* and supervisor *B* each had 25 injuries reported by his people. In a report which shows total injuries rather than frequency rates, their injury experience would appear to be equal. However, when the cases are stated in terms of frequency rates, the supervisor with 100 people has just one-half the rate of the supervisor with 50 people.

Progress and measured results go hand in hand. The various safety reports prepared for supervisors, to be effective, must answer one question, "How am I (the supervisor) doing?" Nevertheless, various arguments have been advanced against the use of total-injury frequency rates as a measure of supervisor safety performance. It is claimed by some that the use of such rates will cause supervisors to discourage the reporting of minor injuries in an effort to make the record look good. Others point out that employees knowing such injuries are counted will be reluctant to report minor injuries and that this will increase the incidence of infection. Perhaps there is some basis for these two claims. Similar claims also might be made with reference to production and quality measurements. For example, the story is told about a large factory which had a river running along one side. The river went dry one summer and over one thousand off-dimension crank shafts were found in the mud. Obviously, several employees were hiding their rejects by tossing them into the river. But the surprising disclosure was not used as a reason for discontinuing the quality-control program. Likewise, a few limitations should not be taken as valid reasons for not using such a useful tool as total-injury statistics. What is needed is a measurement which will tell supervisors how good or how poor a safety job they are doing. The use of total-injury statistics should be considered with the intent of helping supervisors do a better safety job. Hence, a supervisor would be kidding himself and compromising his own integrity to discourage the reporting of minor injuries. Such duplicity would soon be revealed. The supervisor would weaken his own position by his failure to make full use of a valid measure.

A supervisors' accident-prevention performance report (Exhibit 15–2) can be used to implement the use of total-injury statistics. This report lists injuries by *cause* and indicates total-injury frequency rates by supervisors. Such a report will help pin-point the safety problem for each supervisor. The usefulness of these statistics should help convince supervisors that the valid reporting of all injuries will be helpful to them in the long run.

Total-injury-control charts

What is needed is some method for plotting supervisory safety performance which will show at a glance the quality of such performance on a month-to-month basis. Total-injury-control charts are suggested. An injury-control chart is prepared for each supervisor. Such charts contain statistical data as follows:

1. The supervisors' average total-injury frequency rate for the previous year (base year).

SUPERVISORS' ACCIDENT-PREVENTION

PERFORMANCE REPORT

Month *February* Year *1959*

	ACCIDENT CAUSES	BROWN	WHITE	BLACK	GRAY	SMITH	JONES			TOTALS
UNSAFE ACTS	Failure to follow instructions	1	1							2
	Unsafe methods of handling	13	3	2	16	2				36
	Unsafe movements – running, jumping, etc.	30	6	7	10	3	2			58
	Inattention	7		1	1	1				10
	Improper use of tools	4		1	8	1				14
	Failure to use protective equipment	35	2		12	1				50
	Horseplay									
	Other	23	7	4	12					46
UNSAFE CONDITIONS	Defective tools, materials, and equipment	7	3		2					12
	Poor housekeeping	6	2			1				9
	Lack of guards and protective equipment	1			1	1				3
	Ineffective safety equipment	15			1	1				17
	Other				1					1
	Total injuries	142	24	15	64	11	2			258
	Total injury frequency rate	43	41	25	22	21	67			26
	Average safety performance range	41/22	62/38	50/30	48/32	26/14	90/60			31/24
	A = Average range, O = Over, U = Under	O	A	U	U	A	A			A

Prepared by *John Dale* Date *March 10, 1959*

Exhibit 15–2. A sample form for reporting accident statistics on a monthly basis. The arrangement as to spacing, choice of unsafe acts and unsafe conditions, etc., may not be suitable for certain plants and operations. The above form is intended to serve as a guide to the preparation of a more convenient and suitable form as local conditions require. Primarily, it illustrates one way in which major facts of accident occurrence including accident causes and total-injury frequency rates may be listed and reported to supervisors.

2. An average safety-performance range. (This range is the average total frequency rate plus and minus one average deviation. Average deviation is described as the average fluctuation or dispersion of frequency rates about the average frequency rate in the base year.)
3. Total injury frequency rates by months in the current year.

Why an "average safety-performance range" instead of a single average total-injury frequency rate? Mainly because there is nothing fixed or absolute about total-injury frequency rates. A check will usually reveal that these rates fluctuate widely in some sections of the plant and in other sections the fluctuations stay within a rather narrow range. Likewise, narrow fluctuations in total-injury frequency rates might be a factor of chance rather than effort. For example, a supervisor has an average total-injury frequency rate of 100. In January his rate is 90, and in February it is 110. There would be reason to believe he had improved his safety record in January and that the record had become worse in February. The statistician says this conclusion is not valid. In the case of the supervisor with an average rate of 100, a fluctuation of 10, the square root of 100, up or down, could be expected on the basis of chance alone. Hence, average safety performance for each supervisor should be a frequency-rate *range* rather than just the average total-injury frequency rate.

Following calculation of the average total-injury rate for the base year, and the average deviation, these data may be plotted in an injury-control chart as shown in Exhibit 15–3. The straight solid line on the chart is the total-injury frequency rate for the base year. The solid vertical bars indicate the actual total-injury frequency rates by months in the base year and in the current year. The shaded area between the two points marked "upper limit" and "lower limit" is the range of safety performance, that is, the average total-injury frequency rate plus and minus an average deviation. Frequency rates in the current year which fall in the shaded area indicate just average safety performance for the supervisor. Any rates which are above the shaded area indicate an increase in injuries greater than might have resulted from chance alone. Something might be out of control. It might be faulty training, unsafe conditions introduced by a new job or a change in method, worn tools or equipment, or an influx of new people. An analysis must be made to determine the cause, and positive action taken to correct the condition. If, however, the frequency rate goes below the lower limit, the safety efforts of the supervisor may be considered successful.

Reference should now be made to the total-injury-control statistics

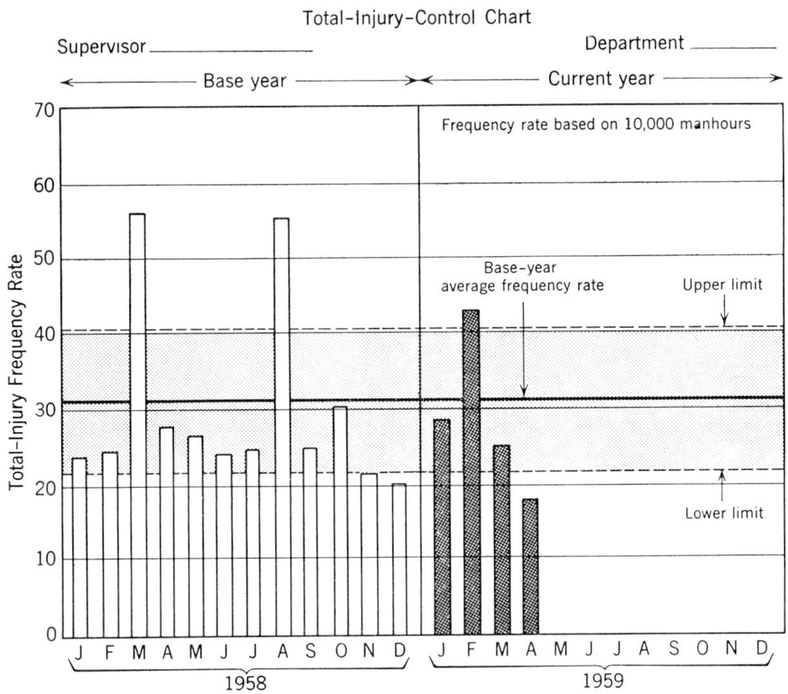

Exhibit 15–3. Injury-control charts are prepared in duplicate. One copy is retained by the safety office and the other one is sent to the supervisor. By the 10th of each month, statistics for the previous month are plotted on the charts. New charts are prepared each year. Shaded area in the above chart is the average safety-performance range.

shown in Table 15–2. These are the actual statistics used to prepare the injury-control chart, Exhibit 15–3. These statistics are used to calculate the average total-injury frequency rate for the base (previous) year and the average deviation.

Column 2 in Table 15–2 shows the total manhours worked each month in the base year. (If there is doubt about a single year being typical, it might be desirable to use two or three years to compute the average frequency rate and the average deviation.) Column 3 shows total injuries by months, column 4 the frequency rate by months, and column 5 the deviation of the month-by-month frequency rates from the annual average total-injury frequency rate, which was calculated to be 31.2. For January, the frequency rate was 24.7; thus the deviation is 31.2 — 24.7 = 6.5, which appears as the first value in the fifth column. In a like manner, the amounts of deviation of all

TABLE 15–2. INJURY-CONTROL STATISTICS

Department—Model Shop | Supervisor—A. L. Brown

Month	Manhours	Total Injuries	Frequency Rate	Frequency-Rate Deviation from Average
Jan.	15,781	39	24.7	6.5
Feb.	14,088	36	25.3	5.9
Mar.	15,228	86	56.4	25.2
Apr.	14,815	41	27.6	3.6
May	14,266	37	26.1	5.1
June	14,073	35	24.7	6.5
July	14,163	36	25.4	5.8
Aug.	15,365	85	55.3	24.1
Sept.	13,944	36	25.4	5.8
Oct.	15,283	46	30.1	1.1
Nov.	13,974	31	22.1	9.1
Dec.	15,132	31	20.4	10.8
Totals	176,112	549		109.5

$$\text{Average frequency rate} = \frac{549 \times 10{,}000}{176{,}112} = 31.2$$

$$\text{Average deviation} = \frac{\text{sum of deviations}}{N \text{ (number of months)}} = \frac{109.5}{12} = 9.1$$

twelve frequency rates have been computed and entered in the fifth column. It should be noted that all deviations, whether above or below the annual average, are taken as positive. The sum of column 5 is the total of the deviations of the twelve frequency rates. This total divided by 12 gives the average deviation.

Had the twelve frequency rates been bunched around the annual average frequency rate to a greater extent, the average deviation would have been smaller. Hence, the so-called "average safety-performance range" would have been narrower than the range shown on the injury-control chart. On the other hand, if the injury rates had fluctuated widely, the safety-performance range would be represented by a much wider shaded area. Hence, the advantages of using a safety-performance range rather than the average total-injury frequency rate are apparent. A safety-performance range takes into consideration the actual injury-rate experience or injury-rate pattern of each supervisor. For example, two supervisors might have exactly the same average frequency rates, but in one case there might be little fluctuation in the rates from month to month and in the other case the fluctuations might be over a wide range. This difference in experience would be reflected in a larger average deviation for the supervisor with the wider fluctuations.

Steps to set up injury-control charts.

1. *Select a base year.* The base year provides comparative data for the current year. It should be one considered typical in production, composition of work force, manhours worked, etc. Usually, the previous year's experience can be used.

2. *Compute the number of injuries per 10,000 manhours for each month of the base year.* Total injuries include disabling injuries, doctor's cases, and all first-aid cases, no matter how slight the injury. Some safety engineers might prefer to use 1000 manhours as the base for this calculation because of the relatively few manhours worked by the employees reporting to a single supervisor. (If a supervisor has fewer than 25 employees reporting to him, it is advisable to compute injury frequency rates by general foreman or superintendents. A wider base produces more meaningful statistics.)

3. *Calculate the safety-performance range.* The safety-performance range is the average total-injury frequency rate of the base year plus and minus an average deviation. This computation establishes the upper and lower control limits on the injury-control chart.

4. *Prepare injury-control charts for each supervisor.* A solid horizontal line shows the average number of injuries per 10,000 manhours worked in the base year. Two broken lines show the upper and lower limits of the supervisor's average safety performance.

5. *Compute monthly total-injury data and plot them.* At the end of each month, supply each supervisor with data which are needed to keep the injury-control chart up to date. Make sure immediate corrective steps are taken when the injury rate goes above the upper control limits.

6. *Set goals for each supervisor.* A realistic goal would be an average total-injury rate for the current year equal to or below the lower control limit. For example, a supervisor's average injury rate is 50. The lower limit is 40. The goal for the current year would be an average total frequency rate of 40 or less.

For many years, disabling-injury frequency rates of one plant or company have been compared with the rates of other establishments. This comparison may have been made without regard to the size of the company, the type of product, and the location of the plant. Where total-injury frequency rates are used, such comparisons should be avoided. It would be impractical and usually unfair to compare the total-injury frequency rate of one supervisor with the rate of a supervisor in another part of the plant. The intent where total-injury statistics are used is to check the current month's injury rate of each supervisor against his safety-performance range. The safety-performance range for each supervisor becomes the standard. But unlike quality control, being on standard is not the goal. The goal is to achieve a total-injury frequency rate which is below the standard. Thus, it is the supervisors who get their rates below the safety-performance range who are doing the better safety jobs, not necessarily the supervisors with the lowest frequency rates. When a total-injury-control program is first started, some safety engineers might wish to disregard the general rule of not comparing the injury rate of one supervisor with that of another. For example, an exception might be made in the case of supervisors who manage sections doing the same kind of work. The rate of a supervisor who has obviously been doing a poor safety job in the past might be compared with that of a supervisor doing the same type of work who presumably has been doing a good job. The safety-performance standard for the supervisor doing the poor job might then be set by use of an average total-injury rate somewhat lower than his actual average rate in the base year. Say, for example, half way between his rate and the rate of the better supervisor, or at any other point which might be indicated by existing facts. But it is well to repeat that generally such comparisons should be avoided.

Finally, there are several reasons for not comparing the total-injury frequency rate of one supervisor with the rate of another supervisor:

1. Minor-injury reporting seems to decrease with distance from the dispensary. (There is agreement that some minor injuries are not reported. An employee close to the dispensary is more apt to report for treatment of a small cut than one who has a long distance to walk.)
2. The possibility of minor injuries varies considerably with jobs.
3. Women are more apt to report minor injuries than men.
4. Workers on light jobs appear to be more consistent in the reporting of minor injuries than workers on heavy jobs. (The millwright is unaware of several minor cuts until he washes up. The draftsman notices immediately a small laceration and goes to first-aid for treatment.)
5. Personalities (the pretty nurse) in the plant dispensary might influence the reporting of minor injuries.

Experience indicates that each section of a plant will have a particular pattern of reporting minor injuries. The basis for measuring supervisor safety performance is this pattern. It is significant that the pattern, or rate, changes quickly once control measures are instituted and a conscientious attempt is made to eliminate the *causes* of *all* accidents.

Conclusions

A marked tendency of modern management is an effort to measure more accurately all industrial results and all forms of effort. In safety work, injury statistics have been used in the past to form judgments rather than as a measurement. In making judgments, things are compared with one another. The injury rates of one supervisor have been compared with the injury rates of other supervisors, and the supervisor with the lowest rate has been adjudged to be doing the best job. Obviously, such a judgment was not always valid.

In making measurements, the basis for comparison is an agreed-upon standard. Thus, for measuring a supervisor's safety performance the standard is the average total-injury frequency rate in the base year plus and minus the average deviation. This calculation establishes the supervisor's safety-performance range. When the data is plotted on an injury-control chart, each supervisor can tell at a glance the scope and the trend of his work-injury problems. With a standard he is able to evaluate the results of his safety efforts. He knows that a frequency rate above the upper limit of the range is an indication that the injury rate is out of control. He must take positive action. A rate below the lower limit indicates that he is preventing accidents. This is tangible evidence of the success of his safety efforts. Of course, there are some who are of the opinion that standards should not be used in safety work. A rather unrealistic argument is advanced that the only standard that can be used is a zero frequency rate. This approach presumes the improbable when total-injury experience is being measured. Besides, the standard is then the same for everyone and the only alternative is to compare supervisors, one with the others. Hence, any evaluation of an individual supervisor's safety performance becomes a judgment and not a measurement.

Over the years, considerable effort has been spent on the development of methods for establishing objectives and measuring the results of supervisory and managerial effort. New safety concepts, new supervisory techniques, and new principles of business organization require a re-examination of the judgments presently used to determine the quality of a supervisor's safety performance. Improved methods for evaluating supervisor safety performance are needed. Total-injury frequency rates used as a basis for establishing standard safety performance appears to be a step in the right direction. Undoubtedly, experience with the statistical methods described in this chapter will lead to refinements which will eventually make total-injury reporting even more practical and useful.

SELECTED REFERENCES

Culbertson, Charles V., "Does the American Standards Methods of Computing Frequency Rates Hide the Truth?," *The Journal of the American Society of Safety Engineers,* May, 1957.

Edwards, D. N., "How Good Is Our Performance," *National Safety News,* August, 1953.

How Good are Our Work Injury Statistics?, New York State Department of Labor, 80 Centre Street, New York 13, N.Y., Special Labor News Memorandum No. 67, 1956.

Howel, J. M., and Lee Johnson, "Statistical Control of Accidents," *Industrial Standardization,* May, 1947.

Leadbeater, T. R., "How Accident Control Charts Can Help Your Safety Record," *Factory Management and Maintenance,* June, 1951.

Lee, Robert E., "A Statistical Control of Industrial Accidents," *The Journal of the American Society of Training Directors,* March-April, 1955.

Miller, H. Gene, "Injury Frequency Rates," *National Safety News,* October, 1953.

Stewart, D. C., "Yardstick for Safety Performance," *National Safety News,* May, 1950.

PART V

THE SAFETY ENGINEER

CHAPTER

16

The safety engineer and the future

Every safety engineer, in order to reach professional status, must not only know the facts of his profession and how to use them, but also progress as an individual personality, with an inordinate curiosity, a measured tolerance, and a compassionate outlook combined with the conscientiousness of the perfectionist.

The basis of the truly professional spirit is ethical, as your own experience will tell you. Each man in each age in living a life as well as a career makes his own choice.

EVERETT W. MARTIN

Liberty Mutual Insurance Company

Perhaps to gain a full understanding of the present and probable future status of safety work, a look at the past will help. At the beginning of the twentieth century, the job of the safety engineer, safety director, or safety inspector was unknown. The specialized knowledge and skill of a safety man had not yet been considered essential to the profitable operation of a business. But early in 1900 there was evidence of a growing interest in industrial safety. Several large companies, especially in the chemical, steel, electrical, and railroad industries, created safety committees or appointed a safety inspector to find work hazards and make suggestions for accident prevention. In 1911, the safety movement, which was then well under way, received added impetus when the Supreme Court declared the Workmen's Compensation Law of the State of Washington constitutional. In the following two years, twenty additional states passed similar laws. These laws focused attention on the direct costs of work accidents. Hence, more and more companies recognized the business as well as the humanitarian needs for an organized safety program. Safety engineers and safety inspectors took their place on the management team, and historically they became the first specialists in the field of personnel administration. However, today many companies feel that safety is not distinctly a personnel function. Many safety men now report directly to the plant manager or they are a part of either the manufacturing or engineering function rather than the personnel function.

The National Safety Council

By 1912 there was enough interest in accident-prevention work to bring over two hundred men to the Hotel Pfister in Milwaukee, Wisconsin, to attend the First Cooperative Safety Congress sponsored by the Association of Iron and Steel Electrical Engineers. Lew R. Palmer, then Safety Director for the Jones and Laughlin Steel Company and chairman of the association's safety committee, was the leading spirit at this first congress. He had seen the need for uniting the efforts of all those interested in safety and furnishing an opportunity for safety experts to exchange experiences.

Delegates at the first congress formed a committee which the following year organized the National Council for Industrial Safety. In 1914, the scope of this committee's activities was broadened and its name changed to the National Safety Council. William H. Cameron, who had been manager of the casualty department of the American Steel Foundries, was appointed as the council's first managing director.

Today, the National Safety Council is the leading safety organization in the United States that is concerned with traffic, home, farm, and school safety as well as industrial safety. It is supported by thousands of dues-paying members from industry, railroads, schools, and local safety councils. The annual Safety Congress, first held in 1912, is still a high point among council activities. Now, in comparison to the 200 men who attended the first congress, over 10,000 safety men and supervisors attend this annual safety function. This vast attendance is an indication of the great interest in safety which has been generated and the rapid growth of the safety movement.

The American Society of Safety Engineers

In New York City in 1911, concurrent with other developments in the safety movement, thirty-five men from insurance companies got together and formed the United Association of Casualty Inspectors. This was the nucleus of an organization which later was to take a prominent part in the safety movement—The American Society of Safety Engineers. The society maintained an independent status for thirteen years. In 1924 it was merged with the National Safety Council as The Engineering Section—American Society of Safety Engineers. This merger was continued until 1947 when the society again became an independent group. Today, the A.S.S.E. has a membership of over seven thousand and active chapters in every part of the United States, Canada, and Hawaii. Under aggressive and tireless leadership of many men who have devoted or are devoting their lives to safety work, the society has become an important influence in the careers of safety engineers. It has advanced fundamental safety knowledge and has made available to everyone the safety-engineering principles developed by its members. The society, through its committee on technical publications cooperates with the National Safety Council in the preparation of Safe Practices Pamphlets and Industrial Data Sheets. The society's Committee on Safety Standards works closely with the American Standards Association in seeing that the society is represented on every important A.S.A. safety-standards-development or standards-revision committee. Other committees include the Committee on Cooperation with Engineering Societies, the Committee on General Publications, which aids in presenting current news and technical developments to the membership, and the Committee on Research, which seeks out and helps direct needed studies that add to the fund of basic safety knowledge. This, then, is a brief sketch of the American Society of Safety Engineers. Its

TABLE 16–1. PAST PRESIDENTS OF THE AMERICAN SOCIETY OF SAFETY ENGINEERS

Year	Name	Affiliation
1946–1947	Roy M. Godwin Manager, Safety Department Philadelphia Electric Company	Utility
1947–1948	John S. Shaw* Safety Director Hercules Powder Company	Chemical
1948–1949	Robert H. Ferguson Assistant Director, Industrial Relations Republic Steel Corporation	Steel
1949–1950	E. C. McFadden Vice President Texas Employers Insurance Association	Insurance
1950–1951	William P. Yant Director, Research and Development Mine Safety Appliances Company	Research
1951–1952	J. C. Stennett Director, Accident and Fire Prevention Division National Association of Mutual Casualty Companies	Association
1952–1953	C. H. Weiser Plant Personnel Southwestern Bell Telephone Company	Telephone
1953–1954	William F. Brown Safety Director Consolidated Edison Company of New York	Utility
1954–1955	W. N. Cox, Jr. Professor of Safety and Industrial Engineering School of Industrial Engineering Georgia Institute of Technology	Education
1955–1956	Edward B. Landry Director of Safety and Health U. S. Post Office Department	Government
1956–1957	Henry B. Duffus Administrator, Accident Prevention Westinghouse Electric Corporation	Electrical Manufacturing
1957–1958	John F. Juli Safety Manager, Consolidated Western Steel Division United States Steel Corporation	Steel

Previous to 1947 the society did not elect a president. The chief officer was a chairman of the Engineering Section of the National Safety Council.

* Deceased.

leaders have come from a wide cross-section of American industry and business, as indicated by the list of the society's presidents, Table 16–1.

Other safety organizations

Other organizations which are identified with the safety movement include, to name a few, the American Industrial Hygiene Association; the American Standards Association; the National Fire Protection Association; Underwriters' Laboratories; the Bureau of Mines; the Division of Safety Standards, Bureau of Labor Standards; the Safety Standards Group, National Bureau of Standards; the Safety Division, American Society of Mechanical Engineers; the National Society for the Prevention of Blindness; the Association of Casualty and Surety Companies; and the National Association of Mutual Casualty Companies.

Safety education

In the late thirties, the need for an educational program to prepare men and women for plant safety jobs was given attention. The Center for Safety Education was established at New York University in 1938. In 1940, the United States Office of Education and the National Committee for the Conservation of Manpower provided a short intensive course in the basic fundamentals of safety engineering which was taken by thousands of people throughout the country. It was part of the Engineering, Science, and Management Training Program. This activity gave impetus to the establishment of safety courses, which are currently available in many colleges and universities throughout the United States. However, there is no school which presently has a curriculum for safety engineering. Many leading safety men feel that establishment of college courses leading to professional degrees in safety engineering would accelerate future progress in the field of accident prevention.

This, then, is a brief look at the history of the safety movement. Much activity has been crowded into a few short years. Thousands of Americans are devoting their lives on and off the job to accident prevention. Numerous safety councils, associations, and societies are now well organized and operating with effectiveness. Basic accident-prevention principles and practices are established; the safety movement is off and running. But what about the future? Many factors point to a different picture in the field of safety in the next thirty years compared to the one in the last thirty years. Changes brought about by automation, new concepts of industrial organization, and new thinking and new methods in the field of industrial accident prevention are sure to affect the direction the safety movement takes in the future. Of course, this does not mean that present practices, which are producing results, should be discarded. But safety engineers and others are concerned. In many companies it is becoming increasingly difficult to achieve further improvement in injury rates. Even an aggressive program produces only minimal results. Hence the question—"Have some safety practices outlived their usefulness?" There are a lot of safety techniques lying around like contests, safety-award dinners, safety committees, mass training methods, and reams of safety booklets. But will all of these gadgets, gimmicks, and projects help much in the big job ahead? They have, of course, been helpful in the past. To originate such activities required imagination and able direction. But as conditions have changed, is it not reasonable to conclude that some of these activities may be unnecessary, especially where the safety program now has top-management support, where supervision understands its function in the safety program, where safety accountability is established, and where the plant safety man is helping the supervisor to do the safety job rather than trying to do it himself? Perhaps some of these activities were necessary in the past because the management team was not applying its supervisory skills to the safety problem, because the first-line supervisor was not assuming full responsibility for safety.

The responsibilities of the safety engineer

In this book a great deal has been said about the safety responsibilities of the supervisor. What then is the job of the safety engineer, safety specialist or safety director?

Safety engineering may be defined as the application of the arts and sciences of engineering and education for the prevention of accidents and the conservation of health, life, and property.[1] It includes the following factors—investigation, research, and analysis of accident and health problems, invention and design of physical means of preventing accidents and occupational illnesses, and the development and direction of educational programs designed to create and maintain safety awareness at every level of the organization.

In keeping with the concept that the safety program must be built

[1] Definition proposed by Nixon de Tarnowsky, Safety Director, The F. & M. Schaefer Brewing Company, Brooklyn, New York.

around line supervisors, some of the specific responsibilities of the safety engineer may be listed as follows:

1. By teaching, counseling, and advising, assist line management to fulfill to the highest degree its responsibility for safety.
2. Provide for periodic safety appraisals to pin-point unsafe work environments and unsafe practices and processes, and report results of such appraisals with sound recommendations for correction. This includes the responsibility for appraising all new and relocated equipment and machines and releasing such equipment to the appropriate line supervisor.
3. Promote and maintain a continuing safety-education program which will help create safety awareness at all levels of the organization and has as a focal point the first-line supervisor's responsibility for safety—specifically teach supervisors to develop safe working conditions, to find the cause of *all* accidents, to use personalized safety training, to promote employee safety participation, and to enforce safety rules.
4. Maintain and interpret accident and injury statistics and accident-cost data.
5. Devise measurements and set standards which provide for an adequate evaluation of accident-prevention performance and loss control for each supervisor at each level of management.
6. Provide for the advancement and dissemination of fundamental safety knowledge, conduct safety research and put existing safety information into usable forms such as safety booklets, data sheets, instruction manuals, and bulletins. Transfer such safety knowledge to the first-line supervisor so it can be used at the place where the action takes place.
7. Maintain liaison with national, state, and local safety councils and take an active part in the activities of such groups.

Dual responsibilities

In relation to the above points, the safety engineer and the plant supervisor have a dual responsibility. That is, to understand and fully appreciate the problems of each other's job. The safety man is part of the service team. He performs a service function. He is in the organization to help the supervisor do a better job of accident prevention. But safety men must realize that accident prevention is just one of the responsibilities of the supervisor, who is also concerned with cost control, production, absenteeism, methods, wage problems, personnel development, quality, community activities, training, labor relations, and many other activities. Hence, it is no wonder, with all of these functions facing him each day, that the supervisor would be willing to surrender his safety responsibilities to anyone willing to take on the assignment—the safety engineer or a safety committee, for example. But one man or a committee cannot do an effective job of controlling accidents. Control requires the collective efforts of every supervisor in the organization. Fortunately, supervisors who are doing a good safety job are the first to insist that safety responsibility belongs to them. They have realized the benefits of integrating safety with their other responsibilities. Better employee morale, improved production, better housekeeping, lower cost, and a greater respect for all rules are just a few of the dividends of their personal and sincere efforts to prevent accidents.

Administration of the safety program

In order to help supervisors discharge their responsibility for accident prevention, functional responsibility for administration of the safety program should be assigned to a single individual. In a small plant this might be a part-time assignment and in a large operation a full-time job. The individual responsible for safety should have a job title consistent with other job titles in the business. This title might be Safety Engineer, Safety Consultant, Safety Supervisor, or Loss Prevention Specialist. If the work to be done is sufficiently technical to call for an engineering background to fulfill the job requirements, then the title Safety Engineer might be preferred. In cases where the individual responsible for safety administration directs the work of other safety specialists and loss-prevention specialists, the title of Safety Supervisor, Safety Director, or Safety Manager might be used.

As previously stated, safety engineers provide for periodic safety appraisals to pin-point unsafe working conditions and unsafe practices. In the future, the practice of making these appraisals at the invitation of the line supervisor rather than as a police action as is sometimes the case will become more widespread. This means the supervisor will be asking for and getting the help he wants. This approach has merit because the safety engineer who goes into a plant unannounced to make a safety appraisal and reports his findings to the boss and the boss' boss generally succeeds in creating a lot of resentment and very little action. But some may contend that the busy supervisor will never get around to extending the invitation for a safety appraisal. If the supervisor is really accountable for safety and needs help, he will be glad to have the qualified safety engineer out there helping him.

Of course, the very nature of safety work makes it necessary for the safety engineer to conduct periodic safety appraisals of certain equipment like power presses, ladders, slings, chains, and electrical equipment on a planned basis. These appraisals would be made on a regularly scheduled basis. An invitation would not be required. However, such appraisals could be announced in advance. This would enable the busy supervisor to adjust his schedule so he will be free when the safety man reaches his area. In these appraisals, the trained safety engineer will be looking for unsafe conditions relating to a specific type of equipment. His special training and skill will help him recognize hazards the supervisor might miss.

Making the safety appraisal of and releasing new and relocated machines and equipment, a key responsibility of a safety engineer, is another function that would not require an invitation. This activity would be an established and accepted routine.

In fulfilling his responsibility for pin-pointing unsafe conditions and unsafe acts, the safety engineer will avoid doing a fire-fighting job, that is, just hunting for hazards on a day-to-day basis. To assure progress, he will establish objectives now for improving job environments on both the short-range and the long-range basis. Thus, in addition to the continuing job of effecting the correction of re-occurring unsafe conditions, the safety engineer will have a goal for the future of higher standards of plant ventilation, lighting and temperature control, lower noise levels, and a better job of factoring the human element into the design of machines and equipment.

Establishing safety responsibility

Safety specialists or safety engineers have another important responsibility—promoting and maintaining a continuing educational program which has as a focal point the first-line supervisor's responsibility for safety.

Where the line supervisor's responsibility for safety has not been firmly established, some type of instruction is needed to clearly define this responsibility. This may well be an assignment for the safety engineer as a part of the safety educational program. In particular, safety engineers must function in a manner which does not become an "open sesame" for the supervisor to duck his safety responsibility. On the contrary, the actions of the safety engineer must always emphasize where safety responsibility belongs. For example, some safety men now have the authority to stop a machine which they consider unsafe. Where the safety man has this authority, the question might be asked, "Who then is responsibile for safety?" If an unsafe machine is not stopped by the safety engineer, then the supervisor is justified in assuming that the machine must be safe for operation. This creates an impractical and a basically unsound situation because the safety man cannot be present every time an unsafe machine is operated. Hence, the only logical solution is to hold the supervisor accountable for stopping equipment considered unsafe. However, in keeping with modern management concepts, the safety engineer in the performance of his duties must have the right to go into any part of the plant, review any operation, and obtain needed facts and information at any time. Hence, the safety engineer is not prevented from *advising* the supervisor that an operation is unsafe and should be stopped. A statement such as the following describing this concept might be included in the safety engineer's job description:

> The safety engineer will bring to the immediate attention of the line supervisor or manager any existing facility or practice that in his opinion is too unsafe for continued operation. Although the safety engineer does not have the authority to shut down an operation or discontinue a present practice, he and the supervisor concerned should find a solution to the immediate safety problem satisfactory to both. If the action taken by the supervisor does not eliminate the hazard, the safety engineer has the responsibility to request action from a higher level of management. If necessary, he may go to the General Manager with a request for action.

Perhaps some safety engineers have retained the authority to stop operations because of a lack of confidence that the supervisor has the ability or the interest to do a good safety job. Where this is the case, it is time to give the safety job back to the supervisor. Then, to implement the basic premise that responsibility for safety rests with line supervisors, the safety engineer should discharge his functional responsibilities by persuasion, teaching, counseling, and advising, relying on the authority of well-marshaled facts rather than the power to command or direct. To render assistance in the true sense of the word, safety men can't be quarterbacks; they must be coaches. This philosophy may be resisted. But after all, resistance to change is not new. It is a common human characteristic. In many plants in the past the safety approach may have been on a fire-fighting, police-action basis. In the future, the emphasis will be on the consultative approach.

Establishing measurements and standards

There is still another area where the safety engineer will perform a service. He will maintain and interpret safety statistical data and establish measurements and set standards to provide for an adequate evaluation of the safety performance of each supervisor.

In determining how well supervisors are fulfilling their safety responsibility, it would be unfair to compare them against each other because of differences in work environments, the nature of the work, the degree of hazards, and the composition of the work force. Hence, as discussed in Chapter 15, standard total-injury rates will be established for each supervisor by the safety engineer. Then, current performance can be compared against the established standard.

In establishing standards and measuring safety performance, a few problems will be encountered. For example, it is common practice after a serious accident not to fix the blame. The contention is that the seriousness of the accident so disturbs everyone that no further action is necessary. Candidly, most supervisors will agree that safety men should not whitewash a bad performance. It is part of the safety engineer's job to insist that supervisors receive an evaluation of the kind of safety job they are doing, good or bad.

In conducting the safety program, the safety engineer performs a distinct service to supervisors. In effect, the safety engineer is the consultant to the line organization. He has a valuable part in the safety program. But carrying out the program is entirely the responsibility of the line organization. When a manager or supervisor is given charge of a plant, a function, or an operation, he also assumes complete responsibility for those reporting to him. It is the duty of each supervisor to strive for results in safety with the same enthusiasm as in production, cost control, and quality on a day-to-day basis. The time, the effort, and the personal attention members of the line organization give to safety matters is an investment that pays dividends. The safety engineer can do much to assure these dividends.

The expanding scope of the safety job

In many companies the position of the safety engineer has received well-earned recognition and status. The safety man is a dedicated person. On and off the job he is teaching safety. He is a man with extraordinary skill in the direction of securing cooperative effort. Safety men, no matter where they are placed in the organization structure, perform a service function which is being recognized as important. Many company presidents, plant managers, and others in top management recognize that the competent, well-qualified safety engineer possesses a unique analytical skill and a philosophy which makes him particularly well suited for a certain type of work—loss

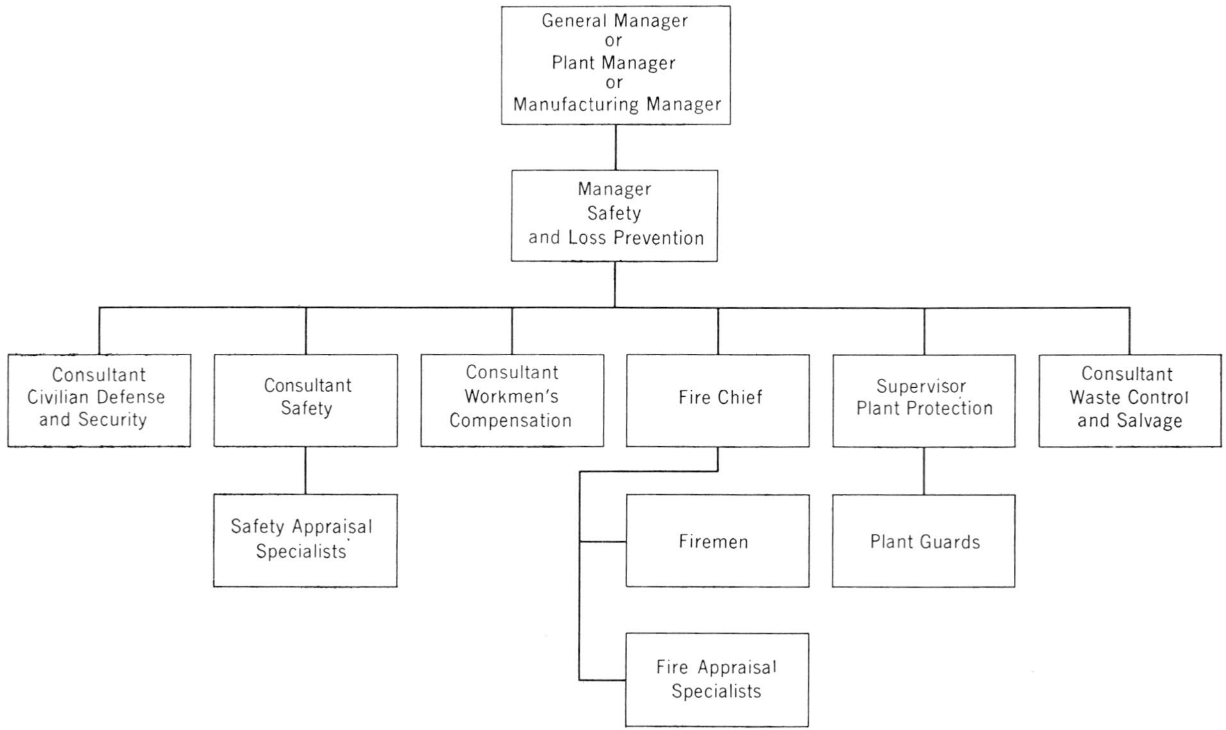

Exhibit 16–1. Proposed organization of safety and loss-prevention functions in a large plant. In smaller organizations functions might be combined or omitted depending on need. Even in a large company some of the above functions might be unnecessary, or perhaps other combinations of functions would be more practical such as plant protection and security, safety and civilian defense, etc. Also, there are some who feel that workmen's compensation should not be considered a loss-prevention function.

prevention. Therefore, it is reasonable to predict that in the future the scope of the safety job in the medium-sized and large companies will expand to take advantage of this special skill. Related activities will be tied together to broaden the scope of the safety job. When such a change is made, safety may not be associated with personnel, but appropriately with plant management or perhaps with engineering or manufacturing executives. Exhibit 16–1 might be a typical organization chart of the future.

Accident prevention, workmen's compensation, fire prevention, waste control, salvage, plant protection, and civilian defense—each of these functions has a common denominator—the prevention of losses. Loss-control techniques are the same whether the loss is injury to a worker, a production delay, a fire, damage to product or property, or wasted materials and supplies.

Safety engineers, by their performances, have demonstrated that the well-trained, experienced safety man furnishes a sound background and a developed skill for managing the various loss-prevention functions found in industry. However, it is usually found that the fire-prevention and plant-protection functions are in manufacturing, the safety function in personnel, workmen's compensation in accounting, waste control in engineering, and civilian defense possibly unassigned. In some respects, this is a hodgepodge. Thus, the suggestion to tie together these loss-prevention functions makes sense. At the moment, some of the functions mentioned when standing alone may have a stepchild status. Under such circumstances the single function is usually regarded as more or less routine with rather low-ceiling possibilities. But with a combined function for loss prevention, each activity should gain a new status. The wide span of responsibility under the proposed consolidation would permit the assignment of a well-qualified person as manager of the loss-prevention activity. The higher pay level which the assignment would permit would attract higher-calibre people. Under such an arrangement, it is more likely that each function would contribute to the profits of the organization.

However, just writing about such a change will not make it so. Present-day safety engineers can do much to further their own progress and the progress of those who will follow them by having the courage, the humility, and the personal integrity to admit their own shortcomings and establish standards and educational requirements for the safety engineer of the future that might be beyond their own qualifications. This would be truly a mark of professional status.

But no matter what changes take place in the future, a tribute must be paid to those leaders and pioneers in the field of safety who have made industrial accident prevention a reality by virtue of their rare sense of dedication, courage, skill, and vision. Much has been accomplished in safety over the past fifty years. But there is no time to relax. Much remains to be done. Each year, if the trend is not reversed, over 40,000 human beings will die in traffic accidents. A great newspaper has called this annual slaughter a national disgrace. Another 30,000 Americans will die in home accidents. Over 14,000 will be killed in work accidents—on the farm, in manufacturing plants, on the railroads, in the woods, mines, and quarries. Accidents each year will cause more deaths to persons between the ages of one and forty-four than cancer, heart disease, or tuberculosis.

Industry, and specifically supervisors and safety engineers, can do something constructive about preventing these off-the-job accidents by their in-plant safety efforts. Maximum results can be anticipated both on and off the job if the safety program is organized and administered to promote the basic concept expressed throughout this book —the first-line supervisor has primary responsibility and accountability for safety.

SELECTED REFERENCES

Andrews, Bill, "Pioneers of 1912," *National Safety News,* July, 1952.

Company Safety Programs, Personnel Policies Forum Survey No. 29, Bureau of National Affairs, Washington, D.C., 1955.

Cutter, Walter A., *Organization and Functions of the Safety Department,* Research Report No. 18, American Management Association, New York, 1951.

Fish, Carmen, "Safety Follow Through," *National Safety News,* October, 1953.

Gidel, Robert D., "The Challenging Decade," *National Safety News,* August, 1957.

Where Is Your Safety Engineer, report on the organizational position of the safety engineer, The Society for the Advancement of Management, New York, 1953.

APPENDIXES

APPENDIX

A

A basic safety program for the prevention of work injuries, property damage, and production losses

I. Introduction

Any safety program established for a large or small establishment must be comprehensive and well integrated so that each part reinforces the other parts, as well as adding effectiveness to the whole program. In order to accomplish this integration, the program must be designed to conform to a set of basic safety principles and sound management practices. This safety-program outline was planned to conform to and implement the basic safety principles which have been discussed in this book.

A. Although top management has major responsibility for establishing definite safety policies, procedures, and safe working conditions, most of what is planned and established must reach the employee on the job by way of the first-line supervisor, who is in frequent and close association with employees.

The first-line supervisor in discharging his responsibility for safety has among his principal duties the following:

1. To teach each employee what the hazards are on his job and how to avoid them. This is personalized safety training and requires the preparation of a job-hazard analysis for each operation.
2. To impart to each employee the understanding that the violation of established safety rules will not be tolerated.
3. To see that needed safety equipment and protective devices are provided for each job.
4. To take prompt corrective action whenever unsafe conditions and unsafe acts are noted.
5. To teach employees that accidents are caused and they can be prevented.
6. To investigate and find the causes of all accidents, even those which result in minor injuries.
7. To see that all injuries are reported and properly treated.
8. To instill a safety awareness in each employee through personal safety contacts and by group safety meetings.
9. To conduct regular safety appraisals of his section. This includes a careful check of all new and relocated equipment before it is placed in operation.
10. To give full support to all safety activities and safety procedures.

B. A safety rule should not be established unless there is a need for the rule, the rule can be followed, and the intention is to enforce it. This means, for example, that personal protective equipment would not be provided unless there were a need for such equipment and employees receiving such equipment would be expected to use it. Enforcement of rules is a necessary step to insure the complete success of any safety program. Disciplinary action should be avoided until management has thoroughly discharged its safety obligations and every effort has been exhausted in securing voluntary cooperation. However, in the final analysis, disciplinary action for failure to follow a rule must be taken or the rule will cease to exist.

C. A safety-observer program, or similar activity, is needed to provide employees a means of participation in the safety program. The purpose of the observer program will be to arouse employee safety interest, create a sense of personal safety responsibility, and enlist voluntary safety cooperation.

D. The safety engineer performs a safety service function with responsibility for helping operating managers and first-line supervisors fulfill their responsibility for safety. Principal duties of the safety engineer include:

1. Pin-pointing unsafe working conditions and unsafe practices and making sound recommendations for correction.
2. Maintaining a continuing educational and safety promotional program for supervisors and employees.
3. Establishing an effective system for measuring supervisor safety performance and maintaining an adequate system for reporting accident and injury statistics.

A specific safety program which will implement the above basic safety principles is outlined in seven sections as follows:

A. Safety rules
B. Plant safety appraisals
C. Safety training
D. Job-hazard analysis
E. The safety-observer program
F. Communication and related activities
G. General administration

II. The Safety Program

A. Safety rules

Safety rule books will be furnished to supervisors by the safety engineer and changes or additions distributed by him to all holders of the book. Suggestions for changes in and additions to the rule book should normally originate with supervisors.

Several considerations will be important in establishing safety rules, including the following:

1. Safety rules will be few in number and always carefully explained to employees. Safe operating practices will not be called "safety rules."
2. Safety rules will have equal application in all sections of the plant.
3. No rule will be published which cannot be enforced.
4. Unnecessary, outdated, and vague rules will be eliminated.
5. Each published rule will be covered by a general instruction signed by the plant manager (or the president of the company, etc.).

B. Plant safety appraisals

1. Safety and housekeeping appraisals.
   a. A safety and housekeeping appraisal will be conducted at least once each month in all plant areas. A safety-appraisal team for each section of the plant will consist of the general foreman and such other persons as the plant manager may designate.
   b. The safety engineer will be the advisory member of each safety-appraisal team.
   c. As unsafe conditions are discovered, the first-line supervisor will be notified and he will immediately set a deadline for corrective action based on the appraisal team's recommendation. The particular supervisor involved will be responsible to his general foreman for meeting this deadline. The safety engineer will serve as a consultant to any supervisor who may desire his services in solving safety problems.
   d. A system will be developed for rating each first-line supervisor based on the results of the safety appraisal. The appraisal team will report the rating to each supervisor.
   e. The results of these safety appraisals will be considered by the general foreman in the annual over-all performance appraisal of each first-line supervisor.

2. Annual safety appraisal.
   a. At least once each year a safety appraisal of the entire plant will be made. The appraisal team might include specialists from outside the company who are particularly qualified in one or more areas of safety knowledge. These areas might include:

      Electrical hazards
      Mechanical hazards
      Chemical hazards
      Fire hazards
      Health hazards
      Security and civil defense

3. Safety appraisal of new and relocated equipment.
   a. The safety engineer will check all new and relocated

machines and equipment for compliance with state and local safety regulations and the adequacy of guards and protective devices.

4. Special safety appraisals.
   a. First-line supervisors will make a daily safety appraisal of their areas.
   b. Periodic safety appraisals by specially trained persons will be made of equipment as follows:

Power presses	2-week intervals
Chains and slings	3-month intervals
Ladders	4-week intervals
Gas-fired ovens	6-month intervals
Portable electric tools, etc.	6-month intervals or whenever tool is returned to crib

(The need for these appraisals will, of course, vary from plant to plant.)

C. Safety training

1. Supervisor safety training.

All supervisors will be required to take a course of safety training. This course will consist of five one-hour sessions designed to increase the supervisor's safety awareness, explain the causes of accidents, and provide techniques and tools for preventing accidents. An outline of the safety training program follows. (*Note:* This is the minimum training required. Other training programs for supervisors will be developed as a follow-up.)

SESSION ONE

Basic Safety Principles

Introduction of participants and purpose of conference
Need for a safety program
1. Improved production
2. Lower cost
3. Better employee and community relations
4. Greater acceptance of supervisory leadership

Definition of an "accident"
What "safety awareness" is

Explanation of disabling-injury frequency and severity rates
The accident flow chart—the anatomy of an accident
1. The immediate causes of an accident
2. The contributing causes of an accident
3. Controlling accidents
Why the supervisor is the focal point of all accident-prevention activities
The functions of the safety engineer
Relation between safety and production responsibilities
Summary of key points of session and assignment for next session

SESSION TWO

Developing Safe Working Conditions

Review key points in session one
Develop four steps supervisors must take to control accidents
1. Develop safe working conditions
2. Personalized safety training
3. Promote employee safety participation
4. Enforce safety rules
Discuss development of safe working conditions in detail
1. Human factors in machine and equipment safety
2. Methods for safeguarding machines
Finding the causes of accidents
1. Unsafe conditions
2. Unsafe acts
3. The accident investigation
How to make a plant safety appraisal
Review key points of session

SESSION THREE

Personalized Safety Training

Review four steps supervisors take to prevent accidents
Discuss various safety training methods
1. Classroom training
2. Posters
3. Safety films
4. Plant safety news
Review results of Dr. G. Roy Fugal's safety-training research[1]
Explain personalized safety training
Need for job-hazard analysis
Practice in making job-hazard analysis
The four-step job-training method

---

[1] G. Roy Fugal, "Relationship of Safety Education to Industrial Accidents," a dissertation, May, 1950, Yale University Library.

G. Roy Fugal, "Reducing Industrial Accidents," *Harvard Business Review*, July, 1951.

Retraining the man on the job
Training new and transferred employees
Ask each participant to make a job-hazard analysis of one job before next session
Review key points of session

SESSION FOUR

Promoting Employee Participation in Safety

Review four steps supervisors take to prevent accidents
Ask three participants to discuss their job-hazard analyses
Discuss need for developing safety awareness

1. Employees must be convinced that accidents are caused
   a. Accident proneness
   b. Your number is up
   c. Law of averages

Safety problems created by resistance to change and resentment of criticism
Methods for promoting employee safety participation

1. The safety-observer program
2. Observer hazard memos
3. Group safety meetings
4. Personal supervisor safety contacts

Review key points of session

SESSION FIVE

Safety Rules and Measuring Safety Performance

Review four steps supervisors must take to prevent accidents
Discuss safety rules that are not followed
Review the reasons rules are not followed

1. Because of the rule
2. Because of the supervisor
3. Because of the employee

Steps supervisors might take to motivate employees to follow rules
Review present rules
Decide which rules should be retained
When disciplinary action should be taken
Procedures for taking disciplinary action
Why there is a need for measuring supervisor safety performance
The injury-control chart
Safety responsibility and accountability
Review high points of course
Close session with request for action: "Safety is a way of life."

The need for building a safety program around the first-line supervisor, rather than the safety engineer, is stressed in the training program.

In an effort to assure continued progress in industrial safety, the line supervisor's responsibility for preventing accidents must be firmly established. He must realize that doing a good job in this area will improve his status as a supervisor.

On the basis of a review of numerous successful safety programs in large and small plants, it is apparent that first-line supervisors must be trained to do a competent job in these four areas:

Development of safe working conditions
Personalized safety training
Promoting employee participation in safety
Enforcement of safety rules

Because safety is so distinctly a supervisory responsibility, it is suggested that line managers, who are qualified conference leaders, be asked to conduct the training sessions for first-line supervisors. The safety or training unit will have the responsibility for training the conference leaders and organizing and administering the program; also, such details as scheduling the meetings, providing training materials, etc., can be handled by one of these units.

D. Job-hazard analysis

1. On a planned basis, first-line supervisors will make a detailed step-by-step job-hazard analysis of each of the jobs they supervise. For existing jobs this should be done by the supervisors working with employees on the job.
2. A copy of the completed analysis should be given the employee for his study and reference, and another kept on file by the supervisor.
3. A job-hazard analysis should be made for every new job and should be used in the training of each new employee.

E. The safety-observer program

1. Each supervisor will appoint a safety observer from among the employees in his group. Participation will be on a voluntary basis.
2. Observers will serve for a period of three months, so in time all individuals in a group will have an opportunity to serve.
3. Safety observers will be granted time off from regular duties

for a period of up to two hours per week to assist the supervisor on safety matters.

4. Once each week the observer will make a formal tour of his area, together with his supervisor, noting and making a record of all hazards found.
5. Safety observers will be given a one-hour indoctrination course at the start of their tour of duty and will be given a button which will identify them as safety observers.
6. The training courses will be established by the safety unit.

F. Communication and related activities

1. Safety posters will be obtained by the safety unit and posted on appropriate bulletin boards throughout the plant. The posters should be approximately 2 feet by 3 feet in size and should be changed at least twice a month. Small-sized posters will be distributed to all supervisors for use in their immediate area.
2. The plant newspaper will be used to inform plant personnel of major safety activities. "Wise Owl" awards and significant statistics will be given publicity through this medium.
3. Accidents and near accidents which offer good lessons for conduct will be appropriately photographed and made into eye-catching posters for display in each supervisor's area where the example is appropriate.
4. Safety memos will be written and distributed to all supervisors as required to call their attention to specific hazards or instructions and to inform them about pertinent company accidents and safety activities.
5. A system of awards will be established.
   a. Manager's award—will be given when a section has achieved one year of work without a disabling injury. The entire section will be taken out to dinner so the accomplishment can be appropriately praised by top management and continued effort requested. Small token awards indicating the accomplishment, or suitably engraved certificates of achievement, might be presented to each employee at the dinner. The dinner award has its principal value as an opportunity to pat everyone on the back, give formal recognition to individuals for various safety achievements, and sell safety one more time. The reason it is suggested that the dinner be held following

the winning of a manager's award rather than a president's award (see below) is two-fold. First, the number of employees in the plant would make a dinner for all employees an unwieldy affair. Second, the purpose of the dinner by sections of the plant is to provide an incentive for the rest of the plant to work for a dinner award too.

b. President's award—will be given whenever the plant achieves a record of 3,000,000 manhours worked without a disabling injury. Each employee will receive a token award as well as an appropriate certificate citing the accomplishment. Adequate publicity in local papers, on radio, and if possible on television will be given to this achievement.

6. Large sign boards will be designed and prominently displayed to tell the running story of each section's safety accomplishments. It will show:
   a. Number of days since last disabling injury in section.
   b. Previous record number of days without a disabling injury in section.
   c. Number of days since last disabling injury in plant.
   d. Number of disabling injuries this year to date.
   e. Number of disabling injuries last year.

G. General administration

1. Any injury requiring medical or first-aid attention will be investigated promptly by the injured employee's supervisor and an accident report prepared within twenty-four hours following the accident.
2. The safety engineer will prepare and maintain an injury-control chart for each supervisor with twenty-five or more people in his work group. Each supervisor will be provided with an injury-control chart which he will be expected to keep up to date.
3. The safety engineer will prepare a quarterly report that goes to all supervisors which tabulates the cause of all injuries reported during the quarter. This report will be prepared by the 10th of the month following the close of the quarter; also, a quarterly report will be prepared containing the following statistics:
   a. An injury-control chart for the plant.
   b. Injury and severity rates by sections of the plant and for the total plant, including:

(1) Number of disabling injuries.
(2) Actual days lost.
(3) Disability time charges.

c. Total injuries.
d. Total-injury frequency rate.
e. Medical expense.
f. Workmen's compensation payments.

(Statistics under b. will be reported for current quarter, last quarter, and year to date.)

4. Management reports.
   a. On an annual basis, management will make an appraisal of each supervisor's safety performance. The appraisal will be made by each section's superintendent, the general foreman, and the safety engineer. Each appraisal will be subject to the approval of the plant manager. Factors which are to be considered in the appraisal, with the range of points allowed for each factor, are shown in the chart on the next page.

SUPERVISOR'S SAFETY-PERFORMANCE APPRAISAL

	Check One			
	Poor 0	Fair 4	Good 8	Excellent 12
Development of Safe Working Conditions:				
General housekeeping				
Condition of machines and equipment, guards, electrical connections, etc.				
Ventilation, lights, and health hazards				
Condition and use of personal protective equipment				
Personalized Safety Training:				
A job-hazard analysis for each job				
Job-hazard analysis reviewed with each employee				
Job-hazard analysis used for instructing all new employees				
Quality of personalized safety training as evidenced by the number of unsafe operating procedures observed				
Promotion of Safety Participation:				
Interest employees have in observer program				
Promptness in handling hazard memos				
Safety-observer activity				
Safety example set by the supervisor				
Enforcement of Safety Rules:				
Action taken when rules are not followed				
Status of rules—are they understood? Are they necessary?				
Supervisor's Total Score				

APPENDIX

B

Color code for portable grinders and grinding wheels[1]

This instruction specifies the requirements for the use of a color code for portable grinders and grinding wheels. *The purpose of this code is safety. It is designed to prevent the use of grinding wheels at speeds in excess of the American Standards Association Safety Code,* Use, Care and Protection of Abrasive Wheels, B 7.1.

I. Basic Rules.

A. All portable grinders shall be painted a specific color according to their rated speed.

B. All grinding wheels shall be grouped according to maximum recommended speed and painted the same color as the grinder on which they may be *safely* used.

C. *No person* shall be permitted to use any wheel on a portable grinder unless the color of the grinder and the color of the wheel are the same.

D. The following color code shall be followed:

---

[1] *Source:* C. E. Harper, "Making Grinding Wheels Behave," *Safety Maintenance and Production,"* October, 1954.

Rated Speed of Grinder	Color
5000 rpm	Blue
6000	Green
9000	Red
12,000	Yellow
18,000	Purple
21,000	White
40,000	Pink

II. Specific Rules. Plant manufacturing service will:

A. Paint all portable grinders according to color code.
B. Group all grinding wheels according to recommended speed and see that they are painted the same color as the grinder on which they may be *safely* used.
C. See that all new grinders or wheels purchased are colored in accordance with the color code before they are issued to operators.
D. Display color-code chart at strategic locations.

III. Other Rules. The manufacturing supervisor will:

A. See that no person is permitted to use a wheel on a portable grinder unless the color of the grinder and the wheel are the same.
B. Instruct each operator in the use of the color code.
C. See that each new employee is properly instructed before he is allowed to use grinding equipment.
D. Furnish a pocket-size copy of the color code to each operator of portable grinding equipment.
E. Make regular checks of the portable-grinding operations in his area to make sure that no grinders are used in violation of the color code.

IV. The supervisor of each manufacturing section should make *periodic* checks to satisfy himself that no person is operating a grinder in violation of the color-code system.

APPENDIX

C

Sources of safety information and educational materials

Following is a list of some organizations which supply safety information and educational materials.

American Gas Association
420 Lexington Avenue
New York 17, New York

American Mutual Alliance
20 North Wacker Drive
Chicago 6, Illinois

American National Red Cross
17th and E Streets, Northwest
Washington 13, D. C.

American Society of Mechanical Engineers
29 West 39th Street
New York 18, New York

American Society of Safety Engineers
425 North Michigan Avenue
Chicago 11, Illinois

American Standards Association, Inc.
70 East 45th Street
New York 17, New York

Association of Casualty and Surety Companies
60 John Street
New York 38, New York

Center for Safety, New York University
Washington Square
New York 3, New York

Factory Insurance Association
555 Asylum Street
Hartford 2, Connecticut

Industrial Hygiene Foundation of America
4400 5th Avenue
Pittsburgh 13, Pennsylvania

Industrial Accident Prevention Associations, General Manager
90 Harbour Street
Toronto, Ontario, Canada

Manufacturing Chemists Association
1625 I Street, Northwest
Washington 5, D. C.

National Board of Fire Underwriters
85 John Street
New York 38, New York

National Bureau of Standards
Connecticut Avenue and Van Ness Street, Northwest
Washington 25, D. C.

National Fire Protection Association
60 Batterymarch Street
Boston 10, Massachusetts

National Safety Council
425 North Michigan Avenue
Chicago 11, Illinois

Superintendent of Documents
Government Printing Office
Washington 25, D. C.

Underwriters Laboratories, Inc.
207 East Ohio Street
Chicago 7, Illinois

United States Department of Labor
14th Street and Constitution Avenue, Northwest
Washington 25, D. C.

United States Public Health Service
1901 Constitution Avenue, Northwest
Washington, D. C.

INDEX